WOMAN
ABUSE
ON
CAMPUS

Sage Series on Violence Against Women

Series Editors

Claire M. Renzetti
St. Joseph's University

Jeffrey L. Edleson
University of Minnesota

In this series. . .

I AM NOT YOUR VICTIM: Anatomy of Domestic Violence
   by Beth Sipe and Evelyn J. Hall

WIFE RAPE: Understanding the Response of Survivors
and Service Providers
   by Raquel Kennedy Bergen

FUTURE INTERVENTIONS WITH BATTERED WOMEN
AND THEIR FAMILIES
   edited by Jeffrey L. Edleson and Zvi C. Eisikovits

WOMEN'S ENCOUNTERS WITH VIOLENCE: Australian Experiences
   edited by Sandy Cook and Judith Bessant

WOMAN ABUSE ON CAMPUS: Results From the Canadian
National Survey
   by Walter S. DeKeseredy and Martin D. Schwartz

RURAL WOMAN BATTERING AND THE JUSTICE SYSTEM:
An Ethnography
   by Neil Websdale

WOMAN ABUSE ON CAMPUS

Results From the Canadian National Survey

Walter S. DeKeseredy
Martin D. Schwartz

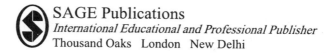

Sage Series on Violence Against Women

SAGE Publications
International Educational and Professional Publisher
Thousand Oaks   London   New Delhi

For information:

SAGE Publications, Inc.
2455 Teller Road
Thousand Oaks, California 91320
E-mail: order@sagepub.com

SAGE Publications Ltd.
6 Bonhill Street
London EC2A 4PU
United Kingdom

SAGE Publications India Pvt. Ltd.
M-32 Market
Greater Kailash I
New Delhi 110 048 India

Printed in the United States of America

Library of Congress Cataloging-in-Publication Data

DeKeseredy, Walter S., 1959–
 Woman abuse on campus: Results from the Canadian national survey
/ by Walter S. Dekeseredy and Martin D. Schwartz.
  p. cm. — (Sage series on violence against women ; v. 5)
 Includes bibliographical references (p.) and index.
 ISBN 0-7619-0567-7 (cloth: acid-free paper). —
 ISBN 0-7619-0566-9 (pbk.: acid-free paper)
  1. Women college students—Crimes against—Canada. 2. Women
college students—Abuse of—Canada. 3. Dating violence—Canada.
 4. Acquaintance rape—Canada. 5. Victims of crimes surveys—Canada. I. Schwartz,
Martin D. II. Title. III. Series.
 HV6250.4.W65D43 1997
 362.88'082—dc21   97-21054

98 99 00 01 02 03 10 9 8 7 6 5 4 3 2

Acquiring Editor:	C. Terry Hendrix
Editorial Assistant:	Dale Grenfell
Production Editor:	Diana E. Axelsen
Production Assistant:	Karen Wiley
Typesetter:	Christina M. Hill
Print Buyer:	Anna Chin

Contents

Preface

Many North Americans view Canada as a "peaceable kingdom": a place where it is safe to walk the streets, go out at night, and in general live a normal life. This perception is partially correct. Compared with their neighbors south of the border, Canadians are less likely to be victimized by predatory street crimes such as robbery or stranger assault. However, at least for women, this safety might not extend to intimate relationships. Here, Canadian men may be the equals of U.S. men. Several widely read and cited representative sample surveys, such as those conducted by the late Michael D. Smith, show that Canadian men are just as, if not more, likely to beat their spouses as American men. However, it is not only women in marital or cohabiting relationships who are in danger of being abused. The research presented in this book shows that the same can be said about women in university and community college dating relationships.

As we shall see in this book, there has been some investigation in the United States as to the extent of woman abuse in postsecondary schools. But how many Canadian female undergraduates are physically, sexually, and psychologically attacked by their boyfriends or dating partners? Prior to the Canadian National Survey (CNS) outlined in this book, several small-scale surveys, which are briefly reviewed in Chapter 1, provided important clues to the answers to this question. The problem was that the results of these studies could not be generalized to the Canadian student population at large. The CNS, a heavily funded federal government project, was an attempt to do for Canada what Mary Koss's famed research into dating violence did in the United States—but also to go beyond these data to provide the answers to many other questions.

An important role of the CNS, then, is to fill this major research gap left by the smaller and local victimization surveys that are not generalizable to the nation's population of college and university students. The CNS also constitutes an attempt to uncover some of the key sources of male-to-female victimization in postsecondary school courtship. The hope of the researchers is that the results of this study will motivate criminal justice officials, policymakers, students, faculty, and campus administrators to struggle to make unsafe learning environments and gender relations in these contexts safer.

Still, there have been strong attacks on the data that have been coming in from across North America indicating that there is a high degree of victimization of women. One of the strongest attacks has been the accusation that women are violent also. "But women do it too!" is the battle cry. "Why do we avoid admitting that women are as violent as men?" One of our discoveries in examining these data is that the question is much more complicated than it seems to many people. Although many women do in fact strike blows against men, we have included in Chapter 3 the CNS data on the meanings and motives of female-to-male violence. Contrary to popular belief, we found that a substantial amount of women's violence was in self-defense, or "fighting back." Such data throw doubt on the argument that dating violence is fully symmetrical or "mutual combat."

Although the purpose behind this book was to explain the major findings of the Canadian National Survey, it seemed to leave too much unsaid to avoid drawing some implications and to avoid making policy recommendations. Thus, in Chapter 5 we have drawn these conclusions and made these suggestions.

We have, individually and together, written journal articles on some of the data generated by the CNS, and we wanted to merge them in one source. This objective could not have been met without the kind and scholarly assistance of Claire Renzetti and Jeffrey Edleson. We are also indebted to Terry Hendrix and Dale Grenfell of Sage, who more or less patiently waited for us to complete this book.

Although we enjoy doing empirical and theoretical work, we knew that behind the statistics scattered throughout this book are female survivors, real people who have endured a terrifying amount of pain and suffering. Analyzing their experiences can be a deeply depressing experience, especially when we thought of the inadequate ways in which most survivors are treated by many campus administrators, police officers, and other agents of social control. Thanks to the support of our families, however, we were able to muster up enough energy to complete a book on one of North America's most pressing social problems. Once again, we are especially indebted to Carol Blum, Patricia, Andrea, and Steven DeKeseredy, Marie Barger, and Eva Jantz. For us, these people personify what social support is all about.

As you can imagine, completing a study like the CNS requires the assistance of many friends and colleagues. Our strongest thanks go out to Katharine Kelly, Daniel Saunders, and Shahid Alvi, who were essential in the analysis of some of the data reported in this book. Molly Leggett was of invaluable support on a wide variety of tasks, and we truly appreciate her very important contributions. The following people went well beyond the call of duty to help CNS researchers gather and analyze data, collect lists of social support services, cope with the antifeminist backlash, and help present the results of this study: Diane Aubry, Bente Baklid, Meda Chesney-Lind, Kim Cook, Dawn Currie, Jurgen Dankwört, Linda Davies, Desmond Ellis, Karlene Faith, Darlene Gilson, Eva Hegmann, Ronald Hinch, Mary Koss, Lisa Leduc, Vera Legasse, Brian D. MacLean, Linda MacLeod, James Messerschmidt, the Ottawa Regional Coordinating Committee to End Violence Against Women, John Pollard and his colleagues and York University's Institute for Social Research, Claire Renzetti, Les Samuelson, the late Michael D. Smith, Betsy Stanko, Noreen Stuckless, Jo-Anne Taylor, Victor Valentine, Barry Wright, and the many wonderful people who worked at Health Canada's Family Violence Prevention Division. Because many of these people disagree with one another, we assume full responsibility for the material presented in this book.

The research reported in this book was supported by a grant from the Family Violence Prevention Division of Health Canada to Walter DeKeseredy and Katharine Kelly. The views expressed in this book, however, are those of the authors and do not necessarily reflect those of Health Canada or Katharine Kelly. Financial assistance to gather information on several sections of this book was provided at Carleton University by the Office of the Dean of Social Sciences and by the Faculty of Graduate Studies and Research, while some of the research and writing was supported by sabbatical leaves provided by Ohio University and Carleton University.

Of course, *Woman Abuse on Campus* would not have been possible without the assistance of the students and instructors who participated in the CNS. Their courage, support, and honesty will always be remembered.

Parts of Chapters 1 and 2 include material adapted from Walter S. DeKeseredy, "Addressing the Complexities of Woman Abuse in Dating: A Response to Gartner and Fox," *Canadian Journal of Sociology* (1994); Walter S. DeKeseredy, "Enhancing the Quality of Survey Data on Woman Abuse," *Violence Against Women* (1995); Walter S. DeKeseredy and Katharine Kelly, "The Incidence and Prevalence of Woman Abuse in Canadian University and College Dating Relationships," *Canadian Journal of Sociology* (1993); and Walter S. DeKeseredy and Martin D. Schwartz, "Locating a History of Some Canadian Woman Abuse in Elementary and High School Dating Relationships," *Humanity and Society* (1994). Some sections of Chapter 3 were adapted from Walter S. DeKeseredy, Daniel G. Saunders, Martin D. Schwartz, and Shahid Alvi, "The Meanings and Motives for Women's Use of Violence in Canadian College Dating Relationships: Results From a National Survey," *Sociological Spectrum* (1997). A few pages of Chapter 4 were adapted from Walter S. DeKeseredy and Katharine Kelly, "Woman Abuse in University and College Dating Relationships: The Contribution of the Ideology of Familial Patriarchy," *Journal of Human Justice* (1993) and Walter S. DeKeseredy, "Woman Abuse in Dating Relationships: An Exploratory Study," *Atlantis* (1989). Some material in Chapter 5 includes reworked material from several pages in Walter S. DeKeseredy, "Making an Unsafe Learning Environment Safer," in C. Stark-Adamec (Ed.), *Violence: A Collective Responsibility* (pp. 71-94), Ottawa: Social Science Federation of Canada (1996). Permission to use or reprint this material is gratefully acknowledged.

To Pat and Carol

1

The Historical, Social, and Political Context of the Canadian National Survey on Woman Abuse in Dating

We have a vision of college here in the United States. You see it in movies: a cultural icon of what college is like. The vision, more or less, includes a beautiful, quiet, rural setting, and in that setting is a small college with perfect buildings, and a kind of idyllic peaceful environment for the pursuit of higher learning. The dorms are comfortable, each has its own dining room, laundry service, and sensitive and caring counselors. Professors, all of whom seem to like each other as well as the students, live in gingerbread houses near the gingerbread village. What could be better. (Schuman & Olufs, 1995, p. 31)

Like their U.S. counterparts portrayed in the quote above, many Canadians share a vision of colleges and universities as peaceful sanctuaries from the "real world." Universities and community colleges are commonly seen as places where students, faculty, administrators, and support staff strive constantly to provide "practical solutions to the problems of the day" (Strong-Boag, 1996, p. 105), while a growing number of people, especially those who hold conservative values and beliefs, view postsecondary schools as little more than "ivory towers" or bastions of political correctness.

To some extent, all of these perceptions are correct. For example, some campuses are beautiful; some members of campus communities try to help policymakers, the media, and members of the general population come to terms with major social, cultural, and economic change. Some faculty, students, and administrators are strong proponents of political correctness. However, colleges and universities consist of a diverse range of people, attitudes, and beliefs. In fact, the campus is a place where "everybody brings something different, seems to expect something different, and often reacts in different ways" (Schuman & Olufs, 1995, p. 17).

Still, every North American university or college, regardless of its philosophy or mission, scholarly and pedagogical approach, reputation, size, and demographic characteristics, mirrors in some ways the broader society in which it exists (Currie & MacLean, 1993). For example, schools rationalize and legitimate ethnic, class, and gender inequality (Curran & Renzetti, 1996; Gomme, 1995). These actions do not make them any different than governments, large corporations, hospitals, police and fire departments, and a host of other formal organizations. This is not only important to understand in the broader sense that every citizen must appreciate certain things about his or her own culture and society. In a narrower and more specific sense, these inequalities have been found to be strongly related to woman abuse in a variety of adult heterosexual relationships (DeKeseredy & MacLeod, 1997). For that reason, many sociologists are not surprised by the fact that the incidence and prevalence rates of woman abuse in university and college dating (which will be described in Chapter 2) are alarmingly high. Unfortunately, for reasons described later, these high figures are *underestimates* and are not likely to decrease unless progressive policy proposals such as the ones discussed in Chapter 5 are implemented throughout society.

Everyone knows that students are taught academic skills, such as reading, writing, and mathematics. However, these students are also exposed to a powerful "hidden curriculum" (Parkinson & Drislane, 1996) that teaches them many other things about society, such as how to maintain racism, sexism, and a variety of other practices within society. Children are not born racists or sexists, and they may or may not learn such attitudes at home. However, from an early age, children learn such things as that boys and girls cannot play together (Thorne, 1993), that sports such as Little League are designed to teach boys that girls are inferior (Fine, 1987), that the Boy Scouts are designed to teach boys that only certain kinds of masculinity are allowed and those are the kinds that harm human relationships (Thorne-Finch, 1992). These lessons and others legitimate and perpetuate the abuse of women in heterosexual relationships.

In another book, we discussed how attitudes on the college campus later serve to promote or at least fail to contradict the physical and sexual abuse of women (Schwartz & DeKeseredy, 1997). For example, it is not unusual for faculty and staff to maintain attitudes that promote acquaintance and date rape. This can be seen in the "boys will be boys" attitudes of fraternity advisers and dorm supervisors who treat serious law violations as minor pranks. This might consist of campus judiciary systems that treat serious felony crimes such as forcible rape as events that might at worst require an apology or, more likely, be dismissed if the victim has not hired a team of investigators to develop the facts to prove her case (Bernstein, 1996; Warshaw, 1988). Sometimes these are not subtle attitudes that professors or administrators pass on to students. Consider Matin Yaqzan, a University of New Brunswick professor who published an article in a student newspaper alleging that "male aggressiveness" and "the male drive for sex" are part of "human nature" and "therefore the reason and need for the so called 'date rape' " (cited in Hornosty, 1996, p. 35). Would male students considering whether to force their dates into sex find any comfort in articles such as this by respected professors? Would they give male students the implicit message that woman abuse is tolerated on college and university campuses (Bohmer & Parrot, 1993; Schwartz & DeKeseredy, 1997)?

Sexist statements and the injurious behaviors described throughout this book foster an atmosphere of fear and insecurity and serve as a powerful means of social control (Hornosty, 1996). Thus, it is no surprise that when asked how safe they felt on campus, many women who participated in the Canadian National Survey on woman abuse in dating relationships (CNS) reported feeling unsafe after dark on their campuses and the immediate surrounding areas. Of the 1,835 women who participated in this study,

- 36.1% felt unsafe and 25.9% felt very unsafe walking alone after dark;
- 35.7% felt unsafe and 12.9% felt very unsafe riding a bus or streetcar alone after dark;
- 34.8% felt unsafe and 38.7% felt very unsafe riding a subway alone after dark;
- 42.5% felt unsafe and 25.7% felt very unsafe walking alone to a car in a parking lot after dark;

- 41% felt unsafe and 31.2% felt very unsafe waiting for public transportation alone after dark;
- 36.3% felt unsafe and 38.9% felt very unsafe walking past men they don't know while alone after dark (Kelly & DeKeseredy, 1994).

Female undergraduates' fear of "stranger danger" and woman abuse in college and university dating are not new problems. Nevertheless, until recently, most North Americans viewed universities and community colleges as "sanctuaries from violent crime and other social problems" (Currie & MacLean, 1993, p. 1). Physical and sexual assaults on female students have generated some concern about women's safety on and near college campuses. However, these offenses are typically seen by most academics, criminal justice officials, campus administrators, and many students as the irregular and infrequent acts of strangers (Currie, 1994). Even such shocking events such as the December 6, 1989, mass murder of 14 women at the University of Montréal, École Polytechnique, did little to challenge the popular notion of universities and colleges as "peaceable kingdoms."

Because very few abusive acts in dating relationships are reported to them, campus officials are able to conclude that women's fear of crime is out of proportion to their risk of assault (Currie, 1994). Further support for this assertion is provided by a few "new generation" feminists (e.g., Roiphe, 1994) and some conservative academics such as John Fekete (1994) and Neil Gilbert (1991, 1994), who argue that the articles and research results published in refereed journals and scholarly books showing high rates of woman abuse on campus have greatly exaggerated the case. These backlash writers have been referred to by the authors of this book as "people without data" because they have no expertise in the area of woman abuse, have never conducted a victimization or self-report survey, and have never (aside from their attacks on research scientists who study rape) revealed any knowledge of this complex area (Schwartz & DeKeseredy, 1994b). In a rather extraordinary argument, Roiphe and Gilbert both assert that they certainly would have heard about it if sexual assault and other abusive acts against women were really widespread. Because they haven't heard about it, it cannot be happening. At the same time they attack findings that as many as 50% of rape victims never told even their best friend about their victimization, conservative writers are upset that rape victims are not confiding in large numbers in people who attack and belittle rape victims.

It is most unfortunate that in the current political atmosphere, which Faludi (1991) terms the "backlash," there is enormous support for campus administrators, conservative authors, politicians, students, academics, and media personnel who mock, taunt, and disregard female survivors of abuse in postsecondary school dating. Such a response is ironic at a time when crime discussions are dominated by calls for support for victims, more prisons and longer sentences, the reinstatement of the death penalty, which was abolished in Canada in 1976, and even caning for minor offenders. However, as in the United States, enormous support remains in Canada for belittling crime victims if they happen to be women. As legal scholars have noted (e.g., Estrich, 1987), this is done by claiming that only certain "facts" constitute "real woman abuse" (Schwartz & DeKeseredy, 1994b).

In other words, if a woman is a victim of the stereotypical crime that people have decided is truly a crime, then her victimization is accepted. For example, in forcible rape, the woman should be attacked by strangers, preferably more than one, should be physically harmed (to show that she wasn't enjoying it), and should report the crime immediately (Adler, 1987). If she was raped by a man she knows, she was probably doing something to deserve it, so it isn't actually rape. Susan Estrich, the law professor who popularized the term *real rape*, points out that when she herself was raped, she was pretty lucky: The rapist stole her car. The police quickly decided that although women might cooperate in being forcibly raped in public by a stranger, they certainly would not agree to having their car stolen. Thus, she was treated like a "real" victim (Estrich, 1987). In stranger rape, there are a number of factors that convince many people that rape is justified, or at least isn't real: The woman was dressed sexily; she used bad language; she was hitchhiking; she was in a place where women should not be (Scully, 1990).

However, the situation is very much worse on campus, where virtually all of the sexual assaults uncovered in surveys are committed by other students, men who not only know the victim but actually just might like the victim (Schwartz & DeKeseredy, 1997). Under these circumstances, where the victim almost always is located in a private place (his or her room, for example), it is very easy for many people simply to dismiss the case as a noncrime, because the victim could have avoided it. Of interest, few people would argue against prosecuting a thief who stole unprotected money or stole a car left unlocked in broad daylight, or against prosecuting someone who badly injured a person he did not like by waiting for the victim to become so intoxicated that he could not effectively fight back. Yet, as the *New York Times* found out at least in the United States, prosecutors commonly dismiss charges against men if the women were foolish enough to enter the room where the rapist was waiting (Bernstein, 1996).

In sum, while thousands of North American female undergraduates are abused each year by their university and community college dating partners, the campus officials, criminal justice personnel, and a host of others fail to recognize, and perhaps contribute to, the pain and suffering of these women. A major consequence is the creation of "a 'chilly climate' for women; that is, universities exhibit a host of conventional practices which communicate a lack of confidence in women, a lack of recognition for women, or a devaluation of their capabilities and successes" (Currie & MacLean, 1993, p. 14).

What, then, is to be done about influencing campus administrators, members of the general population, the media, and the criminal justice system to recognize that the abuse of female undergraduates in dating relationships is widespread, common, and highly injurious? Like many U.S. researchers (Koss & Cook, 1993; Reppucci, 1985), Canadian National Survey (CNS) researchers believe that their work could and should play an important role in the development of public policy. Of course, we and others who helped gather and analyze data generated by the CNS wanted to fill a major Canadian research gap by providing national statistics on the incidence, prevalence, sources, and consequences of woman abuse in the university and college dating population at large. However, the CNS is much more than an empirical enterprise. We hoped that our data would help mobilize resources to curb all forms of male-to-female victimization in postsecondary school courtship. It is to the development of this large-scale study that we now turn.

The Development of the CNS

North American college and university campuses have long been breeding grounds for many different crimes against women, and especially those that take place in dating relationships (Schwartz, 1991). For example, in the United States, Waller (1937) pointed out 60 years ago that many male dating partners are extremely exploitative and competitive. A substantial number of them also physically, sexually, and psychologically abuse their dating partners. However, prior to Makepeace's

(1981) exploratory survey, less than a handful of American studies focused on male-to-female victimization in courtship, and most of this work was conducted by one person, Eugene Kanin.[1] Today there are dozens of U.S. data sets on this problem, which challenge popular notions that dating "was a time of innocent exploration and that intimate violence was more a feature of conflict-ridden married couples" (Sugarman & Hotaling, 1989, p. 3). In fact, a review of the major findings uncovered by these studies and the CNS indicates that female students are abused by their male dating partners at every North American campus, regardless of its size, religious and political affiliation, and location (Bohmer & Parrot, 1993; DeKeseredy & MacLeod, 1997; Schwartz & DeKeseredy, 1997).[2]

The physical, sexual, and psychological abuse of Canadian female undergraduate students had long been recognized as a social problem. However, prior to DeKeseredy's (1988) exploratory survey of southern Ontario male undergraduates, Canadian woman abuse researchers focused mainly on the extent, distribution, correlates, and sources of male physical and psychological attacks on married, cohabiting, and separated/divorced women.[3] The plight of abused female dating partners warrants just as much political, empirical, media, and public attention.

Recognizing the severe lack of data on the extent of woman abuse in postsecondary school dating, in the early 1990s several Canadian researchers conducted small-scale, nonrepresentative sample surveys of university and college students in Ontario, New Brunswick, and western Canada. Table 1.1 presents the results of these studies and the methods used to generate them.[4] Table 1.1 supports the claim that Canadian female students are exposed to a broad range of attacks; indeed, their lives "rest upon a continuum of violence" (Stanko, 1990, p. 95). In a move that is not at all unusual, many frontline workers (e.g., shelter workers) strongly opposed the well-funded survey (the CNS) described throughout this book. These service providers constantly have to search for funding sources, and they experience chronic uncertainty about the survival of their programs. Some practitioners generally feel that research is irrelevant to providing services (National Research Council, 1996). Others are deeply disturbed by what they see as competition: the allocation of scarce funds for research that could have been better spent on frontline services for abused women (Doob, 1995). For example, as one woman who participated in the September 1992 Toward Women's Safety Forum[5] told Walter DeKeseredy, "We don't need more statistics. No one has to tell me that a lot of women are beaten, raped, and emotionally brutalized by men. The money should go to those who are trying to save their lives!" This woman's concerns reflect those of many other frontline workers, and they are to a large extent justified because throughout North America, many shelters, rape crisis centers, and other social support services for abused women have been or are at great risk of being shut down because of funding cuts (DeKeseredy & MacLeod, 1997). Worse, typically funding agencies want quick results and do not want researchers to slow down and adequately consult with practitioners. When the research is completed, the researchers move on to other tasks and fail to bring the new knowledge back to help practitioners (National Research Council, 1996).

There is no question that much more money must be devoted to providing more and better services to women (and occasionally men) who are abused in a variety of intimate relationships, including those who are victimized by their lesbian or gay partners.[6] This funding should be made permanent, so that shelters do not have to put such an incredible amount of their energy into writing grants and fund-raising, which seriously depletes the amount of time available for direct services.

The problem is that this increased funding will not be forthcoming without better data. It is extremely unlikely that any funding body will become convinced that the problem is widespread and dangerous because frontline workers tell executive and legislative leaders that they "know" that many women are abused. One of the reasons more reliable data are necessary is that the statistics presented in Table 1.1 cannot be generalized to the undergraduate student population at large. This methodological shortcoming is hardly a trivial concern. An entire survey can be discredited if researchers, policymakers, the media, and members of the general population cannot distinguish whether the women who reported having been abused are representative of all abused women in the sample (Smith, 1994). In fact, most campus administrators either ignored the surveys described in Table 1.1 or claimed that the findings were unreliable because they tell us little about the "true" extent of dating abuse in the university and community college student population (DeKeseredy, 1996a).

Struggles for effective social support services and prevention and control strategies are also hindered because unreliable data decrease the probability of mobilizing resources to curb dating abuse and other threats to women's safety on campus. Unfortunately, many government officials and members of the general population do not listen to women's accounts of their pain and suffering. When they do listen, these reports

(text continued on p. 13)

TABLE 1.1 Woman Abuse in University and College Dating Surveys

	Description of Surveys			Abuse Rates		
Survey	Survey Location	Sample Description	Interview Mode	Measure(s) of Abuse	Incidence Rate(s)	Prevalence Rate(s)
DeKeseredy (1988)	Southern Ontario	308 male university students	Self-administered questionnaires	CTS[a] and two modified SES[b] items	70% reported physical and/or psychological abuse, 69% stated that they engaged in psychological abuse, 12% reported being physically abusive, 2.6% admitted to having been sexually aggressive	Not examined
Barnes, Greenwood, & Sommer (1991)	Manitoba	245 male university students	Self-administered questionnaires	CTS, VBN,[c] and CRA[d] Abuse Index	Not examined	42% reported using violence, 92.6% stated they emotionally abused women

(continued)

TABLE 1.1 Woman Abuse in University and College Dating Surveys (Continued)

	Description of Surveys			Abuse Rates	
Survey	Survey Location	Sample Description	Interview Mode	Measure(s) of Abuse	Incidence Rate(s)	Prevalence Rate(s)
DeKeseredy, Kelly, & Baklid (1992)	Eastern Ontario	179 female and 106 male university and college students	Self-administered questionnaires	CTS and SES	13% of the men reported using physical violence, 68% reported psychological abuse, 8% indicated being sexually aggressive; 26% of the females indicated being physically abused, 69% said they were psychologically victimized, 28% stated that they were sexually abused	18% of the men stated they used physical violence, 75% psychologically abused women, 12% reported acts of sexual aggression; 32% of women reported experiencing physical violence, 78% indicated being psychologically attacked, 40% stated they were sexually abused

	Description of Surveys				Abuse Rates		
Survey	Survey Location	Sample Description	Interview Mode	Measure(s) of Abuse	Incidence Rate(s)	Prevalence Rate(s)	
Elliot, Odynak, & Krahn (1992)	University of Alberta	1,016 undergraduate students (men and women)	Self-administered questionnaires	Modified SES	Not examined	44% of the students who reported an unwanted sexual experience while registered at the U. of A. stated that the offender was a romantic acquaintance and 18% said that the perpetrator was a casual or first date[e]
Finkelman (1992)	University of New Brunswick and St. Thomas University	447 undergraduate students (men and women)	Self-administered questionnaires	SES	Approximately 34.4% of the 127 respondents who reported one or more unwanted sexual experiences were victimized by a boyfriend/ girlfriend or date[e]	Not examined

a. Conflict Tactics Scale (Straus, 1979).
b. Sexual Experiences Survey (Koss & Oros, 1982).
c. Violent Behavior Inventory (Domestic Abuse Project, cited in Gondolf, 1985).
d. CRA Abuse Index (Stacy & Shupe, 1983).
e. Gender variations in victimization are not reported in this study.

BOX 1.1.

The Conflict Tactics Scale (CTS)

The Conflict Tactics Scale (CTS) will be described many times in this book, but a very quick introduction seems to be in order as soon as possible. First used in a national sample of couples in the 1970s (Straus, Gelles, & Steinmetz, 1981), the CTS tells people that couples in times of conflict often use various tactics to deal with these problems. Although the CTS may be used in many ways, it is most typically used to ask both male and female members of these couples to describe what tactics they had used in the past year. The nature of the disputes is not discussed—only the tactics used in the conflict situation.

The CTS is set up in a linear fashion, with the presumption being that events at the top of the scale are less serious than those at the bottom of the scale. The complete set of CTS items, as well as response data, can be found in Table 2.9 in this book. Most of the discussion on the CTS has been about the physical abuse section. In this section, there are nine sets of behaviors for the respondent to choose from. At the top, in the "minor" violence section, persons are asked about whether they threw something at a family member; pushed, shoved, or grabbed the person; or slapped him or her. In the "severe" violence section, people are asked whether they had hit, bit, punched, hit with an object, beat up, choked, or used or threatened to use a knife or gun.

There have been a number of attacks on the CTS. It measures acts almost completely divorced from context, for example. To too many researchers, two gunshot wounds count the same as being hit twice with a teddy bear. There is usually no question about who started the trouble, or whether the violence was simply malicious evil or pure self-defense, and it does a poor job of differentiating different types of attacks (Barnett, Miller-Perrin, & Perrin, 1997). Murray Straus, who developed the instrument, agrees with much of this criticism; it is difficult to compare being hit with a pillow with being hit with a brick, he argues. However, he simply challenges those researchers who find context important to add questions that ask about the context in which they are interested (Straus, 1990b).

Straus's call is taken up in this book. The researchers here agree that the CTS is the most reliable and valid instrument available for the limited range of questions it asks, but finds that other questions are essential to understand some of the meaning of the data. The CTS has been used as the basis of many more than 100 professional journal articles and several books, although it is, unfortunately, more rare than it should be that researchers have asked the meaning, context, and motive questions that are missing.

are often interpreted or dismissed as products of fantasy or "vindictive artifice." Rigorous qualitative studies are also dismissed because they are viewed as being nonrepresentative of a larger population (Bart, Miller, Moran, & Stanko, 1989, p. 433).

Will rigorous quantitative studies move governments toward action? It is naive to assume that accurate statistics derived from large- or small-scale representative sample surveys generally motivate government agencies and campus administrators to devote more resources to the development of prevention and control strategies. Nevertheless, according to Bart et al. (1989), "the principal questions that organize policy efforts are ultimately quantitative—how many are there, who are they, where are they, how bad are the consequences, how much will it cost?" (p. 433). Accurate data can help influence university and college administrators to consider implementing progressive polices and offering more adequate social support services (Currie, 1994; DeKeseredy, 1994; Smith, 1994). Further, once these administrators decide to take action, they will still need to make a number of decisions. As the National Research Council's (1996) Panel on Research on Violence Against Women points out, "Policy decisions—such as how many resources to allocate to service delivery—require solid data about the incidence and prevalence of violence against women" (p. 39). One of the most solid data findings, for example, is that the biggest problem on campus for women is not stranger rape but violence by dates, friends, and acquaintances. The National Research Council, then, suggests that these data should be used by policymakers to divert scarce resources away from programs dealing with stranger attack and toward programs dealing with violence by intimates and acquaintances.

BOX 1.2.

The Sexual Experiences Survey (SES)

The Sexual Experiences Survey (SES) is an important part of this book and will be covered again and again. A brief introduction is in order at this point.

Although Mary Koss used various versions of the SES in earlier work, the most famous use of it was as part of a project known as the Ms. Magazine Campus Project on Sexual Assault, which was funded by the National Institute of Mental Health. In 1985, Mary Koss and her coworkers gathered information from students across the United States, including asking thousands of women 10 questions about various degrees of sexual aggression. These questions asked about the victimization of these women through coercion, threats of bodily harm, advantage taken of a woman who was unable to defend herself, and actual violence.

In repeated administrations of the SES in many forms and places (see, e.g., Schwartz & DeKeseredy, 1997, for a review of its use), the survey has become famous for showing that at least one quarter of college women have been the victims of rape or attempted rape. It has also been the object of extensive attack by backlash critics, as discussed in this book, who worry that the changes in society seemingly called for by such shocking figures would require too much changing.

An example of SES questions, as well as response data, can be found in this book in Table 2.7.

To overcome the methodological limitations of previous North American surveys (especially those described in Table 1.1), to challenge campus administrators' assertion that female students' fear of crime is irrational, and to help people mobilize resources to curb woman abuse in dating, Walter DeKeseredy and Katharine Kelly conducted the CNS, the first national representative sample survey of Canadian university and community college undergraduate students. Shortly after all the data were gathered, several other researchers, including Martin Schwartz, Daniel Saunders, and Shahid Alvi, analyzed and coauthored several publications on the data presented throughout this book. The work of DeKeseredy and Kelly in gathering the data for the CNS, as well as several other major Canadian studies, such as Statistics Canada's national Violence Against Women Survey[7] (VAWS) and Randall and Haskell's (1995) Women's Safety Project, were commissioned and funded by Health Canada's Family Violence Prevention. Additional funding for the CNS was provided by Carleton University's Faculty of Graduate Studies and Research.

The CNS was explicitly designed to do the following:

- Overcome or minimize the limitations of previous North American surveys on woman abuse in dating
- Provide accurate estimates of the extent of male-to-female victimization in Canadian elementary school, high school, and university/college dating
- Compare Canadian national survey data with those generated by U.S. surveys
- Determine the key risk factors associated with woman abuse in Canadian dating
- Identify the contexts, meanings, and motives of female-to-male violence in Canadian postsecondary school courtship
- Test several theories of woman abuse in dating

To meet these key objectives, DeKeseredy, Kelly, and others involved in the development of the CNS used four strategies. It is to the first, preparatory research, that we now turn.

Preparatory Research

Most North American dating abuse surveys have only used either modified versions of the Conflict Tactics Scale (CTS) (Straus, 1979)[8] or the Sexual Experiences Survey (SES) (Koss, Gidycz, & Wisniewski, 1987). There are many advantages to such an approach, such as the fact that the various studies using the same instruments can be easily compared with each other. On the other hand, Sugarman and Hotaling (1989) argue that such an approach fosters "methodological parochialism" because it ignores other valuable means of obtaining data on abusive acts committed by male, heterosexual intimates. Furthermore, the CTS and SES exclude many physically, sexually, and psychologically threatening behaviors.

To develop questions that adequately address the complexities of woman abuse in dating, the CNS research team included a "preparatory component of qualitative investigation" (MacLean, 1996). This involved in-depth interviews with male and female students, members of the Ottawa Regional Coordinating Committee to End Violence Against Women, researchers, friends, family members, and peer counselors. The valuable information provided by these people sensitized the research team to the multifaceted nature of woman abuse in courtship and influenced them to construct several supplementary open- and closed-ended questions that reflect these experiences, such as those described in a subsequent section of this chapter. This preparatory research also contributed to the development of a broad definition of woman abuse. This definition is similar to the one employed in a recent British left-realist local survey on domestic violence in North London (Mooney, 1993a, 1993b).[9]

Broad Definition of Woman Abuse

Most surveys on the "dark side" (often called the hidden side) of heterosexual courtship conceptualize abuse in narrow terms. A review of the literature shows that most researchers use operational definitions that include only one, or sometimes both, of the following behaviors: physical assault and sexual abuse. Psychological or emotional mistreatment (e.g., public humiliation, put-downs, and so on) is typically given short shrift, and thus a substantial number of fear-inducing events are ignored (Schwartz & DeKeseredy, 1991; Smith, 1994).

Some researchers use narrow definitions because they contend that "lumping all forms of malevolence and harm-doing together may muddy the water so much that it might be impossible to determine what causes abuse" (Gelles & Cornell, 1985, p. 23). Others do not examine psychological victimization because they regard it as "soft-core" abuse and argue that researchers who combine "what is debatably abusive with what everyone agrees to be seriously abusive . . . stand to trivialize the latter" (Fox, 1993, p. 322). There are also those who define psychological assaults as either simply "unwanted interactions" (Fekete, 1994) or "early warning signs" of physical and sexual attacks rather than being abusive in and of themselves (e.g., Kelly, 1994).

These viewpoints do not reflect the brutal reality of many women's lives. For example, Kirkwood (1993) found that some of her respondents were drawn into a web of long-term terror through a barrage of psychologically abusive events that many North Americans are likely to term minor. Physical violence might not ever be used on some of these women who were nevertheless severely abused emotionally. In many ways, the actual problem involved is emotional abuse. Anyone who has worked with battered women knows how amazingly strong many of these women are and how little they worry about a few slaps or a punch here and there. However, it is very hard for anyone with feelings to be physically beaten up and not to be simultaneously emotionally battered. Physical battering is emotional battering. Except in the case of those women who are afraid for their lives, it is rare to hear women complain about a black-and-blue mark or pain. Rather, they complain about their terror of being robbed of their lives, their friends, and everything dear to them and their fear for their children. What is rarely recognized out of this is that some men have the power to induce this terror and psychological abuse without ever physically harming the woman. People who work within the criminal justice, medical, and social service communities and even members of the general public too often measure a woman's problems by what has been called the "stitch rule." This wry piece of humor refers to the tendency of most people to judge how badly abused a woman is by how many stitches are needed in the emergency room. The presumption is that a woman who does not need stitches was not abused, which Kirkwood and others have found is simply not the case. A growing number of qualitative studies show that emotional or verbal abuse can be equally or more injurious than physical and sexual victimization (Chang, 1996; DeKeseredy & MacLeod, 1997; Fitzpatrick & Halliday, 1992; MacLeod, 1987; National Research Council, 1996; Walker, 1979).

Researchers have not yet carefully studied and documented all of the ways in which psychological abuse and other types of assault adversely affect female students' academic performance and the quality of their educational experience (Currie & MacLean, 1993). However, it is fair to assume that many survivors of psychological abuse drop out of school, earn low grades, miss classes, or transfer to other institutions (DeKeseredy, 1996b).[10] For example, an emotionally abused first-year U.S. college student, interviewed by Gamache (1991), stated,

Lots of times he told me I deserved it. Most of the time he said that I deserved to be treated that way because I was such a whore, such a bitch and stuff. So he almost gloated. It made him feel really powerful. I started feeling real inadequate. My grades went down dramatically. I missed classes a lot, because I felt sick—stomach stuff, real nervous stuff. I always felt like a nervous wreck. It was probably a deep depression, but I started feeling sleepy all the time, all I wanted to do was stay in bed. It just seemed like everything just kept going down, down, down. (p. 75)

Rather than reproduce definitions that ignore many female students' subjective experiences or create an inaccurate and undesirable "hierarchy of abuse based on seriousness" (Kelly, 1987), the CNS used a broad definition that views any intentional physical, sexual, or psychological assault on a female dating partner as abuse. This definition coincided with many women's real-life experiences and minimizes the problem of underreporting by uncovering high levels of injurious acts (Smith, 1994). However, it should be noted in passing that for descriptive or theoretical purposes, it is occasionally best to conduct separate analyses of abuse types.

Minimizing Underreporting

As Smith (1987) correctly points out, "Obtaining accurate estimates of the extent of woman abuse in the population at large remains perhaps the biggest methodological challenge in survey research on this topic" (p. 185). There are a wide variety of reasons that both abused women and male offenders might not disclose incidents. These include embarrassment, fear of reprisal, "forward and backward telescoping," deception, and memory error (DeKeseredy & MacLean, 1991; Kennedy & Dutton, 1989; Smith, 1987, 1994). Others suggest that underreporting can come from the reluctance or inability to recall traumatic incidents and the belief that violent or psychological assaults are too trivial or inconsequential to mention (Smith, 1994; Straus et al., 1981). Finally, Rae (1995) suggests that many batterers are involved in a complex status process of attempting to remain in control of relationships. They may not be ashamed of their violence because of the pain it caused, but they might be ashamed of the violence because it represents a last-ditch action needed to compensate for their inability to maintain control through the use of masculine authority. The problem is no different when studying abused men or persons abused in gay or lesbian relationships.

These problems are difficult to overcome and are not likely to be eliminated in the near future (DeKeseredy & MacLean, 1991). However, attempts to minimize these sources of underreporting are necessary because of the problems described previously in this chapter (e.g., that campaigns for effective social support services are hindered if surveys show significantly less abuse than is taking place). Therefore, feminist and profeminist researchers have developed several techniques of eliciting more accurate estimates of abuse, such as the multiple measures of abuse included in the CNS instruments. It is to these contributions that we now turn.

Multiple Measures of Abuse

To enhance the reliability and validity of social variables, several methodologists promote the use of multiple measures (Bohrnstedt, 1983; National Research Council, 1996; Smith, 1994). Even so, as noted previously in this chapter, most researchers engaged in courtship surveys disregard this recommendation and only use modified versions of either the CTS or the SES. These are reliable and valid measures (Koss & Gidycz, 1985; Smith, 1987; Straus, 1990a, 1990b), and they are widely used in Canada and the United States. Nevertheless, these measures ignore many injurious acts, such as suffocating, squeezing, stalking, and scratching, and, in the case of the CTS, sexual assault.

Another problem with using only the CTS or the SES is that respondents are not given additional opportunities to disclose abusive experiences. At the outset, people may not report incidents for reasons described previously (e.g., embarrassment, shame, fear of reprisal). However, if respondents are probed later by an interviewer or asked to complete self-report, supplementary, and/or open- and closed-ended questions, some silent or forgetful participants will reveal having been victimized or abusive (DeKeseredy et al., 1992; Hanmer & Saunders, 1984; Junger, 1987, 1990; Kelly, 1988; Roberts, 1989). For example, Smith (1987) found that some silent or forgetful female victims ($N = 60$) changed their answers when asked again in different words by a telephone interviewer. Belated responses increased the overall violence prevalence rate by approximately 10%, and 21 belated disclosures increased the severe violence prevalence rates.[11]

Heavily influenced by Smith (1987) and other advocates of multiple measures, the CNS research team used a modified version of Straus and

Gelles's (1986) CTS, a slightly revised rendition of Koss et al.'s (1987) SES, as well as several supplementary open- and closed-ended questions to minimize underreporting. In the questionnaire administered to men, these questions were modified to elicit accounts of their abusive behaviors.

The first supplementary question focused on the impact of exposure to pornographic media:

> Thinking about your entire university and/or college career, have you ever been upset by dating partners and/or boyfriends trying to get you to do what they had seen in pornographic pictures, movies, or books?[12]

Those who answered "yes" were then asked to respond to the second supplementary question:

> If you were upset, can you tell us what happened? Please provide this information in the space below.

The third supplementary question was located at the end of the questionnaire:[13]

> We really appreciate the time you have taken to complete this survey. And we'd like to assure you that everything you have told us will remain strictly confidential. We realize that the topics covered in this survey are sensitive and that many women are reluctant to talk about their dating experiences. But we're also a bit worried that we haven't asked the right questions.
>
> So now that you have had a chance to think about the topics, have you had any (any other) experiences in which you were physically and/or sexually harmed by your dating partners while you attended college or university? Please provide this information in the space below.

In addition to giving respondents more opportunities to disclose events, supplementary open-ended questions build researcher-respondent rapport. According to Smith (1994),

> For one thing, an open format may reduce the threat of a question on violence, because it allows the respondent to qualify her response, to express exact shades of meaning, rather than forcing her to choose from a number of possibly threatening alternatives. For another, open questions may reduce the power imbalance inherent in the interviewer

situation (the relationship between researcher and researched parallels the hierarchical nature of traditional male-female relationships) because open questions encourage interaction and collaboration between interviewer and respondent. . . . The less threatening the question and the more equal the power relationship, the greater the probability of rapport and, in turn, of eliciting an honest answer to a sensitive question on violence. (p. 115)

Open questions were not the only useful means of obtaining in-depth information on abusive experiences. The same can be said about closed-ended measures of the contexts, meanings, and motives of violence in university and community college courtship.

Context, Meaning, and Motive Measures

As in Canada, dating violence research is a relatively new subject of social scientific inquiry in the United States. Even so, there are at least 30 data sets on either the incidence (events that took place in the year before the study) or prevalence (a much longer time period, such as "ever") of this variant of intimate abuse. Almost all of them have used modified versions of the CTS, which asks a person to report which of a series of reported tactics were used by themselves or a partner during a conflict situation. These tactics could range from pushing and shoving to shooting. Unfortunately, it is rare that a study combines the CTS with any question of meaning, motive, or outcome (e.g., injury). Thus, shoving someone down a flight of stairs or shoving out of the way of someone blocking your escape might be counted as equally violent acts. Being kicked with an open-toed sandal might count equally with having your kneecap shattered by the steel toe on a work boot. Sugarman and Hotaling's (1989) comprehensive review of prevalence studies shows most of them have found that, on average, women report using (with this definition) somewhat higher rates of physical aggression than men (39.3% versus 32.9%). Stets and Henderson's (1991) national survey of "never-married" people between the ages of 18 and 30 produced similar CTS-based results. These CTS data have led many people to conclude that female dating partners are the primary aggressors, or at least relatively equal aggressors. However, CTS data alone provide a "slender basis" for the "sexual symmetry" or "mutual combat" thesis (Dobash, Dobash, Wilson, & Daly, 1992).

For example, the last nine CTS items were designed specifically to measure only the extent of various types of physical violence. Because there is no information on the subject, the answers here can never by themselves help explain why, for example, women assault their male partners (DeKeseredy, 1993). Although CTS data typically show that women hit men as often as men hit women, these findings are not sufficient to demonstrate "sexually symmetrical motivation" (Dobash et al., 1992). There has never been any doubt that some women physically abuse their male dating partners. What is most relevant here is that research specifically on the contexts, meanings, and motives of intimate violence shows that, regardless of their severity, many female-to-male assaults are acts of self-defense (Saunders, 1986, 1988; Schneider & Jordon, 1978).[14] Of course, this presumes that the researcher cares. The National Research Council's (1996) Panel on Research on Violence Against Women points out that one could design research that equates self-defense and aggressive violence, although, because they discuss this in the form of a rhetorical question, it is unclear just what their stance might be on this subject. We will discuss this more later, but data pictures in this area are made more fuzzy by the fact that males are more likely than females to underreport engaging in violence toward their partners (Browne, 1987; DeKeseredy, 1993; Ellis, 1995). This would show more symmetry than actually exists.

A few U.S. surveys have tapped undergraduates' reasons for using dating violence (Bookwala, Frieze, Smith, & Ryan, 1992; Follingstad, Wright, Lloyd, & Sebastian, 1991; Makepeace, 1986). However, prior to the CNS, no comparable Canadian studies were conducted. To fill this research gap and to avoid inaccurate interpretations of CTS violence data, three questions that asked male and female respondents to explain why they used dating violence since leaving high school were included in the CNS's version of the CTS. Developed by Saunders (1986), these questions were asked twice; one set followed the first three violence items and the second set followed the last six violence items. These two groups constitute what Straus et al. (1981) refer to as the "minor violence index" and the "severe violence index."

The responses to the following questions are presented in Chapter 3:

On items . . . what percentage of these times overall do you estimate that in doing these actions you were primarily motivated by acting in self-defence, that is, protecting yourself from immediate physical harm?

TABLE 1.2 Demographic Characteristics of the Sample

Ethnicity	Men (%)	Women (%)
Central American	.2	.1
Scandinavian	1.1	1.0
French Canadian	27.0	22.4
English Canadian	46.0	47.9
British[a]	4.3	5.5
West European[b]	2.9	3.2
East European[c]	2.9	3.2
South European[d]	4.9	5.5
Far Eastern[e]	5.0	5.3
African[f]	1.9	1.6
Caribbean	1.0	1.6
Middle Eastern[g]	1.0	1.4
Latin American	.3	.3
Aboriginal	1.9	1.8
Black	.2	.1
Jewish	.2	.1
Other	1.0	.7
Refugee	1.7	.7
Recent immigrant	4.3	3.8

SOURCE: Adapted slightly from DeKeseredy and Kelly (1993a).
a. Wales, Scotland, Northern Ireland, England.
b. France, Germany, Holland, and so on.
c. Russia, Poland, Baltic States, Hungary, and so on.
d. Italy, Spain, Portugal, Greece, and so on.
e. Japan, China, India, Hong Kong, and so on.
f. North, Central, or South.
g. Israel, Lebanon, Iraq, and so on.

On items . . . what percentage of these overall do you estimate that in doing these actions you were trying to fight back in a situation where you were not the first to use these or similar tactics?

On items . . . what percentage of these times overall do you estimate that you used these actions on your dating partners before they actually attacked or threatened to attack you?

These questions and other CNS methods have several limitations. However, one central finding presented in Chapter 3 continues to stand: Much of the violence by undergraduate women is in self-defense and should not be labeled "mutual combat" or "male partner abuse." Furthermore, in Chapter 3, a profile is provided of the women who are most victimized and most likely to try to defend themselves. The discovery that there are distinctly different groups in terms of their likelihood to use self-defense can be used to guide service programs and future research.

Theory Testing

Most courtship abuse surveys are not designed to test theories (DeKeseredy & Hinch, 1991). Instead, the majority of these studies have focused primarily on the collection of incidence and prevalence data and the discovery of "risk markers" (Hotaling & Sugarman, 1986). A risk marker is any attribute of a couple, victim, or abuser that is associated with an increased probability of abuse (Smith, 1988). It may or may not be a causal variable.

The CNS moved beyond simply trying to identify key risk markers. It was explicitly tailored to test hypotheses derived from several theoretical perspectives, such as DeKeseredy and Schwartz's (1993) male peer support model, radical feminist accounts of women's fear of crime (e.g., Hanmer & Saunders, 1984; Radford, 1987; Stanko, 1987, 1990), and feminist perspectives on the influence of familial patriarchal ideology (Dobash & Dobash, 1979; Millett, 1969; Smith, 1990a). The empirical evaluations of these theories are described in Chapter 4.

Following in the methodological path broken by Smith (1987, 1994), in designing the CNS great care was taken both to implement feminist techniques and to address one of the primary objectives of mainstream survey research: eliciting valid and reliable data from a representative sample. The data analyzed so far and presented throughout this book show that some of the strategies described here enhance the quality of survey data on a sensitive topic. Even so, every study has limitations, and of course, the CNS is no exception. Given time and budget restraints, Walter DeKeseredy, Katharine Kelly, Martin Schwartz, and others involved in the development of this large-scale project (e.g., Health Canada, the Institute for Social Research, and the Ottawa Regional Coordinating Committee to End Violence Against Women) tried to develop a survey that meets the highest disciplinary standards, overcomes the shortcomings of previous dating abuse surveys, and takes feminist concerns seriously. Nevertheless, future survey research on male-to-female victimization in courtship needs to overcome several shortcomings of the

CNS. Before we discuss these limitations, it is first necessary to describe the sample, data collection techniques, and definition and measurement of woman abuse.

Sample and Data Collection

Because the sampling and data collection techniques are described in Appendix A, they will only be briefly discussed here. The data reported in this book are derived from a Canadian national representative sample survey of community college and university students conducted in the autumn of 1992.[15] A research team administered two questionnaires, one for men and another for women, in 95 undergraduate classes across Canada, from the Maritimes to British Columbia. Both French and English language versions were administered. Response rates were very high, with less than 1% of the participants refusing to answer.

The sample consists of 3,142 people, including 1,835 women and 1,307 men. The median age of female respondents is 20, and the median age of males is 21. As described in Table 1.2, although members of many different ethnic groups participated in the CNS, most of the respondents identify themselves as either English Canadian or French Canadian, and the majority of them (81.8% of the men and 77.9% of the women) have never married. All respondents were carefully and repeatedly warned, however, that all questions in the survey referred only to events that took place in dating (nonmarital relationships). The sample is composed mainly of first- and second-year students, and a sizable portion (42.2% of the women and 26.9% of the men) are enrolled in arts programs. Approximately 2% of the women are members of sororities, and 3% of the men belong to fraternities.

Under the research protocol, the Institute for Social Research at York University was contracted to develop a sample design that ensured that students chosen to participate were representative of university and college students across Canada. Within a multistage sampling strategy, specific classes were chosen for participation. Students in these selected classes were asked by a research team member to participate in a study on problems in male-female dating relationships. They were also told that participation was completely voluntary and anonymous, and that all information they provided would be kept strictly confidential. Additionally, students were told that they did not have to answer any question they did not want to and that they could stop filling out the questionnaire at any time. This information was also printed on the cover of the instrument that respondents were asked to read before starting.

Following each administration, debriefings were conducted. These debriefings discussed the objectives of the survey, existing information on the frequency and severity of woman abuse in dating, and the roles that peers play in perpetuating this type of intimate female victimization. All respondents were given a list of local (on- and off-campus) support services for survivors and offenders. Participants were also encouraged to ask the research team questions and to discuss the survey. These debriefing techniques are similar to those used by Koss et al. (1987) in their national sexual assault survey.

Definition and
Measurement of Woman Abuse

A review of the literature reveals that the definition of "woman abuse" is the subject of much debate.[16] The CNS research team, like Straus et al. (1981), were well aware of the fact that "no matter what definition we opted for there seemed to be hundreds of reasons for not using the definition" (p. 20). Nevertheless, a decision had to be made, and as stated previously in this chapter, woman abuse was defined as any physical, sexual, or psychological assault on a female by a male dating partner. The term *abuse* was used instead of terms such as *battering* and *violence* because it implies that women are victims or survivors of a wide range of injurious behaviors in a variety of social contexts (Okun, 1986). Indeed, many studies demonstrated that male-to-female victimization in intimate relationships is "multidimensional in nature" (DeKeseredy & Hinch, 1991).

Again, physical and psychological abuse were measured using a modified rendition of Straus and Gelles's (1986) CTS. Given the sharp attacks on this measure and its many limitations, why did the CNS research team decide to use it? Perhaps the rationale for employing it is best described by Smith (1994), who argues that the attacks on the CTS are

apt but also misplaced. The CTS is not flawed simply because it is unidimensional; rather studies employing the CTS are flawed if they used the CTS as the sole measurement of violence, without any attempt to explore the multidimensionality of violence through other measures. The weakness of such studies is that they *conceptualized* the violence as one-dimensional. (p. 114)

Based on this argument and for reasons described in a previous section of this chapter, we did not rely on the CTS as the only indicator of abuse.

Another key reason for using the CTS is that a paramount concern was determining whether Canadian dating relationships are more or less abusive than those in the United States. For example, because the majority of the surveys of psychological and physical abuse in dating done south of the border used the CTS, it was essential to include it to make adequate comparisons.

The problem of eliciting honest and accurate responses from men also motivated the CNS research team to use the CTS. Indeed, the male incidence and prevalence rates reported in all surveys on female victimization in intimate, heterosexual relationships are underestimates for the reasons described previously, such as social desirability factors. For example, the past 20 years have witnessed a significant increase in public, criminal justice, media, and clinical attention to male-to-female abuse in North America. More people recognize that this type of behavior is unacceptable (Kine, Campbell, & Soler, in press; Straus & Gelles, 1986). Therefore, many men will not reveal their abusive behavior to researchers for fear of stigmatization, even when researchers guarantee anonymity and confidentiality (DeKeseredy, 1988).

The CTS minimizes this problem by presenting the instrument to respondents in the contexts of disagreements and conflicts that "all couples experience," and by categorizing items on a continuum from least to most severe so that tactics least likely to be seen as socially undesirable are presented first (Kennedy & Dutton, 1989). However, in analyzing CTS data, it is incorrect for researchers to assume that this continuum correctly shows abuse severity. The scale may show that a punch is worse than a slap, but a slap can break teeth (Smith, 1987). Further, researchers cited earlier in this chapter found that many women state that psychological mistreatment hurts them more than acts of physical or sexual violence. Thus, one must be especially careful not to presume that what we have called the "stitch rule" of woman abuse is being used: "If she didn't need stitches, she was not hurt."

The CTS used in this study was introduced as follows:

We are particularly interested in learning more about your dating relationships. No matter how well a dating couple gets along, there are times when they disagree, get annoyed with the other person, or just have spats or fights because they're in a bad mood or tired or for some other reason. They also use many different ways to settle their differences. Below is a list of some things that you might have done to your girlfriends and/or dating partners in these circumstances. Please circle the number which best represents your answer in each of the following situations. Please note that the items are repeated twice. The first set is for the past 12 months; the second set covers all of your experiences since you left high school.

IF YOU ARE OR HAVE BEEN MARRIED, PLEASE NOTE THAT THESE QUESTIONS REFER ONLY TO DATING RELATIONSHIPS.

Sexual abuse was operationalized using a slightly reworded version of Koss et al.'s (1987) SES and some supplementary open- and closed-ended questions. The 10 items in the CNS version of the SES can be examined both in their totality and as subdivided into four types of sexual abuse: unwanted sexual contact, sexual coercion, attempted rape, and rape. Widely used in Canada and the United States, the SES is a reliable and valid measure (Koss & Gidycz, 1985).

The Limitations of the CNS and
Suggestions for Further Empirical Work

Unfortunately, one survey cannot answer everyone's scientific concerns, and thus a long list of methodological improvements could easily be described here. Indeed, several prominent survey researchers have published articles, book chapters, and books on the issue of enhancing the quality of survey data on woman abuse (e.g., DeKeseredy, 1997; Koss, 1993; Schwartz, 1997; Smith, 1994). We will focus mainly on two key concerns typically ignored by most of the previous surveys on postsecondary school dating abuse: racial/ethnic participation and psychological abuse.

Racial/Ethnic Participation

Racial and ethnic experiences are generally missing from data elicited from undergraduate students because most North American surveys, including the CNS, include only or mainly white students (DeMaris, 1990). Consider the racial/ethnic data presented in Table 1.2. This table shows that of the 3,142 people who participated in the CNS, most identified themselves as either English Canadian or French Canadian. Given that this table also reflects the proportion of minority students attending college or university in Canada, it is obvious that these communities make up a small percentage of the somewhat elite status of "college student." Perhaps the reason for this is that many members of visible minority groups cannot afford to go to a college or university. Thus, their experiences are excluded because of their low socioeconomic status rather than racist empirical techniques (Ellis & DeKeseredy, 1996). It has been suggested that in "open admission" environments, foreign students with limited skills in either English or French might have trouble filling out complex questionnaires, and that this would further limit the number of visible minorities in the final sample.

According to Jones, MacLean, and Young (1986), normal sampling techniques will not, in an atmosphere such as those on most college campuses, generate a sufficient number of ethnic minorities to allow for a complex, multivariate analysis of the patterns of woman abuse. To overcome this problem, Jones and his colleagues oversampled Asian and Afro-Caribbean people who lived in the London Borough of Islington. Similarly, North American researchers should develop ethnic minority "booster samples" of university and college students (Jones et al., 1986). If the problem is, for example, a lack of representation from the foreign community, this goal could be achieved by contacting campus officials for lists of foreign students and those who have difficulty speaking either English or French.

In very specific situations, where there are obviously a large number of students who speak a language other than English or French, it will be necessary to translate questionnaires. This procedure is costly, but it can minimize underreporting. For example, although not on a college campus, a substantial number of Italian women refused to be interviewed in Smith's (1986) first woman abuse survey because they claimed that his questions were unintelligible (Northrup, 1985). In response to this problem, Smith (1987) used a translated instrument in his second survey, and this approach resulted in "a somewhat improved response rate." Unfortunately, he does not state the degree of improvement.

Enhancing the Quality of Survey Data
on Psychological Abuse

In another important area, more reliable measures of psychological abuse are needed (Kasian & Painter, 1992). In fact, very little work has been devoted to operationalizing psychological mistreatment in courtship of any kind (Sugarman & Hotaling, 1989). To fill this research gap, the coinvestigators of the CNS, Walter DeKeseredy and Katharine Kelly (1993a, 1993b), added a six-item index. Four items were taken directly from the CTS and two were used by Statistics Canada in their pretest for the national Violence Against Women Survey.

Male respondents were asked to report how many times they engaged in the following behaviors, and female participants were asked to state the number of times they were victimized by these acts:

- Insults or swearing
- Put her (you) down in front of friends or family
- Accused her (you) of having affairs or flirting with other men
- Did or said something to spite her (you)
- Threatened to hit or throw something at her (you)
- Threw, smashed, or kicked something

Despite strong evidence of concurrent validity and internal consistency (Straus, 1990a, 1990b), the above index is viewed by some critics as an ambiguous or invalid measure of psychological abuse because it does not clearly reveal whether female respondents regard the six items as injurious (Fox, 1993; Gartner, 1993). For example, in response to DeKeseredy and Kelly's (1993a) interpretation of the psychological abuse incidence and prevalence data described in Chapter 2, Gartner (1993) contended that "apparently, their judgment, as researchers, as to what constitutes abuse is more valid than judgments based on the lived experiences of their respondents" (p. 315).

Although CNS data do not show that most of the female participants perceive insults, swearing, put-downs, and the like to be painful, Gartner and Fox have no way of showing that they do not. As Straus (1990b) points out in response to critics of the CTS, perhaps in-depth qualitative research can help provide more accurate data on the outcomes of psychological abuse. This does not mean that quantitative researchers should not attempt to measure psychological abuse in future surveys, because there are reliable means of eliciting such data.

For example, to measure the extent of psychological abuse in university dating relationships, Kasian and Painter (1992) administered a modified version of Tolman's (1989) Psychological Maltreatment of Women Inventory (PMWI) to 1,625 (868 females and 757 males) introductory psychology students. Their results show that this 40-item measure is useful in identifying those who psychologically abuse their dating partners. Examples of Kasian and Painter's PMWI items are as follows:

- My partner tried to turn my friends and family against me.
- My partner blamed me for his violent behavior.
- My partner blamed me when upset even if I had nothing to do with it.
- My partner treated me like his personal servant.
- My partner insulted or shamed me in front of others.
- My partner monitored my time and made me account for my whereabouts.

Additional Limitations of the CNS

In addition to providing some problematic psychological abuse data and inadequate information on the injurious experiences of members of various ethnic/racial groups, the CNS suffers from several other limitations. For example, despite attempts to minimize or overcome under-reporting, because (for ethical reasons) the CNS was announced to each class at some date prior to the administration of the questionnaires, an unknown number of students may have "skipped class" to avoid "potential embarrassment, guilt, shame or other reactions that might arise from questions dealing with the sensitive topic of dating violence or from prior unpleasant events in the individual's life" (Hay, 1993, p. 59). Other students, regardless of whether they had abusive dating experiences, may not have participated in the CNS because they did not attend class that day, whether for good or bad reasons.

Last, but certainly not least, like many other quantitative woman abuse surveys, the CNS cannot tell us much about the following issues:[17]

- The many and diverse survival strategies women use to cope with or escape abusive dating relationships.
- Why men join and stay with male peer groups that perpetuate and legitimate woman abuse in dating.
- The long-term psychological and physical damage caused by abuse (Kirkwood, 1993).

- Discrete and often overlapping abusive events that take place over a long period of time (Dobash & Dobash, 1992).
- The many and complex ways in which broader social forces (e.g., patriarchy and capitalism) influence men to victimize women.
- The subtle and overt types of abuse women experience in dating relationships (Hippensteele, Chesney-Lind, & Veniegas, 1993).

Innovative ways of overcoming or minimizing these and other limitations of the CNS and other woman abuse surveys are necessary given that woman abuse in dating is a "never-ending and constantly evolving issue" (Ledwitz-Rigby, 1993, p. 93). It should also be noted that, regardless of the methods used, survey researchers will always have to face the fact that some respondents simply refuse to disclose abusive experiences (Smith, 1994). Perfect woman abuse surveys are not possible (Babbie, 1973), but good ones can and should be done (Hay, 1993). The methods used in the CNS constitute an important step toward achieving this goal.

Chapter Summary

Contrary to popular belief, North American universities and colleges are not "ivory towers" or "havens in a heartless world" (Lasch, 1977). Rather, they are mirrors of the role of men and women in broader society (Schuman & Olufs, 1995). Indeed, if women hold unequal status in the paid workforce and in marital/cohabiting relationships, the same can be said about their status on campus. For example, a large empirical literature shows that females are less valued by many professors, are given less attention in lecture halls and seminars, and their experiences and achievements are largely left out of curriculum material or are treated in a sexist fashion (Reynolds, 1995). Furthermore, men and women are taught a "hidden curriculum," one that perpetuates and legitimates woman abuse, which is a terrifying symptom of gender inequality. In a society characterized by gross gender inequality, this is not surprising because patriarchal beliefs, attitudes, and behaviors are bound to spill over into postsecondary schools.

According to Henslin and Nelson (1996), "The first criterion for a good education is security, to guarantee students' physical safety and freedom from fear" (p. 498). Unfortunately, like their U.S. counterparts, the studies presented in Table 1.1 show Canadian universities and colleges have done little, if anything, to meet this criterion. Nevertheless, because the data generated by these surveys are gleaned from nonprobability samples, they are only suggestive of the incidence and prevalence of woman abuse in the Canadian postsecondary student population at large (DeKeseredy & Kelly, 1993a). Consequently, many campus administrators, criminal justice officials, and members of the general population claimed that they were unreliable.

The CNS was developed and administered in response to the need for more accurate survey data on woman abuse in university and community college courtship. An equally, if not more, important objective was to collect representative sample survey data that have a high probability of mobilizing resources to curb *all* forms of abuse in university and college dating. The results presented throughout this book challenge the popular notion of Canada as a "peaceable kingdom" and show that various forms of woman abuse are quite common in campus dating. Furthermore, a comparison of the incidence and prevalence data presented in Chapter 2 with those generated by Koss et al.'s (1987) national U.S. data and estimates reviewed by Sugarman and Hotaling (1989) show that the problem of male-to-female victimization in courtship is just as serious in Canada as it is in the United States.

Although the Canadian federal government did not respond to the data presented in this book by creating new legislation or allocating more funds to make female undergraduates' lives safer (MacIvor, 1995), we believe that the CNS has shown many doubtful people that a large number of women in university and college dating relationships "suffer in silence" (Pizzey, 1974). Moreover, the results of this study have raised the level of public awareness about courtship abuse and support Renzetti's (1995) assertion that "the experience of violent intrusion—or the threat of such intrusion—is a common thread in the fabric of women's everyday lives" (p. 3).

Notes

1. These were sexual assault studies conducted by Kanin (1957, 1967a, 1967b, 1969) and Kirkpatrick and Kanin (1957).
2. See Currie and MacLean (1993), Ellis and DeKeseredy (1996), and Pirog-Good and Stets (1989) for comprehensive reviews of U.S. survey data on woman abuse in postsecondary school courtship.

3. See DeKeseredy and Hinch (1991), DeKeseredy and MacLeod (1997), Ellis and DeKeseredy (1996), and Ellis and Stuckless (1996) for reviews of these studies.

4. This is a slightly modified version of a table constructed by DeKeseredy and Kelly (1993a).

5. The forum was cosponsored by the Ontario Ministries of Correctional Services and Community and Social Services, and the Ontario Women's Directorate. The published proceedings can be obtained by writing to Ontario Women's Directorate, Wife Assault Prevention Unit, 12th Floor, 2 Carleton Street, Toronto, Ontario, Canada, M5B 2M9.

6. See Renzetti (1992) for a rich study and in-depth review of the social scientific literature on partner abuse in lesbian relationships.

7. See the *Canadian Journal of Criminology* (Vol. 37, No. 3, 1995) and Johnson (1996) for data uncovered by this survey.

8. See Breines and Gordon (1983), DeKeseredy and MacLean (1990), and Dobash et al. (1992) for detailed critiques of the CTS.

9. Left realism is one of the most important new developments in critical criminology. See DeKeseredy and Schwartz (1991a, 1991b), Lea and Young (1984), Lowman and MacLean (1992), MacLean and Milovanovic (1991), and Schwartz and DeKeseredy (1991) for the history and major principles of this school of thought.

10. Bohmer and Parrot (1993) found that many sexual assault survivors dropped out of college or transferred to other schools.

11. Smith defined *prevalence* as the percentage of women who reported ever having been physically abused.

12. This is a modified version of a question developed by Russell (1982).

13. This is a modified version of one of Smith's (1987) supplementary questions.

14. See DeKeseredy, Saunders, Schwartz, and Alvi (1997), Dobash et al. (1992), and Schwartz and DeKeseredy (1993) for comprehensive reviews of these studies.

15. See Pollard (1993) for more details on the sampling procedure and other technical aspects of the CNS, or Appendix A in this volume.

16. See DeKeseredy and Hinch (1991), DeKeseredy and MacLeod (1997), and Ellis and DeKeseredy (1996) for comprehensive reviews of the major debates surrounding definitions of woman abuse.

17. This list was compiled by DeKeseredy and MacLeod (1997).

2

The Incidence and Prevalence of Woman Abuse in Canadian Courtship

I went to the drive-through window at the bank to cash a check and he followed me in his car. He got out and started telling me what a cunt I was and how nobody would ever love me. I was really embarrassed. Everyone was watching me through the bank window. When they sent my money out, he took it and my driver's license. We argued, and he called me names. I grabbed my driver's license as he started to crack it, and I turned to run. He grabbed me by the hair and slammed my head into the top of his car. A bunch of my hair ripped out. I fell back against the car. Everything was blurry. He shook me, saying, "Why do you make me hurt you." (Stone, 1991, p. 30)

Each of us has been extensively involved in the profeminist male movement on woman abuse for many years, both as activists and as scholars. Having written more than two dozen pieces on courtship violence, together and separately, we view some of the research presented in this chapter as a logical extension of our evolving views that students do not come to college or universities as "clean slates" but, too often, as highly experienced abusers of females. For example, the vicious and extremely injurious behaviors described in the quote above were committed by a high school student.

The word *evolving* is important because, prior to analyzing data generated by the CNS, most of our theoretical and empirical work was in the area of male peer support for woman abuse among college-aged men.[1] We originally (as does much of the literature) saw certain college institutions as key factors in the development of such abuse. However, we heard from many people interested in the topics addressed in this book—students, parents, colleagues, and others—who suggested that proabuse attitudes start much earlier than college.

For example, it was a subject of great derision and joking that in 1996 two elementary school boys were in trouble for allegedly sexually harassing their female schoolmates. It was an illegitimate use of the legal system to deal with the typical boyhood behavior of children, the argument generally went. Now, we have no facts on the specifics of these cases, and an argument can certainly be made that there are other venues than the courtroom to deal with these problems. However, the real problem was the ready tendency to dismiss the seriousness of such events simply because the participants were children.

It is interesting that people seem to think that most views are rooted in childhood behavior, but have a blind eye when it comes to violence against women. We force children to go to church and Bible study against their will, so that they will learn the habit early. We do what we can to make them respect their elders, keep their language clean, study hard, and in general start to develop the habits we wish to see in them as adults. When they beat up girls, denigrate them, devalue them, make fun of them, exclude them, make them cry, play pranks on them, scare them, and chase them home, however, they are just boys being boys. Why is it that we would not assume that boys would learn lessons from their own behaviors?

These behaviors may even be taught to little boys. Gary Alan Fine (1987), for example, studied Little League baseball and found that this organization was particularly detrimental to boys who might wish to develop normal relations with girls. To be less than a star was to be like a girl. Actually, quite a number of approved organizations and outlets provide the same messages: Men must be sexually aggressive, girls love it that way; boys cannot show emotion; any failure (especially at sports) is girl-like, if not homosexual. The media generally, the military, a wide variety of sports outlets, and even a great number of parents pass on these messages. Mariah Burton Nelson (1994) points out that a large number of coaches make fun of athletes who may not have performed at the approved level of aggression by putting bras, tampons, or sanitary napkins in their lockers. What is it about not only colleges but society in general that would demand a coach be fired immediately for using the word *nigger* but allows coaches across the country to refer regularly to their male players as *cunts?* What does it tell us about our attitudes about women and girls?

What we then find is that boys do engage in sexual harassment of girls from a very early age, certainly starting in elementary school. It may start as gender harassment (nothing sexual about it, just constant harassment of girls), combined with the lessons boys are learning long before they get out of elementary school about the importance of avoiding close relationships with girls and about portraying oneself as sexually aggressive.

Thus, in addition to presenting data on the incidence and prevalence of woman abuse in Canadian college and university courtship in this chapter, we present data showing that identified woman abuse in college relationships has some roots in earlier dating relationships.

Locating a History of Some Canadian Woman Abuse in Elementary and High School Dating Relationships

Again, woman abuse in dating does not start only after high school. In some ways, few people have argued this specific point. However, most of the literature on the subject takes this view. The most reprinted articles in the field are those that suggest that fraternities and sports teams are to blame for campus sexual assault. Presumably, if fraternities and sports teams are to blame, then in the absence of these organizations, campus sexual assault would not take place or would not be as widespread. The opposite argument is that high school boys can be as violent or more than college men and may in fact be headed off to college looking for mechanisms that will facilitate their abusive behaviors. As pointed out in our earlier work (see Schwartz & DeKeseredy, 1997), momma's perfectly innocent little altar boys don't go to college and just happen to come under the influence of aggressive fraternity men, who teach these new students a brand-new set of college values based on the exploitation and victimization of women. For example, in Rae's (1995) study, a middle school boy told her what society had taught him: "One of the big messages, [and] I don't think it's a visible message, like nobody gets up and *says* it, is that men rule and all men are leaders and men have to be violent, like soldiers and stuff" (p. 70).

What several small-scale surveys, summarized in Table 2.1, show is that many Canadian men while in high school have also physically, sexually, and psychologically abused their female dating partners. Moreover, the patterns usually associated with wife abuse appear in high school dating relationships, and often for similar reasons. For example, Mercer (1988) argues that there is great pressure among adolescent girls to "get" a boyfriend. These girls often internalize ideologies that assign relationships as "women's work" and blame women for the failures of men. Thus, it is understandable that there are many young women who are under intense pressure to "think positively and to forgive him," even if he is physically violent. Still, while we knew much about such behavior locally, there were no national estimates of the extent of such behavior either in Canada or in the United States.

So far we have talked about the need for national high school data. The same can be said about reliable estimates of the extent of woman abuse in North American elementary and middle school dating relationships (grades 1 to 8). Because many elementary school girls date heterosexual boys (Holmes & Silverman, 1992), albeit to a much lesser extent than their high school and college counterparts, it is fair to hypothesize that some of them are abused. Even at young ages, boys have been found to have developed strong masculinist and pro-woman abuse attitudes (Connell, 1995; Hobbs, 1994). They are heavily influenced by the ideology of familial patriarchy, which has been found to be a key determinant of woman abuse in later dating contexts. According to Mercer (1988),

> Adolescence is clearly not a period when young people reject the traditional gender roles for which they have been groomed. It is characteristically a time when they act them out—sometimes to their worst extremes. The alarming revelations about this process testify to the grave personal implications that male power has for females long before they become adults. (p. 16)

For example, Davis, Peck, and Storment (1993) found that 60% of surveyed high school boys approved of forcing sexual activities on a girl at least in some circumstances. Unfortunately, one of the disadvantages of this sort of research is that it does not let us know for sure whether those who hold such attitudes would ever act them out. One of the problems of much experimental research into such things as the effect of

TABLE 2.1 Description of Surveys of Woman Abuse in Canadian High School Dating

Survey	Survey Location	Sample Description	Interview Mode	Prevalence Rates
Mercer (1988)	4 metropolitan Toronto high schools	217 female and 87 male high school students	Self-administered questionnaires	Of the total number of female respondents, 11% stated that they were physically abused, 17% reported having been verbally abused, and 20% disclosed having been sexually abused
Jaffe, Sudermann, Reitzel, and Killip (1992)	4 London, Ontario, high schools	358 female and 379 male high school students	Self-administered questionnaires	23.6% of the females and 16.4% of the males experienced verbal abuse[a]
Sudermann and Jaffe (1993)	2 London, Ontario, high schools	790 female and 757 male high school students	Self-administered questionnaires	Of the female respondents, 44.5% stated that they experienced verbal abuse, 13.5% disclosed experiencing physical abuse, and 14.2% indicated having experienced sexual abuse; 25.2% of the males reported having experienced verbal abuse, 4.4% disclosed experiencing physical abuse, and 3.7% stated that they experienced sexual abuse[a]

a. There is no way of determining how many of these respondents were victims or offenders because they were not asked to provide such information. Rather, they were only asked to disclose having "experienced" abuse.

39

pornography on behavior is that we do not know whether these attitudes ever leave the laboratory settings (Schwartz, 1987).

Still, there is a great deal of reason to worry about such findings. First, some unknown number of these boys might indeed be currently engaging in forcing girls into sexual activity. Or they might be willing under certain future circumstances to force a woman physically. Second, boys who hold these attitudes often provide the atmosphere that encourages and gives permission to others to engage in sexual aggression, even if they themselves never move beyond verbal support for such behavior (Schwartz & DeKeseredy, 1997).

Some researchers have commented that the injurious behaviors described here as taking place in elementary and high school dating relationships will continue in subsequent intimate relationships (Girshick, 1993; Roscoe & Callahan, 1985). However, such conclusions have been based on comparing completely different college and high school samples. This means that the data are not directly relevant to their arguments. Using CNS data, we tried to overcome this and other methodological problems related to empirical work on woman abuse in elementary and high school courtship. Before we describe our findings, however, it is first necessary to discuss the ways in which the CNS generated these data.

Definition and Measurement of Woman Abuse in Elementary and High School Courtship

As pointed out in Chapter 1, the CNS used a broad definition of woman abuse, one that refers to this problem as any intentional, physical, or psychological assault on a female by a male dating partner. Four measures were used to measure the prevalence of this problem in elementary school courtship (grades 1 to 8), and different wording was used for male and female respondents. For example, men were asked to report their abusive behavior, while women were asked to disclose victimization. Below are the female questions; for each one, respondents were asked to circle "yes" or "no":

In elementary school, did a male dating partner and/or boyfriend ever . . .

- threaten to use physical force to make you engage in sexual activities?

- use physical force in an attempt to make you engage in sexual activities, whether this attempt was successful or not?
- intentionally emotionally hurt you (i.e., insult, say something to spite you)?
- intentionally physically hurt you?

The same questions were asked about woman abuse in secondary school courtship, except the words "high school (grades 9 to 13)" were included in the preamble.

Abuse that occurred in college and university dating relationships was measured through the use of modified relevant questions from Koss et al.'s (1987) Sexual Experiences Survey and Straus and Gelles's (1986) Conflict Tactics Scale. The items included in these measures are described later in this chapter.

Results

The Prevalence of Woman Abuse in
Elementary School Courtship

Of the men who answered the elementary school questions (and said that they dated before the ninth grade),

- 1.7% ($N = 12$) stated that they threatened to physically force their partners to engage in sexual activities,
- 1.5% ($N = 11$) disclosed having physically forced women to engage in sexual activities,
- 18.6% ($N = 133$) reported having been emotionally abusive, and
- 3.6% ($N = 26$) admitted to having been physically abusive.

As we anticipated, women reported rather higher rates of victimization:

- 3% ($N = 25$) stated that their partners threatened to physically force them to engage in sexual activities,
- 4.3% ($N = 36$) revealed that they were physically forced to engage in sexual acts,
- 23.7% ($N = 198$) said their partners emotionally hurt them, and
- 7.2% ($N = 60$) disclosed having been physically hurt.

Are Canadian women more likely to be abused in elementary school courtship than their U.S. counterparts? Unfortunately, because the above findings are, to the best of our knowledge, the first of their kind, this question cannot be answered. However, some Canadian-U.S. comparisons can be made with the figures described below.

The Prevalence of Woman Abuse in High School Courtship

Given that high school students spend more time dating than those in elementary school, we anticipated higher rates of disclosure from both men and women because they spend greater "time at risk" of abuse (Ellis & DeKeseredy, 1996). For the women, 89% said they dated in high school, while 38.2% said they dated in elementary school. For the men, the equivalent figures are 87.1% in high school and 48.3% in elementary school. However, this increased rate in dating did not result in an increased rate of self-reported abuse, except for an 80% increase in reported emotional abuse:

- 1% ($N = 11$) stated that they threatened to use physical force to make their partners engage in sexual activities,
- 2.3% ($N = 25$) reported having used physical force to make women engage in sexual activities,
- 33.4% ($N = 362$) disclosed having emotionally hurt their dates, and
- 1.4% ($N = 15$) admitted to having physically hurt their dates.

On the other hand, all of the estimates from females support the hypothesis that the more time at risk, the more likely women were to have been the objects of violence in dating in high school. In the first three questions, the high school rates are significantly higher than the elementary school rates, while the rate is slightly higher in the fourth area (physical harm):

- 8.3% ($N = 131$) stated that their partners threatened to physically force them to engage in sexual activities,
- 14.5% ($N = 228$) revealed that their dates physically forced them to engage in sex acts,
- 49.7% ($N = 780$) reported having been emotionally hurt, and
- 9.1% ($N = 143$) stated that their partners physically hurt them.

Table 2.2 shows that the above statistics are markedly lower than the U.S. physical and sexual violence data uncovered by Bergman (1992)—although her questions are much broader in their scope—and approximate those generated by Henton, Cate, Koval, Lloyd, and Christopher (1983). Comparisons with Roscoe and Callahan's (1985) U.S. study cannot be made because the authors do not present data on gender variations in acts committed by and against men and women.

Trying to make comparisons of these findings with previous U.S. and Canadian high school prevalence data is problematic for at least three reasons. First, different measures of abuse were used. This actually makes it almost impossible to compare statistics from study to study. For example, U.S. researchers Henton et al. (1983) and Roscoe and Callahan (1985) used modified versions of Straus's (1979) Conflict Tactics Scale. Another U.S. scholar, Bergman (1992), employed four closed-ended questions that are more specific but broader in scope than those used in the CNS,[2] and she used one open-ended question. Second, the samples in the studies reviewed in Tables 2.1 and 2.2 are all local, rather than being national, representative samples. Further, the questions are less well crafted than those used in the study described in this book. Finally, because all of the participants described in the other studies summarized in Tables 2.1 and 2.2 were not told to focus only on heterosexual dating abuse, it is possible that a considerable number of them reported acts that occurred in gay or lesbian relationships. This is not to discount the harm from these abusive acts but only to point out that the studies may be measuring different things.

Although they involve different samples and measures, three previous Canadian surveys on high school abuse have been conducted (see Table 2.1). It is difficult to compare our CNS findings to any of the three. First of all, the other studies ask questions directly of high school students. Later, we will discuss the methodological advantages and disadvantages of this approach, but here it is important to note that the CNS asked university and community college students about their experiences in high school. Obviously, then, students who did not go on to tertiary education are eliminated from the CNS sampling frame.

Jaffe et al. (1992) did not ask respondents to report whether they were victimized by or engaged in physically or sexually abusive behaviors, and Sudermann and Jaffe (1993) only asked high school students to indicate whether they had "experienced" these two types of behaviors and verbal or emotional abuse, leaving open the possibility for each individual respondent that they were *either* an offender or a victim. Jaffe

TABLE 2.2 Description of Surveys of Woman Abuse in U.S. High School Dating

Survey	Survey Location	Sample Description	Interview Mode	Prevalence Rates
Henton, Cate, Koval, Lloyd, and Christopher (1983)	5 Oregon high schools	351 male and 293 female high school students	Self-administered questionnaires	Of all respondents, 12.1% reported that they were involved in a violent dating relationship. In 71.4% of the violent relationships, each partner had been both a victim and an offender at some point in time. Of the remaining 28.6% of those involved in violent relationships, 12.9% were victimized women, 1.4% were male offenders, 8.6% were male victims, and 5.7% were female abusers.[a]
Roscoe and Callahan (1985)	1 midwestern senior high school	96 male and 108 female high school students	Self-administered questionnaires	Of all participants, 9% stated that they experienced violence in a dating relationship: 5% disclosed having been violent to a dating partner and 4% stated that they had been in a relationship in which both partners were violent to each other. Females were more likely (65%) to experience violence than were males (35%),[b] and females were more likely to be victims of violence.[c]
Bergman (1992)	3 midwestern high schools	337 female and 294 male high school students	Self-administered questionnaires	15.7% of the girls and 4.4% of the boys stated that they were victims of sexual violence; 15.7% of the girls and 7.8% of the boys disclosed having been victimized by physical violence; 24.6% of females and 9.9% of the males stated that they were targets of "severe violence" (a combined category of sexual and physical violence); 32% of the females and 23.5% of the males reported being victimized by any violence (verbal, sexual, and physical violence).

a. It is unclear whether these women acted in self-defense or out of fear of being attacked.
b. The researchers do not define the term *experience*; therefore, it is unclear whether they are referring to offenders, victims, or both.
c. The researchers do not present data in support of this assertion.

et al. (1992), however, did ask their respondents if they used "verbal force" on a dating partner and if their dating partners had victimized them in such a way. A substantially lower number of their male respondents (14.1%) reported using verbal force, and a much smaller number of women reported being victimized by this conduct (23.6%).

It is unclear how Mercer (1988) measures abuse because she does not report her questions. Even so, a review of her findings described in Table 2.1 reveals the following differences:

- A markedly higher percentage of her high school male respondents admit to having been sexually abusive (12%), while 16.4% of CNS female respondents report being sexually abused in high school, a bit lower than Mercer's 20%.
- Mercer's male and female physical abuse figures are very similar to those produced by the CNS.
- CNS male (33.3%) and female (49.7%) psychological abuse self-reports are markedly higher than Mercer's (17% male, 13% female). This could be because she seems to have limited psychological abuse to something called "verbal" abuse, although we cannot be sure because the question is not reported or discussed by Mercer.

The Relationship Between Postsecondary School Dating Abuse and Elementary and Secondary School Dating Abuse

Although the number of men who admit to the physical, sexual, and psychological victimization of women in elementary and high school dating is fairly small, it is large enough for us at least to look to see if these are the same people who admit to similar victimization in college and university dating relationships. In other words, do men establish these patterns early? Do men begin patterns of victimization in elementary and high school and bring them to college?

Additional measures. To speak to these questions, we must first explain how the questions asked about college and university experiences differed from those explained above that discussed elementary and high school experiences. Because the main purpose of the CNS was to obtain data on postsecondary dating experiences, the questions here are deeper and more complex.

For reasons described in Chapter 1, physical and psychological abuse were measured using a modified version of Straus and Gelles's (1986)

Conflict Tactics Scale (CTS). The psychological abuse component of the CTS consisted of six items, four of which are part of the Straus and Gelles verbal aggression subscale: "insulted or swore at her"; "did or said something to spite her"; "threatened to hit or throw something at her"; and "threw, smashed, or kicked something." Two new items were added to this subscale that were used in Statistics Canada's pretest for the national Violence Against Women Survey.[3] These measures are "put her down in front of friends and family" and "accused her of having affairs or flirting with other men." Previous research shows that these items are related to male-to-female violence in marital contexts (Smith, 1990a), so there was some reason to investigate whether they were also related to such violence in dating violence.

The physical abuse component of the CTS consisted of nine items used by Straus and Gelles: "threw something at her"; "grabbed or shoved her"; "slapped her"; "kicked, bit, or hit her with your fist"; "hit or tried to hit her with something"; "beat her up"; "choked her"; "threatened her with a knife or a gun"; and "used a knife or a gun on her." The last six items in this subscale constitute Straus et al.'s (1981) operational definition of "severe violence."

It should be noted in passing that one version of the CTS used in the CNS, including the preamble described in Chapter 1, was tailored to elicit women's reports of their victimization, and the other was designed to elicit men's accounts of their abusive behavior. In other words, different wording was used for male and female respondents.

Sexual abuse was operationalized using a slightly reworded version of Koss et al.'s (1987) Sexual Experiences Survey (SES), and different wording was used for male and female respondents (e.g., men were asked to report abusive behavior and women were asked about their victimization). In designing the CNS, Walter DeKeseredy and Katharine Kelly chose the SES because it has been used widely in the field as a standard instrument for sexual victimization on campus both in the United States and in Canada. The 10 items in the CNS version of the SES can be examined in their totality, for one measure of sexual abuse. Or, following Koss et al. (1987), they can be subdivided into four types of sexual abuse:

- *Sexual contact* includes unwanted sex play (fondling, kissing, or petting) arising from menacing verbal pressure, misuse of authority, threats of harm, or actual physical force.
- *Sexual coercion* includes unwanted sexual intercourse arising from the use of menacing verbal pressure or the misuse of authority.

- *Attempted rape* includes attempted unwanted sexual intercourse arising from the use of or threats of force or from the use of drugs or alcohol.
- *Rape* includes unwanted sexual intercourse arising from the use of or threats of force and other unwanted sex acts (anal or oral intercourse or penetration by objects other than the penis) arising from the use of or threat of force or from the use of drugs or alcohol.

Making the comparison. There are some indicators that a pattern exists showing that men who are admitted victimizers often have some earlier experience as precollege victimizers in each of the three areas of physical, sexual, and emotional abuse.[4] Table 2.3 and subsequent tables only look at that part of the sample that began dating in elementary school, because that is the group relevant to the question being discussed here. Although most physical abuse obviously takes place after high school, of the 31 men who claim that they were intentionally physically abusive in elementary and high school dating relationships, 17 (54.8%) also admit to similar acts after high school. Earlier, we had predicted that the increased rate of dating in college and university life would increase the time at risk for being abusive. On the other hand, it is worth pointing out that two thirds of these men were in the autumn term of their first year (39.2%) or second year (27.9%) at the time of the survey. Thus, the time at risk as college or university students (measured in months) is not very long for some of these students.

A similar pattern can be seen in Table 2.4 with the small number of men who admit the use of force to make a dating partner engage in sexual activities. When those who admit to using such force in high school and/or elementary school are compared with those who admit to using such force after high school, 8 (32%) of the 25 elementary and/or high school admitters also disclose similar forced sexual behavior in college. If one takes a retrospective look, 8 (34.85%) of the 23 men who admit to using force in college also admit to having used it in the elementary and/or high school dating relationships.

Finally, Table 2.5 shows the strongest pattern, and the one where the admitted behavior of male offenders most approximates the reported victimization of women. A bit less than half of all the men (48.1%) admit to abusing women emotionally in any of the ways covered by the survey questions. However, virtually all of the men who admit such abuse in elementary and high school also admit similar abuse after high school (96.1%). Perhaps most interesting of all, especially considering that a strong majority of the men are first- and second-year students, is that

TABLE 2.3 Physical Abuse: Comparison of Precollege With College Men

		Admitted Abuse Precollege	
		yes	no
Admitted Abuse After High School	yes	17 54.8%	109 17.4%
	no	14 45.2%	516 82.6%
	Total	31 100%	625 100%

NOTE: χ^2 = 26.62; df = 1; p = .0000; phi = .201; gamma = .704.

TABLE 2.4 Sexual Abuse: Comparison of Precollege With College Men

		Admitted Abuse Precollege	
		yes	no
Admitted Abuse After High School	yes	8 32%	15 2.4%
	no	17 68%	607 97.6%
	Total	25 100%	622 100%

NOTE: χ^2 = 61.37; df = 1; p = .0000; phi = .308; gamma = .900.

85.3% of all the men who had dated since elementary school admit being emotional abusers since high school.

Of course, as we pointed out earlier, women in this survey and in many others report much more victimization than men report being victimizers. Whether this is because women, or victims, are more likely to disclose or whether it is because there is a small number of men who victimize many women each is impossible to tell from this methodology (or any other methodology currently in use).

Women not only report more victimization than men, but the patterns are also the same. Table 2.6 shows that, retrospectively, 31.6% of those women who report being sexually assaulted since high school had

TABLE 2.5 Emotional Abuse: Comparison of Precollege With College Men

| | | Admitted Abuse Precollege | |
		yes	no
Admitted Abuse After High School	yes	273 96.1%	294 77.2%
	no	11 3.9%	87 22.8%
	Total	284 100%	381 100%

NOTE: $\chi^2 = 46.56$; $df = 1$; $p = .0000$; phi $= .265$; gamma $= .760$.

TABLE 2.6 Sexual Assault by Force: Comparison of Precollege With College Women

| | | High School or Elementary Victimization | |
		yes	no
Victimized After High School	yes	50 31.6%	82 13.2%
	no	108 68.4%	537 86.8%
	Total	158 100%	619 100%

NOTE: $\chi^2 = 30.21$; $df = 1$; $p = .0000$; phi $= .197$; gamma $= .504$.

a similar experience earlier. Due to space constraints, we have not reproduced the similar tables here for physical and emotional abuse, but of those women who were physically harmed in college, 25.4% report similar episodes in high school. The pattern on emotional abuse matches that for male admitted offenders. Slightly less than two thirds of all college and university women (64.5%) report being emotionally abused in some way since high school. However, virtually all (95.7%) of the women who report abuse in high school or elementary school report that it happened again after high school.

Summary of Precollege Information

The above statistics add to the small amount of data on woman abuse in North American high school dating relationships and mark the start of the development of a numerical database on the physical, sexual, and psychological victimization of females in elementary school courtship. The data presented here also constitute an exploratory attempt to determine whether abuse in these two educational contexts persists into university and college dating relationships.

We know that high school boys, even more than college men, believe in rape myths and assign blame to sexual assault victims (Blumberg & Lester, 1991). It is generally accepted that these attitudes play a role in the abusive behavior of some men and that these myths permeate virtually all levels of society (Schwartz & DeKeseredy, 1997). Of interest, Metz (1993) argues that white, upper-middle-class girls are particularly at risk of sexual assault on dates. In other words, looking to isolate the causes of the abuse of women in one segment of society is not useful. Further, these data suggest that many men come to college with the full armory of ideology and behaviors necessary to engage in sexual, physical, and emotional harm of women. As we have suggested, this idea is important because there is a literature centering on fraternities that leaves the impression that men learn to abuse women after arriving at college (e.g., Martin & Hummer, 1993; Sanday, 1990). Although such learning patterns may be true in many cases, it may also be true that many other men arrive at college fully prepared to abuse women with no additional learning required.

It appears that men are much less likely to report having been abusive and women are much less likely to report having been abused in Canadian elementary and high school dating relationships. We would suggest that there are several reasons for this difference.

First, younger students spend more time at home with their parents and thus their contacts with dating partners are less frequent. In other words, their routine activities place them at lower risk of offending or being victimized. In comparison, many college and university students live away from their parents in residences, houses, and apartments, which criminologists have sometimes termed "hot spots" of female victimization (Ellis & DeKeseredy, 1996).

Perhaps the relatively low rates of assault in elementary and high school courtship uncovered by the CNS are functions of the methodological pitfalls discussed in Chapter 1. Again, some of the major factors that contribute to underreporting are

- embarrassment,
- fear of reprisal,
- deception,
- the belief that some events are too trivial or inconsequential to mention,
- "reverse telescoping," and
- the reluctance to recall traumatic events (Kennedy & Dutton, 1989; Smith, 1987, 1994; Straus et al., 1981).

Another factor that may contribute to low disclosure rates is the absence of multiple measures, such as those used to generate data on abuse in university and college dating (see Chapter 1). Unfortunately, because the main objective of the CNS was to elicit rich data on college and university students' experiences, time and financial constraints meant that we could not include additional open- and closed-ended questions on abuse in elementary and high school courtship. Perhaps future surveys will attempt to do so.

Underreporting also could have been minimized by administering the questionnaire to high school and elementary school students. This strategy might have decreased the chance of memory error. As Bradburn (1983) correctly points out, the longer the time period examined, the greater the chance that people will forget various life events. This argument is well taken. However, it is extremely difficult, if not impossible, to administer well-worded questionnaires on sexual abuse to these students because few, if any, Canadian school boards are amenable to such research (Lenskyj, 1990; Marlies Sudermann, personal communication). In the United States, human subjects research boards typically require that academic researchers obtain written permission from the parents of each student under 18 years old before the questionnaire can be administered. Obviously, it would be impossible to obtain an adequate sample for questionnaires. As a result of such restrictions, other researchers have decided not to ask direct questions on sexual behavior, which are the ones that could most easily be compared with the data now being gathered on college campuses. For example, rather than ask high school students in London, Ontario, to report abusive acts committed by or committed against them, Sudermann and Jaffe (1993) asked them if they had "experienced" abuse in teen dating relationships.

To obtain a better understanding of woman abuse in elementary and high school courtship, and to prevent and control injurious behaviors, more than just accurate prevalence data are required. Future representative sample surveys need to discover the major factors associated with male-to-female assaults in elementary and high school dating, such as attachment to dominant ideologies, male peer support, level of intimacy, educational status, or many others. This type of analysis can provide information on who is at risk of being abused or of being abusive. Such correlational research also assists the development of theories and practical, progressive policies that might keep men from becoming abusive in university/college dating relationships (DeKeseredy & Kelly, 1993a).

Jealousy

Although Canadian researchers Gagné and Lavoie (1993) did not measure the incidence and prevalence of violence in adolescent dating relationships, their nonprobability survey of young people's views on the causes of this problem warrants some brief attention here. In April 1992, they administered a questionnaire to 151 grade 11 students in a private secondary school in Quebec City, Quebec, and found that the majority of their male and female respondents consider jealousy to be the most important cause of psychologically and physically abusive behavior among couples of their age. Moreover, one quarter of the female respondents believed that violent boys are motivated by a desire to intimidate their partners. Similarly, in the United States, two small-scale high school surveys found that most of the respondents view jealousy as the most common cause of dating violence (Roscoe & Callahan, 1985; Roscoe & Kelsey, 1986).

Many adolescents view jealousy as a sign of love (Lavoie, Vezina, Piche, & Boivin, 1993). However, the story described in Box 2.1 as well as a growing body of research show that jealousy is often an expression of domination, control, and psychological abuse (Gagné & Lavoie, 1993). For example, according to Gamache (1991),

> An abusive boyfriend seeks greater and greater control over his victim in the name of love. He loves her so much that he can't stand for her to spend time with others, especially other guys. He's jealous of her friends and her family; he wants to have her all to himself. Teens often feel flattered by these demands and view them as proof of passion, a view

reinforced in our society. Jealousy is often accepted as an excuse for abusive behavior in relationships. In cases involving so-called crimes of passion, sympathy and sometimes leniency are accorded to the perpetrators, particularly when victims, usually female, have engaged in behavior likely to arouse sexual jealousy. (p. 77)

BOX 2.1.

The Brutal Nature of Jealousy and Possessiveness

I was sure that he loved me. He often showed it through displays of extreme jealousy and possessiveness. I couldn't talk to another boy. In fact, David wanted me all to himself, to the point that he resented my girlfriends and family. All we needed was each other, he said. He did a lot of subtle things to discourage me from spending time with anyone else. And if he chose to go out with his friends or not bother to call me, I was still to sit home alone and wait by the phone for his call. If I wasn't there, I was interrogated about where I was, who I talked to, even what I wore. The hassle wasn't worth it. I became more and more isolated, more dependent on David as my sole source of support. Actually, I was a little frightened of David's temper if I didn't do what he wanted me to do. The confusing part was that his expectations frequently changed. . . . It seemed that I could do nothing to please him. The more I failed to please him, the more I felt like a failure myself.

I felt it was up to me to make this relationship work. You see, we had become sexually involved by this time. To me, that meant commitment. I had to protect my image of myself as a "nice girl." Our sexual intimacy seemed to create a strong bond of ownership. I was now "his" to control and to use as he wished. My boundaries began to disintegrate as I relinquished my self-identity to become a part of David.

We began to fight a lot. That is, David fought. He was often very angry for little or no reason at all. I'd try to calm him down. He'd smash his fist into a wall or destroy something. That also frightened me. Sometimes he'd swear at me or call me names. That hurt a lot. I'd cry. Then he'd cry and hold me close, begging me to forgive him. He promised not to act that way again. I was the only one who could help him change, he always said. He needed me so much, and he was so afraid of losing me. That was why he acted the way he did. So I forgave him . . . and tried to forget.

We played the "if only . . . " game. If only we could get married and be together all the time, we'd be happy and wouldn't fight. If only his dad wasn't so abusive, David wouldn't be so angry. If only I was more loving and caring, he wouldn't feel so bad. The game went on and on. The cycle of abuse had begun, although we were both too entrenched in denial to see the reality of it all. I needed to deny what was happening to protect my shaky self-esteem. He needed to deny his actions to avoid taking responsibility for changing his behavior.

SOURCE: Jenson (1991, pp. 45-49).

The Incidence and Prevalence of Woman Abuse in Canadian University and College Dating

Unlike fine wine, some things don't improve with age, and the incidence and prevalence data reported in the next few sections of this chapter support this assertion. *Incidence* refers here to the percentage of women who stated that they were abused and the percentage of men who indicated that they were abusive in the past 12 months. *Prevalence* is, since they left high school, the percentage of men who reported having been abusive and the percentage of women who indicated having been abused.

Results

Prior to the CNS, many Canadian people thought that the phenomenon of high rates of woman abuse in dating was unique to the United States, that the U.S. violent crime rate (much higher than Canada's) in some way influenced the rate of sexual assault and other variants of woman abuse in courtship on campus (Schwartz & DeKeseredy, 1997). This perception is due in part to Canada's proximity to the United States. For example, approximately 90% of the Canadian population lives within 200 miles of the U.S. border, so that the U.S. media are influential in shaping concern about crimes in the street and private domains (MacLean, 1992; Surette, 1992). Although the precise number is unknown, it is fair to state that a substantial portion of the Canadian population watch popular television shows such as *Oprah, America's Most Wanted,* and *Top Cops* that feature stories about woman abuse and other highly injurious behaviors (DeKeseredy & MacLean, 1993). As Taylor (1983) correctly points out,

> Day in and day out, these programs portray an image of urban life in North America as a dangerous human jungle, where the prospect of criminal assault and homicide is almost random and immediate. Human life is seen to be threatened in particular, by the presence (especially "on the street" but also in everyday business and personal relationships) of psychopathic individuals intent on murder and general mayhem. (p. 92)

As will be reported in this book, the CTS and SES data generated by the CNS and analyzed by DeKeseredy and Kelly (1993a) show that woman abuse in postsecondary school courtship is not restricted to the United States. Further, the findings support the United Nations's (1995) view of Canada as a country where many heterosexual women experience a substantial amount of physical and psychological pain in a variety of intimate and domestic relationships.

The Incidence and Prevalence of Sexual Abuse

The responses to each of the items in the SES are presented in Tables 2.7 and 2.8. DeKeseredy and Kelly (1993a) found the following:

- Of the female participants, 28% stated that they were sexually abused in the past year, while 11% of the males reported having sexually victimized a female dating partner during the same time period.
- As was expected, the prevalence estimates are significantly higher, with 45.1% of the women stating that they had been abused since leaving high school and 19.5% of the men reporting at least one incident in the same time period.
- Except for the male prevalence figure, these data approximate DeKeseredy et al.'s (1992) pretest estimates.
- Despite some methodological differences, the data presented in Tables 2.7 and 2.8 are consistent with Koss et al.'s (1987) U.S. national data.

TABLE 2.7 Sexual Abuse Incidence Rates

Type of Abuse	Men (N = 1,307)		Women (N = 1,835)	
	%	N	%	N
Have you given in to sex play (fondling, kissing, or petting, but not intercourse) when you didn't want to because you were overwhelmed by a man's continual arguments and pressure?	7.8	95	18.2	318
Have you engaged in sex play (fondling, kissing, or petting but not intercourse) when you didn't want to because a man used his position of authority (boss, supervisor, etc.) to make you?	.9	10	1.3	21
Have you had sex play (fondling, kissing, or petting but not intercourse) when you didn't want to because a man threatened or used some degree of physical force (twisting your arm, holding you down, etc.) to make you?	1.1	13	3.3	54
Has a man attempted sexual intercourse (getting on top of you, attempting to insert his penis) when you didn't want to by threatening or using some degree of physical force (twisting your arm, holding you down, etc.), but intercourse did not occur?	.6	7	3.9	67
Has a man attempted sexual intercourse (getting on top of you, attempting to insert his penis) when you didn't want to because you were drunk or high, but intercourse did not occur?	2.5	29	6.6	121
Have you given in to sexual intercourse when you didn't want to because you were overwhelmed by a man's continual arguments and pressure?	4.8	55	11.9	198
Have you had sexual intercourse when you didn't want to because a man used his position of authority (boss, supervisor, etc.) to make you?	.8	9	.5	8
Have you had sexual intercourse when you didn't want to because you were drunk or high?	2.2	25	7.6	129
Have you had sexual intercourse when you didn't want to because a man threatened or used some degree of physical force (twisting your arm, holding you down, etc.) to make you?	.7	8	2.0	34
Have you engaged in sex acts (anal or oral intercourse or penetration by objects other than the penis) when you didn't want to because a man threatened or used some degree of physical force (twisting your arm, holding you down, etc.) to make you?	.3	3	1.8	29

TABLE 2.8 Sexual Abuse Prevalence Rates

Type of Abuse	Men (N = 1,307)		Women (N = 1,835)	
	%	N	%	N
Have you given in to sex play (fondling, kissing, or petting but not intercourse) when you didn't want to because you were overwhelmed by a man's continual arguments and pressure?	14.9	172	31.8	553
Have you engaged in sex play (fondling, kissing, or petting but not intercourse) when you didn't want to because a man used his position of authority (boss, supervisor, etc.) to make you?	1.8	24	4.0	66
Have you had sex play (fondling, kissing, or petting but not intercourse) when you didn't want to because a man threatened or used some degree of physical force (twisting your arm, holding you down, etc.) to make you?	2.2	25	9.4	154
Has a man attempted sexual intercourse (getting on top of you, attempting to insert his penis) when you didn't want to by threatening or using some degree of physical force (twisting your arm, holding you down, etc.), but intercourse did not occur?	1.6	19	8.5	151
Has a man attempted sexual intercourse (getting on top of you, attempting to insert his penis) when you didn't want to because you were drunk or high, but intercourse did not occur?	5.5	6.3	13.6	244
Have you given in to sexual intercourse when you didn't want to because you were overwhelmed by a man's continual arguments and pressure?	8.3	96	20.2	349
Have you had sexual intercourse when you didn't want to because a man used his position of authority (boss, supervisor, etc.) to make you?	1.4	17	1.5	24
Have you had sexual intercourse when you didn't want to because you were drunk or high?	4.7	55	14.6	257
Have you had sexual intercourse when you didn't want to because a man threatened or used some degree of physical force (twisting your arm, holding you down, etc.) to make you?	1.5	18	6.6	112
Have you engaged in sex acts (anal or oral intercourse or penetration by objects other than the penis) when you didn't want to because a man threatened or used some degree of physical force (twisting your arm, holding you down, etc.) to make you?	1.4	16	3.2	51

These findings yield several conclusions. Perhaps the most important one is that a substantial number of Canadian women are sexually abused by their university/college male dating partners. There are, however, large gender differences in reporting the incidence of sexual abuse, and the reporting gap widens for the prevalence data. What accounts for these discrepancies? In Box 2.2, we provide some answers to this question.

BOX 2.2.

What Accounts for Gender Discrepancies in Reporting Sexual Assault in Postsecondary School Dating?

One argument popular in conservative men's quarters is that the data here are wrong: "Women do lie about sexual assault, and do so for personal advantage or some other personal reason, which is pretty well why anybody lies" (Fekete, 1994, p. 54). The problem is that such critics almost never have any evidence to offer on this score, other than a deep-seated mistrust of women generally. The debate is similar to earlier ones on marital rape, where large numbers of men without any evidence argued that the law should not allow a husband to be prosecuted for raping his wife, because women are natural liars (Schwartz, 1982). It is similar to debates over rape law itself, which until fairly recently made it almost impossible to obtain a rape conviction in most jurisdictions because the state had to overcome a presumption written into law that women lie (Schwartz & Clear, 1980; Tong, 1984). In each of these cases, rape law was changed virtually everywhere in North America to remove the presumption that all women are liars. On the college campus, however, and in the backlash literature, this presumption continues to exist.

In fact, there is no reason to believe that survey data generated by measures such as the SES exaggerate the extent of sexual assault on college campuses. Rather, it is much more likely that such surveys underestimate the problem. Many survey participants do not report incidents because of embarrassment, fear of reprisal, reluctance to recall traumatic memories, deception, memory error, and many other factors (Kennedy & Dutton, 1989; Smith, 1994). A great number of women report on such surveys that they have lived for years without telling a single person about their victimization and are revealing the fact for the first time on an anonymous questionnaire. It would be naive not to believe that there are additional women (how many is, of course, unknown) who continue to keep their secret, even when given this questionnaire opportunity.

Thus, it is unlikely that men and women report differently because large numbers of women are lying. Some researchers have argued that a more likely explanation is that social desirability plays a key role in shaping male responses (Arias & Beach, 1987; DeKeseredy & Kelly, 1993a; Dutton & Hemphill, 1992). It is already difficult to obtain honest and complete responses from male perpetrators (Smith, 1987). One worry is that to the extent that we become successful in getting the message out that sexual assault in college settings is illegitimate and illegal, it will become less likely that men will admit to doing it, even when researchers guarantee anonymity and confidentiality.

The Incidence and Prevalence of Physical Abuse

The CNS physical abuse data summarized below and in Tables 2.9 and 2.10 are alarming examples of "when 'I love you' turns violent" (Johnson, 1993). For example, DeKeseredy and Kelly (1993a) found that the male physical abuse incidence rate (13.7%) approximates those generated by previous Canadian and U.S. incidence studies that employed similar measures (DeKeseredy, 1988; DeKeseredy et al., 1992; Makepeace, 1983). Even so, this estimate is considerably lower than the CTS incidence rate (37%) uncovered by White and Koss's (1991) U.S. national survey of college students. The CNS female estimate (22.3%) is also markedly lower than that of White and Koss (32%). These differences may be the result of using different psychological abuse measures.

Table 2.9 shows that every type of violence was reported by at least one respondent; however, what many people regard as "less lethal" forms of physical abuse apparently occurred more often. This is consistent with most of the earlier North American research (see Sugarman & Hotaling, 1989).

WOMAN ABUSE ON CAMPUS

TABLE 2.9 Psychological and Physical Abuse Incidence Rates

Type of Abuse	Men (N = 1,307)		Women (N = 1,835)	
	%	N	%	N
Psychological:				
insults or swearing	52.7	623	52.5	857
put her (you) down in front of friends or family	18.9	233	30.7	491
accused her (you) of having affairs or flirting with other men	29.3	350	37.2	614
did or said something to spite her (you)	57.7	350	37.2	614
threatened to hit or throw something at her (you)	6.1	71	10.6	174
threw, smashed, or kicked something	25.4	304	25.5	433
Physical:				
threw something at her (you)	3.5	40	5.1	85
pushed, grabbed, or shoved her (you)	11.7	132	19.6	319
slapped her (you)	2.9	30	5.5	85
kicked, bit, or hit her (you) with your (his) fist	1.7	16	3.9	61
hit or tried to hit her (you) with something	1.9	20	3.3	54
beat her (you) up	.9	7	1.4	21
choked you (her)	1.0	10	2.1	32
threatened her (you) with a knife or gun	.9	9	.5	9
used a knife or gun on her (you)	1.0	8	.1	2

As expected, the prevalence data presented in Table 2.10 also show that "less severe" types of violence occur more often. For example, almost 35% of the women reported having been physically abused and 17.8% of the men stated that they were violent since leaving high school. These prevalence estimates are similar to the pretest results (DeKeseredy et al., 1992). Even so, the male figure is much lower than Barnes et al.'s (1991) rate (42%). This inconsistency probably reflects differences between the versions of the CTS employed by the other two Canadian studies. For example, Barnes et al.'s version included a sexual assault item, and several other items were distinct from those used in the CNS version. National representative sample survey data on the *prevalence* of physical abuse were not gathered by White and Koss (1991). Therefore, at this point in time, it is extremely difficult to make Canadian-U.S. comparisons using similar samples.

Again, we find gender variations in reporting. In our opinion, the reasons for these discrepancies are found in Box 2.2.

TABLE 2.10 Psychological and Physical Abuse Prevalence Rates

Type of Abuse	Men (N = 1,307)		Women (N = 1,835)	
	%	N	%	N
Psychological:				
insults or swearing	62.4	747	65.1	1105
put her (you) down in front of friends or family	25.9	322	44.2	742
accused her (you) of having affairs or flirting with other men	40.9	495	52.6	901
did or said something to spite her (you)	65.2	773	72.2	1216
threatened to hit or throw something at her (you)	8.0	97	20.6	346
threw, smashed, or kicked something	30.6	373	37.3	652
Physical:				
threw something at her (you)	4.3	50	10.6	185
pushed, grabbed, or shoved her (you)	15.8	182	31.3	529
slapped her (you)	4.9	53	11.1	186
kicked, bit, or hit her (you) with your (his) fist	2.8	28	8.0	135
hit or tried to hit her (you) with something	2.9	33	8.0	136
beat her (you) up	1.0	8	3.9	63
choked you (her)	1.0	9	4.6	80
threatened her (you) with a knife or gun	.9	9	2.4	41
used a knife or gun on her (you)	1.0	9	.5	8

The Incidence and Prevalence of Psychological Abuse

Men and women provided similar incidence rates. For example, 74.1% of the men stated that they were psychologically abusive, and 79.1% of the women stated that they were abused this way in the past year. The male incidence figure is higher than other Canadian estimates produced by DeKeseredy (1988) and DeKeseredy et al. (1992). The women's estimate is also higher than DeKeseredy et al.'s. However, White and Koss (1991) obtained higher male (81%) and female (88%) figures. Furthermore, the CNS male prevalence statistic is 12% lower than that reported by Barnes et al.'s (1991) Canadian male respondents (92.6%). These differences probably reflect the use of different measures.

The responses to the psychological abuse items presented in Tables 2.9 and 2.10 show that there is considerable congruency in male and female reporting. This is particularly true of "insults or swearing"; "throwing, smashing, or kicking something"; and "doing something to spite a partner." However, there were inconsistent responses to the following items:

"threatening to throw something at her," "putting her down in front of friends and family," and "accusing her of having affairs or flirting with other men."

Summary of the College and University Data

The incidence and prevalence data described here show that for many Canadian women, college and university dating relationships are indeed "dangerous domains" (Johnson, 1996). Furthermore, based on the assumption that most of the students who participated in the CNS come from the more affluent sectors of Canadian society, these data challenge the popular notion that those who engage in woman abuse are economically disadvantaged—an inaccurate perception unfortunately supported by flawed police statistics (Hinch, 1996). Although these figures are high, as is the case with *all* survey statistics on woman abuse, they should be read as underestimates. As pointed out in Chapter 1, the problem of underreporting affects *all* woman abuse surveys; however, the CNS, like other Canadian surveys (e.g., Johnson, 1996; Smith, 1987), included methods specifically designed to overcome or minimize this shortcoming.

The CNS data described here yield two more important conclusions. First, a comparison of the incidence and prevalence figures with those reviewed by Sugarman and Hotaling (1989) show that the problem of college dating abuse is just as serious in Canada as it is in the United States. Second, like their U.S. counterparts, while Canadian female undergraduates have a "well-founded fear" of being attacked by strangers in public places (Hanmer & Saunders, 1984; Kelly & DeKeseredy, 1994), they have more to fear from their male dating partners. In fact, as Gibbs (1994) correctly points out, "What people think of 'real rape'—the assault by a monstrous stranger lurking in the shadows—accounts for only 1 out of 5 attacks" (p. 206). Unfortunately, many people's ideas of what constitutes woman abuse are based on the myths and stereotypes transmitted by the media (e.g., pornography, feature films, and rock videos) and sexist male social networks (DeKeseredy & Schwartz, 1993; Koss & Cook, 1993; Schwartz & DeKeseredy, 1997).

Chapter Summary

In this chapter, we presented data on the unknown or "dark side" of courtship. Unfortunately, for several reasons described in Chapter 1 and in other sources (e.g., DeKeseredy & MacLeod, 1997), the estimates of women's pain and suffering described here probably constitute only the tip of the iceberg. Even so, these statistics suggest that male psychological, physical, and sexual assaults on female dating partners "happen with alarming regularity" (Lloyd, 1991).

Some of the research reported here also adds to the small amount of data accumulated on woman abuse in North American high school dating relationships and marks the start of the development of a numerical database on the physical, sexual, and psychological victimization of females in elementary school dating. Furthermore, the CNS constitutes an exploratory attempt to determine whether abuse in these two educational contexts persists into university/college dating relationships.

Some conservative critics, however, contend that the CNS is an example of a "serious case of distorted science in Canada" (Christensen, 1995). Similarly, others, such as Fekete (1994), one of Canada's premier "media darlings of the anti-feminist backlash" (Renzetti, 1997), contend that by labeling some of the acts listed in the CTS and SES, the CNS research team has "disrespected and discounted" respondents' interpretations of these events. Fekete asserts that the CNS would have generated considerably lower estimates if respondents were asked to describe their interpretations of their own experiences. In his opinion, the CNS research team has learned that if women are explicitly asked if they have been abused, the incidence and prevalence estimates described in this chapter would be much lower than those generated by the CTS and SES.

We and others who were involved in the development and administration of the CNS do not derive any pleasure from eliciting alarmingly high rates of abuse, and the CNS research team did not manipulate the questionnaires to guarantee the generation of "big numbers." Rather, like other survey researchers, the CNS team was well aware of the fact that most female and male members of the general public do not identify intimate forms of victimization as "rape," "abuse," or "violence." Unlike most crimes in which right and wrong are reasonably clear to most people (e.g., armed robbery), date rape and other examples of intimate abuse are problems that often "muddy the normative waters" (Fenstermaker, 1989).

What Fekete and other conservative critics of the CNS fail to recognize is that the bulk of the abusive events listed in the CNS instruments are violations of the Canadian *Criminal Code.* Simply because many women who experience these behaviors do not realize that their dating partners have committed a crime does not mean that they view the outcome of their partners' behaviors positively or even neutrally (Koss & Cook, 1993). In fact, 50% of the rape victims in Koss et al.'s (1987) national sample of college students defined their experiences as rape or some crime similar to rape, and only 10% stated that they did not feel harmed by this experience (Koss & Cook, 1993). In addition, several studies show that many women who did not initially view their experiences as rape contacted researchers later on to disclose events they now define as rape after the legal criteria were explained to them (Koss & Cook, 1993; Russell, 1990; Wyatt, 1992).

Fekete, Christensen, and other conservative "people without data" have also tried to discredit CNS findings by saying "but women do it too" (DeKeseredy & MacLean, 1997; Stanko, 1995). Of course, there has never been any question that women strike their male dating partners, sometimes with the intent to injure. That there are battered male dating partners should not be a subject for disagreement (Schwartz & De-Keseredy, 1993). The points of contention between conservative critics of the CNS and us are whether female dating partners *primarily* use violence as a means of self-defense and whether the presence of some male victims mitigates or changes the meaning of the conclusion that women are the overwhelmingly predominant victims of dating abuse. This debate played a central role in the development of the CNS, and an attempt to resolve it is described in Chapter 3.

Notes

1. See Schwartz and DeKeseredy (1997) for a comprehensive review of our work on this topic.

2. Bergman provides examples of injurious behaviors in each question.

3. In all cases of the data analysis that follows, definitions of physical, sexual, and emotional abuse in university and college dating relationships follow those used by DeKeseredy and Kelly (1993a, 1993b).

4. There are several comparisons that could be made here, because college sexual victimization was measured using the Sexual Experiences Survey (SES). Much of the victimization uncovered by the SES comes from questions about unwanted sex while the woman is drunk or high. Although we are clear that this constitutes sexual assault (see Schwartz & Pitts, 1995), in this case the decision was made to limit the table to cases in which the question clearly asks whether or not physical force was used.

3

"But Women Do It Too"

The Meanings of and Motives for Women's Use of Violence

> Women in relationships with men commit comparatively as many or more acts of physical violence as men do, at every level of severity. It is not a case of a friendly slap against vicious beating. It is slap for slap, beating for beating, knifing and shooting for knifing and shooting, on the evidence of women's own *self*-reports. (Fekete, 1994, p. 88, emphasis in original)

The CNS data presented in Chapter 2 and other parts of this book challenge an idea found throughout society that violence is mainly found in marital relationships. The "discovery" of extensive violence on the college campus has been used to argue that government and campus officials need to devote more attention, time, and funds to the development of effective prevention and control strategies (Currie, 1995).

However, a backlash response has broken out (Renzetti, 1994; Stanko, 1995) featuring arguments such as in the Fekete quote above. As the result of dozens of studies all pointing in the same direction, it is now widely accepted that in intimate, heterosexual relationships, men are the primary aggressors. Yet a number of faculty, journalists, and others have

65

attempted to challenge this finding. Anyone, for example, subscribing to any of dozens of computer discussion groups or newsletters that relate to this topic is completely familiar with the argument that "women do it too." Conservative writers, columnists, and news magazines have similarly raised this issue, suggesting that this information is kept secret because there is a "political agenda" to destroy the career of anyone who brings this information forward (Versagi, 1996).

Thus, the nature of one public battle seems to be that if men beat nonviolent women, then men are at fault. If we find that women hit men, however, then the conclusion can be reached that both sides are at fault. Murray Straus, for example, has argued that we must give serious attention to any minor violence by women (such as slapping the face of a husband who is verbally abusive), because such minor violence can be seen as setting the stage for and legitimizing (at least to the men) violent and highly injurious assaultive behavior later. Thus, we need to divert attention from men's (extensive) violence to pay attention to women's (minor) violence (Schwartz & DeKeseredy, 1993).

Part of the problem seems to be that at times the issues are symbolic rather than real. For example, some researchers are truly concerned about how many men are physically harmed in attacks by women. There is no question that even if 95% of all intimate violence is committed by men, this means that there are still some men being violently attacked by women. We know very little about these men. For example, many counselors claim that a great many of the men who claim to be battered are in fact uninjured and unthreatened. What they are is *angry* that the women they were beating fought back, perhaps even effectively. Although counselors who deal with such men regularly make such claims (Versagi, 1996), we actually do not have very much solid empirical information about these men.

However, not all of the writers in this field are motivated by a genuine concern for learning more about battered men. Too often, the concern is to defend men against attacks that would seem to undermine man's natural role as unquestioned family leader. If men as a group are dangerously violent in intimate situations, there is a serious problem that requires some important societal intervention. If, on the other hand, men and women are equally violent, we can pretty much ignore the issue or at least move it down our list of concerns. Such researchers may not find it important to look at the actual nature of the facts (Goode & Ben-Yehuda, 1994). Any fact developed by any researcher with any methodology is enough to justify their views.

Taking the issue seriously does not automatically make things simple. Even those engaged in honest and legitimate debate over "facts" often have little agreement on what they are or how to count them. For example, we may wish to study how violent women are. Some have decided to view any blow struck by a woman as a form of offensive attack. If this method is to be used, then the conclusion one seeks can be found fairly simply: by counting up the total number of blows struck by men and comparing it with the total number of blows struck by women. This methodology has been the hallmark of most of the studies that use the CTS, and most who use it tend to find that the number of blows struck by women is fairly equal to the number struck by men. This is why many people have declared that men and women are equally violent.

Others have been troubled by this for a number of reasons. One is that a simple trip to the emergency room of any major hospital will reveal that, although it is common to find women there severely injured by their male partners, it is fairly rare to find a man there injured by a female partner. Often this is explained away by arguing that men simply are stronger than women. From the first major book on the subject (Straus et al., 1981), theorists have argued that men and women may have equal intent but that the men actually are able to inflict injury while women are not very good at this. This does bring up a problem that has been almost completely ignored in the field. If this is true—women are the ones who are injured in intimate violence, not men—then why would we be so quick to dismiss the problem because women and men begin with equal intent? The argument seems to take the following form: Men can and do terrorize, beat, and seriously injure women. Women try but are unable to harm or scare men. Therefore, the state of affairs is equal.

Even among those women who are in fact violent, there is a question in the minds of many counselors and researchers as to whether their violence can legitimately be compared with men's violence. Of course, *some* women's violence can certainly be compared quite accurately with men's violence. However, there has long been a suspicion in the field that women's violence can be very different than men's. Although it is possible that many women are striking in pure aggression, it is also likely that many women are striking partially, or mainly, in self-defense. CTS surveys ask, for example, if the man ever did something to the woman, and the woman ever did something to the man. If, for example, a man chased a woman around the house for half an hour swinging a baseball bat, finally hitting her once and breaking her arm, he would be guilty of one violent act. If, in an attempt to get out of the house, she threw a table lamp toward him, and distracted him, and then raced out of the door while he chased after her threatening to kill her, then she is guilty of one violent act (throwing). Adding up the acts of violence our simple survey has uncovered, then, the man and woman are equally violent—except that she may have just saved her life and may right now be at the hospital having painful surgery on her broken arm. He wasn't even hurt.

In this chapter, we will look at the question of whether this example above is a wild and outlandish one or, instead, is a more common statement of the problem. Simply put, how much of women's violence, at least in courtship relationships, is in self-defense or retaliation rather than being aggressive (first-strike) violence? This research is important to the nature of much current public debate. There is an important battle being waged over the nature of women's behavior and its role in woman abuse.[1]

As we have said, there is no doubt that some women strike men or that some of these acts clearly seem to be abusive. Few in the field would argue that there are not battered men or abusive women. However, when looked at more carefully, much female violence in courtship seems to be primarily or at least partially in self-defense (e.g., Makepeace, 1986). Given the small amount of research on this subject, it has been premature before this study to make any conclusions about the motives for women's use of violence within Canadian college couples.

CNS researchers tried to develop a more comprehensive under-standing of these motives. For example, the authors of this book along with Daniel Saunders and Shahid Alvi examined the proportion of times that female dating partners report their use of violence as "defensive," "retaliatory," or "first strike." Although the results will be covered later in this chapter, it might be pointed out here that this team wanted to know whether female student CNS respondents distinguished acts of "self-defense" from violence labeled "fighting back." Sometimes, al-though we think that we can make a distinction between these two, the women themselves do not make this distinction. Saunders (1986) found that the battered women in his sample did not make such a distinction.

Gender Differences in Dating Violence

Why do Canadian women use violence in courtship? Prior to the CNS, the Canadian social scientific community had not conducted studies designed specifically to answer this important question. Instead, those interested in dating violence focused primarily on the incidence and prevalence of physical assaults.

In fact, as we pointed out in Chapter 1, prior to the nonprobability sample surveys conducted in the late 1980s and early 1990s (see Table 1.1), there was an absence of data on the physical abuse of female students in Canada. Thus, not only was there no information on why women used violence, there was virtually no information on women's experiences of violence in dating, whether as victims or perpetrators. In the United States, too, dating violence is a relatively new topic of social scientific inquiry. Nevertheless, there are at least 30 existing data sets on the extent of this variant of intimate abuse. Almost all of them have used modified versions of the Conflict Tactics Scale (CTS) (Straus, 1979). We have discussed in some detail that the data generated by this measure have led many people to conclude that dating violence is sexually symmetrical (women beat men as often as men beat women). Our complaint was that for the most part these studies did not combine the CTS with any question of meaning, motive, or outcome (e.g., injury).

In Chapter 1, we identified some other limitations of CTS data, and just why it is that we have reason to doubt any conclusion that findings of sexual symmetry might accurately represent what is happening in male/female relationships. For example, a number of studies have uncovered a tendency on the part of men to underreport their own violence (Dutton, 1986; Edleson & Brygger, 1986; Ellis, 1995; Jouriles & O'Leary, 1985): "Men consistently have been found to report their own use of violence as less frequent and less severe than their female partners report it to be" (National Research Council, 1996, p. 32). If this is generally the case, then findings that men and women are equally violent are inaccurate—men would in fact be more violent in true counts. In fact, some have argued that the situation is even worse: At the same time that men are underreporting their violence, women are more likely to report their minor acts of violence. This would further confuse the picture.

Another problem with using only the CTS to determine sex variations in violence is that the CTS only focuses on conflict-instigated violence. It is generally introduced with the following: "No matter how well a couple gets along, there are times when they disagree on major decisions, get annoyed about something the other person does, or just have spats or fights because they're in a bad mood or tired or for some other reasons." Of course, many people use violence to "resolve" what they define as conflicts, and that would be fully covered by this question. However, men are far more likely than women to use *control-instigated* violence, a situation excluded from the above preamble (Ellis, 1995). If there is no disagreement or "spat" but, instead, one person who wants to make a violent point, punish the other, or force the other into doing something, this might not be reported by that person in a CTS survey. Worse, it is widely recognized that many male assaults "come out of the blue." Some violence is used in a conflict situation to achieve an instrumental end, such as winning an argument, and this is what is measured in the CTS. Other violence, as noted above, is used for instrumental reasons when there is no disagreement or conflict situation (such as to proclaim dominance or to punish the other person). However, a substantial number of women are beaten for no apparent reason (Browne, 1987; Schwartz & DeKeseredy, 1993). Lillian Rubin (1976) has interviewed a number of young men who simply are angry much of the time. Their violence might not be covered in CTS-oriented studies, if respondents do not recognize it in terms of disagreements or spats.

Last, but certainly not least, the CTS excludes acts of sexual violence. Many small- and large-scale studies, including the CNS (see Chapter 2) and Koss et al.'s (1987) national survey, show that women are sexually assaulted in a variety of ways by their male college dating partners. Although there have not been many good studies on this, it is the experience of many counselors working with battered women that these women are also sexually assaulted. In fact, in shelters that we have worked with extensively, virtually all women admitted as victims of battery turn out to be victims of sexual violence also. What this suggests to us is that there is a serious problem in measuring violence by using only a CTS survey that does not ask about sexual violence. If questions on sexual violence were added, it would become clear that men commit the overwhelming majority of violent attacks in intimate relationships. This would be true even if one ignores all of our other criticisms. If our other criticisms are taken into account also, the scale would be tipped even more strongly in favor of men being the primary aggressors.

In sum, CTS data alone may not reflect the reality of dating violence. As yet, there are no good alternatives for the questions that the CTS or the new CTS^2 asks, but several U.S. researchers have recognized the limitations of the CTS and included questions about motivations to supplement CTS items. For example, Makepeace (1986) examined six different motives for using violence and found that female violence, "even when for the conscious purpose of causing harm, is predominantly self-defensive" (p. 385). As an indirect indicator of self-defensive violence, Bookwala et al. (1992) found that the most powerful risk factor for the use of violence by dating women was whether or not they had been the recipient of violence themselves. Women who received violence were most likely to use it. Follingstad et al. (1991) used a more comprehensive list of motives and showed that the need to protect oneself, retaliation for being emotionally hurt, and retaliation for being hit were common motivations for women's violence.

A Study of Women's Use of Self-Defense

Informed by these studies and U.S. spousal abuse research showing self-defense as a frequent motive of battered women, our research team (ourselves plus Saunders and Alvi) hypothesized that much of the violence that women use in Canadian college dating relationships comes in situations that the women consider self-defensive. We also hypothesized that there would be a positive correlation between women's reports of "fighting back" and self-defense, as found in previous research (Saunders, 1986).

Because not all women would be expected to attribute their violence to self-defense, our analysis of CNS data was also designed to explore the predictors of different types of women's dating violence, specifically to answer the question: What are the differences between women who use and do not use self-defensive violence? How might attitudes, beliefs, alcohol use, and victimization experiences explain their behavior? The following hypotheses were developed to test differences between defensive and nondefensive uses of violence:

1. Violence used in self-defense would be related to a history of victimization in dating relationships, including more severe physical violence sustained, more medical help-seeking, and higher rates of sexual abuse.
2. Violence not used in self-defense would be related to more traditional sex role beliefs, approval of violence in dating relationships, and a greater frequency of alcohol use.

The hypothesis on alcohol use stemmed from previous research on dating violence, which has typically found such a relationship (Sugarman & Hotaling, 1989). However, our hypothesis refined these previous results by predicting that the relationship would hold primarily for women who are not using violence to defend themselves.

We tested these hypotheses using data generated from 1,835 female respondents of the CNS. The sample and data collection procedures, of course, were fully covered in Chapter 1 and Appendix A on methods. Dan Saunders did much of the data analysis in this chapter and is responsible for many of the tables.

Measures

The Prevalence of Physical Violence

The prevalence of physical violence was measured using the slightly expanded version of the CTS described in the first two chapters. For example, female respondents were asked to report if *they have ever* used one or more of the nine violent acts described in Table 3.1 with boyfriends or dates since leaving high school. The first three of these acts are often described as "minor" acts because they are viewed as less dangerous (Straus, 1990a), although at times the consequences can be severe. The last six make up what Straus et al. (1981) refer to as a severe violence subscale. The respondents were carefully warned to limit their answers to dating relationships and to exclude any events that might have taken place in marital relationships.

Motives for Dating Violence

Two identical sets of slight modifications of the questions developed by Saunders (1986) were placed in different sections of the CTS. One set followed the first three items described in Table 3.1 and the other followed the last six. It seemed possible that the results would differ based on the level of severity (although the division, as we shall see, is somewhat arbitrary).

After each motive question, there was a line with 0% at one end and 100% at the other end, marked at every 10 percentage points. Respondents were asked to mark anywhere on the line. They were not asked to divide a total of 100% among the three motivation items but, instead, to assign a percentage score to *each* type of motivation. In other words, the three forms of motivation (e.g., self-defense, fighting back, and initiated an attack) were not stated in mutually exclusive terms. The last question on initiation of an assault could, when a respondent feared for her safety,

TABLE 3.1 Violence Use Prevalence Rates

Type of Abuse Engaged In	Women (N = 1,835)	
	%	N
Threw something	21	230
Pushed, grabbed, or shoved	34.9	550
Slapped	23.6	370
Kicked, bit, or hit with a fist	16.1	292
Hit or tried to hit with something	16.4	256
Beat up	1.3	21
Choked	1.1	17
Threatened with a knife or gun	1.3	21
Used a knife or a gun	.1	1

be self-defensive but, as was the case in Saunders's (1986) study of battered women, this was not clearly defined in our research.

Victimization

Victimization since leaving high school was measured with the slightly modified version of the CTS described previously in this book. For example, items were added to expand the psychological abuse section (e.g., "put you down in front of friends and family" and "accused you of having affairs and flirting with other men"). In an attempt to find out mathematically how the various victimizations were related to each other, we performed a principal components factor analysis with varimax rotation. Here we found that the various victimizations sorted themselves out into three "factors": (a) psychological abuse, which included items on insulting, public put-downs, accusing, spitting, throwing, and smashing objects (violent threats and pushing, grabbing, and shoving overlapped with this factor and the next one); (b) physical abuse, which included items on violent threats; throwing and smashing objects; throwing objects; pushing, grabbing, shoving; slapping; kicking, biting, or hitting with a fist; beating up; and choking; (c) severe violence, which included items on choking, threats with a weapon, and use of a weapon.

This analysis suggests that the categories of "minor" and "severe" violence arbitrarily chosen by Straus (1979) do not hold with this sample. For example, beatings are in the same factor as throwing objects and slaps. The question has been raised with us as to why we have continued, given this finding, to use the categories chosen by Straus. Unfortunately, this analysis was completed on the data we collected using the original divisions. As seen above, some of the key questions depend on the original division. This places us in the difficult situation of basing all of our analysis on a division between minor and severe violence with which we do not totally agree. Our "solution" has been to place the terms *minor* and *severe* in quotation marks in this chapter to indicate their arbitrary nature.

Sexual Abuse

This form of abuse was measured with a version of Koss et al.'s (1987) SES described previously in this book. Respondents were asked whether or not they had experienced 10 forms of abuse in dating since high school. This scale has an internal reliability coefficient of .74 (alpha).

Medical Help

Medical help-seeking was measured with a single item requesting a "yes" or "no" response: "Did you turn to a medical professional for help?"

Relationship Intensity

The seriousness of the relationship was measured with a series of single items asking for "yes" or "no" responses regarding "casual dating (i.e., a good time with no future commitment or obligation on the part of you and your dating partner)," "serious dating (i.e., involving a great deal of commitment and intimacy)," and "moved in with or lived regularly with a boyfriend." These questions referred to relationships within the past year. In addition, a question about current marital status referred to "living with male partner."

Patriarchal Beliefs

The ideology of familial patriarchy is defined as a discourse that supports the abuse of women who violate the ideals of male power as well as control over women in intimate relationships. Women's adherence to this ideology was measured using a six-item scale (Smith, 1990b). Below are a few examples of items included in this scale:

- A man and his wife/partner should have equal say in deciding how to spend the family income.
- A man has the right to decide whether or not his wife/partner should go out in the evening with her friends.
- A man has the right to have sex with his wife/partner when he wants, even though she may not want to.

Four response categories were allowed: "strongly agree," "agree," "disagree," and "strongly disagree." The internal reliability was .72 (alpha).

Approval of Dating Violence

Eight situations, developed from Smith (1990b), were used to measure the approval of violence, specifically the approval of "a man slapping his dating partner or girlfriend." For each of the following situations, female respondents were asked to circle "yes," "no," "depends," and "don't know":

Now we would like to ask you a few questions about your attitudes for each of the following situations. Please tell us if you would approve of a man slapping his dating partner or girlfriend. Would you approve if . . .

- she won't do what he tells her to do?
- she insults him when they are home alone?
- she insults him in public?
- she comes home drunk?
- she is sobbing hysterically?
- she won't have sex with him?
- he learns that she is dating another man?
- she hits him first when they are having an argument?

Once again, a mathematical analysis was run (principal components factor analysis with varimax rotation) to see which of these answers were related to each other. Two groups emerged, which are called "factors": (a) refusal, with items like "she won't do what he tells her to do" and "she won't have sex with him," and (b) transgression, with items like "she comes home drunk," "she hits him first when they are having an argument," and "she insults him in public." Factor scores were used for the variables.

Analysis

Out of the 1,835 women respondents to the CNS, 705 reported that they had engaged in "minor" forms of violence and 356 in "severe" forms of violence. These two groups were further divided into (a) those who reported that their violence was never in self-defense, (b) those who reported that their violence was self-defensive 1% to 49% of the time, (c) those who used it 50% to 99% of the time, and (d) those who reported that their only use of violence was in self-defense (100%). One-way analysis of variance and chi-square analysis were the primary mathematical or statistical means of comparing the four groups. Pairwise comparisons between groups in the analysis of variance were tested with the Student-Newman-Keuls range test, a standard and fairly conservative post hoc test for comparing means (Klockars & Sax, 1986).

Results

Table 3.1 shows the percentage of women who engaged in any type of physical violence since leaving high school. Almost half of all women reported using violence (46.1%), although most of the acts reported were at the upper (more "minor") end of the CTS scale. Only one woman reported using a weapon on a dating partner.

Women were asked how often they used three motives for violence. Table 3.2 shows the number of women who reported (a) self-defensive violence, (b) "fighting back," or (c) initiating an attack. In each case, the three motives are broken down into four levels of frequency and two levels of severity. The first finding from this table is that only a distinct minority of women reported that they had ever (1%-100% of the time) initiated an attack: 37% of the women who used "minor" forms of violence initiated an attack at some time, and 43% initiated "severe" violent acts at least once. However, only 7.3% of the women who used "minor" violence always (100% of the time) attacked first, and only 9.9% of the women who reported using "severe" violence were always the ones

TABLE 3.2 Percentage of Women Using Different Motives for Violence by Frequency of Violence

Motive	N	0%	1%–49%	50%–99%	100%
"Minor violence":					
self-defense	678	62.3	20.1	10.7	6.9
fighting back	677	53.6	23.2	16.1	7.1
initiate attack	663	63.3	19.7	9.7	7.3
"Severe violence":					
self-defense	367	56.5	21.6	13.4	8.5
fighting back	359	48.9	26.7	15.2	9.2
initiate attack	359	56.8	20.9	12.4	9.9

who initiated an attack. Unfortunately, many women did not claim any of the three motives asked in the question.[3] The most logical explanation for this lack of response is that there are other motives for women's violence, unaccounted for in the literature and in these questions.

Thus, a substantial amount of the total violence reported was in self-defense, even though Table 3.2 shows that a majority of women did not report using "minor" (60.9%) or "severe" acts (56.5%) of violence in self-defense. We can also see that many women were "fighting back." Although not *most* of the acts, *much* of women's acts of violence are either self-defensive or "fighting back." Within each level of violence severity, self-defense and "fighting back" were positively and significantly correlated with each other ($r = .67, p = .000$ for "minor" violence; $r = .72, p = .001$ for "severe" violence). Initiating an attack, however, was very weakly and nonsignificantly correlated with either self-defense or "fighting back" ($r = .05, p = .07$ for self-defense; $r = -.05, p = .18$ for "fighting back").

One of our hypotheses is that women use self-defense more when they are themselves more victimized by physical violence. As hypothesized, Table 3.3 ("nonsevere" violence by the women) and Table 3.4 ("severe" violence by the women) show that generally there is a linear relationship: The higher the frequency of women's victimization, the higher the use of self-defense violence. The differences were especially marked for nearly all forms of physical abuse, including threats, although less so for psychological abuse. With psychological abuse there is still a strong difference, but it is not linear. Rather, the difference here is between any form of defensive violence and no use of defensive violence. Threats with weapons and the actual use of weapons were experienced

(text continued on p. 80)

TABLE 3.3 Comparisons Among Women Using Different Levels of Defensive "Nonsevere" Violence: Abuse Sustained Since High School (Means)

	1 Non- defensive 0% n = 422	2 Some Defensive 1%–49% n = 137	3 Mostly Defensive 50%–99% n = 72	4 All Defensive 100% n = 47		
Abuse			Mean		*F*	*SNK*
Insulted/ swore	2.8	3.6	3.6	3.9	14.7***	4, 3, 2>1
Put down	1.5	2.3	2.5	3.0	20.5***	4, 3, 2>1; 4>2
Accused of affair	2.0	2.9	2.7	3.2	10.8***	4, 3, 2>1
Spit	2.8	3.4	3.6	3.9	11.3***	4, 3, 2>1
Threat to hit/throw	.5	1.5	2.3	2.4	51.1***	4, 3, 2>1; 4, 3>2
Threw, smash, kick object	1.4	2.0	2.6	3.1	21.9***	4, 3, 2>1; 4, 3>2
Threw at	.2	.8	1.0	1.5	28.8***	4, 3, 2>1; 4>3, 2
Pushed, grabbed, shoved	.9	2.0	2.6	3.1	57.1***	4, 3, 2>1; 4, 3>2
Slapped	.2	.7	1.1	1.4	25.5***	4, 3, 2>1; 4, 3>2
Kicked, bit, hit with fist	.2	.6	.8	1.4	26.4***	4, 3, 2>1; 4>3, 2
Hit or tried to hit— object	.1	.5	1.0	1.5	35.8***	4, 3, 2>1; 3>2; 4>3
Beat up	.03	.3	.4	.9	29.4***	4, 3, 2>1; 4>3, 2
Choked	.04	.3	.5	.9	24.2***	4, 3, 2>1; 4, 3>2; 4>3
Threat with weapon	.01	.1	.2	.3	12.5***	4, 3, 2>1; 4>3, 2
Used weapon	.00	.06	.05	.01	1.8	

*p ≤.05; **p ≤ .01; ***p ≤ .001.

TABLE 3.4 Comparisons Among Women Using Different Levels of Defensive "Severe" Violence: Abuse Sustained Since High School (Means)

Abuse	1 Non-defensive 0% n = 205	2 Some Defensive 1%–49% n = 75	3 Mostly Defensive 50%–99% n = 45	4 All Defensive 100% n = 31	F	SNK
	Mean				F	SNK
Insulted/ swore	3.1	3.7	4.2	4.3	10.5***	4, 3, 2>1
Put down	1.6	2.2	2.8	3.6	12.7***	4, 3, 2>1; 4>2
Accused of affair	2.3	3.0	2.6	4.0	9.0***	4, 2>1; 4>3, 2
Spit	3.0	3.3	3.7	4.3	6.3***	4>1, 2
Threat to hit/ throw	.8	1.8	2.6	3.0	28.5***	4, 3, 2>1; 4, 3>2
Threw, smash, kick object	1.7	2.5	2.9	3.7	15.0***	4, 3, 2>1; 4>2
Threw at	.3	1.0	1.5	1.8	19.3***	4, 3, 2>1; 4>3, 2
Pushed, grabbed, shoved	1.1	2.3	2.9	3.5	34.5***	4, 3, 2>1; 4, 3>2
Slapped	.3	.8	1.4	2.0	27.7***	4, 3, 2>1; 4, 3>2; 4>3
Kicked, bit, hit with fist	.3	.9	1.0	1.8	17.8***	4, 3, 2>1; 4>3, 2
Hit or tried to hit— object	.2	.9	1.0	2.0	25.1***	4, 3, 2>1; 4>3, 2
Beat up	.01	.3	.4	1.5	35.6***	4, 3, 2>1; 4>3, 2
Choked	.07	.3	.4	1.3	20.3***	4, 2>1; 4>3, 2
Threat with weapon	.02	.03	.2	.6	15.3***	4>3, 2, 1
Used weapon	.01	.0	.0	.3	7.3***	4>3, 2, 1

*p ≤ .05; **p ≤ .01; ***p ≤ .001.

more frequently by women who always used "severe" violence in self-defense.

Thus, among those women who used violence at all, the ones who report higher levels of self-defensive violence also report higher levels of violence committed against them. When analyzed using percentages, and looked at in the reverse way, close to half of those women who experienced violence reported that their own violence was committed in self-defense. This can be seen most clearly by looking only at those women who claim that 100% of their violence was in self-defense. Here one can see very high rates of victimization: About three fourths had been threatened, and over 85% had been pushed, grabbed, or shoved. Over half the women who used "severe" violence to defend themselves had been choked, kicked, or hit with a fist. Roughly one fourth of these women had been threatened with a weapon.

Further, women using self-defensive violence have experienced much higher rates of sexual abuse than other women in the survey.[4] Although the differences are at times minimal between categories, strong differences can be found between the women at the two extremes: those who report never using self-defensive violence, and those who always report that any violence they used was only used in self-defense. For example, we can look at what is commonly considered the most serious form of sexual abuse: "Have you had sexual intercourse when you didn't want to because a man threatened or used some degree of physical force (twisting your arm, holding you down, etc.) to make you?" Of those women who *never* used defensive violence, 4.8% reported such victimization, as compared with 37.7% of those women who reported that *all* of their violence was in self-defense. As another example of the same phenomenon, another question from the survey presented in Chapter 1 asks women whether they had been made upset because their partners tried to get them to engage in behavior they had seen in pornography. The women who report that their violence was always in self-defense were about twice as likely to claim that they were made upset (25.9%) as were the women who said their violence was never in self-defense (13.1%).

The effects of separate types of abuse and their combinations were also analyzed. Evidently, if the only abuse the woman received was psychological abuse, she was less likely to respond with self-defensive violence. Rates of psychological abuse as the only abuse the woman received were much higher among those who were *not* responding with self-defense—over 80% in the most recent episode. Looked at in another way, however, those who receive multiple types of abuse are the most likely to engage in self-defensive violence. Looking at victimization since high school, those who experienced psychological abuse, threats, and physical abuse in combination were much more likely to respond with self-defensive violence—about 80% compared with 36% to 42% of all other victimized women.

The seriousness of the violence experienced by those who used self-defense is revealed in their help-seeking behavior. Rates of calling the police and women's centers increased significantly (chi-square = 21.6, $p < .001$; chi-square = 11.1, $p < .05$) as the amount of self-defensive violence increased. For example, 24% of those who always used self-defensive violence called the police, compared with only 3% of those who never did.

The types of violence used by these women and some of their other motives are shown in Tables 3.5 and 3.6. The groups did not differ significantly on the most serious forms of violence: choking, threats with weapons, and use of weapons. The groups also did not differ among women using "severe" defensive violence on the items "push, grab, shove" and "slapped." The highest frequencies of violence tended to be among those who used self-defense violence some or most of the time (but not all of the time). Whether the women were using "nonsevere" or "severe" violence, the more they used self-defense, the more they reported "fighting back." In only one comparison did the groups differ on the percentage of time they initiated violence. Those who used "nonsevere" violence most of the time for self-defense also initiated the violence an average of 28% of the time, compared with about 16% of the time for those who never or sometimes used "nonsevere" self-defense.

Tables 3.7, 3.8, 3.9, and 3.10 show some of the comparisons for the demographic and belief variables. Older women, who are more likely to be married, divorced, or separated, are the most likely to use self-defense all of the time.[5] The word *older* is merely relative here; only college students are in the sample. For example, those who always used self-defense were the oldest, averaging 27 years old among those using "severe" violence. These women also tended to be separated or divorced. Those using any frequency of self-defense were more likely to be living with a partner currently or in the past year. For those using "nonsevere" violence, the frequency of drinking alcohol with one's partner was higher for those who never or sometimes used defensive violence. Patriarchal beliefs and attitudes approving of dating violence did not differ significantly among the groups.

TABLE 3.5 Comparisons Among Women Using Different Levels of "Nonsevere" Defensive Violence by Violent Acts Women Report Committing

	1 Non-defensive 0% n = 422	2 Some Defensive 1%–49% n = 137	3 Mostly Defensive 50%–99% n = 72	4 All Defensive 100% n = 47		
Abuse		Mean			*F*	*SNK*
Threw at partner	1.2	2.1	1.9	.9	5.8***	2>4, 1; 3>1
Pushed, grabbed, shoved	2.4	3.3	3.9	2.6	6.4***	3, 2>1
Slapped	1.1	1.8	2.8	1.0	11.4***	3>1, 2, 3; 2>1
Kicked, bit, hit with fist	.8	1.6	1.7	1.8	6.1***	3, 2>1
Hit or tried to hit—object	.8	1.2	2.1	1.2	7.5***	3>2, 1
Beat up	.03	.23	.08	.08	2.4	2>1
Choked	.11	.20	.06	.04	.5	
Threat with weapon	.02	.06	.06	.06	.9	
Used weapon	.0	.0	.0	.0	—	

*p ≤ .05; **p ≤ .01; ***p ≤ .001.

Discussion

The CNS data presented in this chapter show that many Canadian female respondents reported using violence against their heterosexual dating partners. However, only a small percentage reported using violence that was likely to cause serious injuries, such as "beating up" or "using a weapon." This finding is consistent with data from Saunders's (1986) sample of battered women and two national U.S. dating violence studies: Stets and Henderson (1991) and White and Koss (1991).

TABLE 3.6 Comparisons Among Women Using Different Levels of "Severe" Defensive Violence by Violent Acts Women Report Committing

	1 Non- defensive 0% n = 205	2 Some Defensive 1%–49% n = 75	3 Mostly Defensive 50%–99% n = 45	4 All Defensive 100% n = 31		
Abuse		Mean			F	SNK
Threw at partner	1.7	2.6	2.7	1.2	3.6**	2>1
Pushed, grabbed, shoved	3.3	4.0	4.3	2.3	2.6	
Slapped	1.6	2.4	2.5	1.3	2.4	
Kicked, bit, hit with fist	1.8	2.9	3.1	2.5	3.2*	2>1
Hit or tried to hit—object	1.8	2.2	2.9	1.4	2.6*	3>1
Beat up	.06	.49	.0	.12	3.5*	2>1
Choked	.19	.54	.03	.06	1.6	
Threat with weapon	.04	.11	.12	.08	1.0	
Used weapon	.0	.02	.0	.0	1.7	

$*p \le .05$; $**p \le .01$; $***p \le .001$.

The most important feature of the research reported here is its focus on the women's motives for violence. Although many women are indeed violent in dating relationships, a common motive for violence was self-defense; a majority of women did not initiate an attack. Furthermore, as predicted in our first hypothesis, the concepts of self-defense and "fighting back" tend to be closely related.

Some of the women who reported initiating violence may have sensed impending violence from their partners and thus initiated an assault to stop the overwhelming buildup of tension (Gelles, 1974; Lewis, 1981). For example, according to Walker (1979), physically abused

(text continued on p. 86)

TABLE 3.7 Age, Beliefs, and Alcohol Use of Women Using Different Levels of "Nonsevere" Defensive Violence

Characteristics	1 Non- defensive 0% n = 205	2 Some Defensive 1%–49% n = 75	3 Mostly Defensive 50%–99% n = 45	4 All Defensive 100% n = 31	F	SNK
		Mean				
Age	21.7	22.3	23.3	24.8	7.3***	4>1, 2; 3>1
Drinking alcohol with partner	3.1	3.0	2.6	2.9	4.3**	1, 2>3
Sex role beliefs	3.8	3.8	3.8	3.9	1.6	

*$p \le .05$; **$p \le .01$; ***$p \le .001$.

TABLE 3.8 Background of Women Using Different Levels of "Nonsevere" Defensive Violence

Background	1 Non- defensive 0% n = 205	2 Some Defensive 1%–49% n = 75	3 Mostly Defensive 50%-99% n = 45	4 All Defensive 100% n = 31	Chi-sq.
		Percentages			
Lived with partner past year	24.6	29.8	41.8	33.0	8.7*
Marital status:					
never married	75.7	66.7	64.5	52.2	
married	7.0	5.4	7.5	8.4	
live with	13.3	22.4	23.0	24.1	
separated	1.6	2.7	1.9	8.8	
divorced	2.4	2.9	3.1	6.5	25.4**
Alcohol use with partner in past year, "often" or "very often":					
	33.2	17.1	16.6	24.7	

*$p \le .05$; **$p \le .01$; ***$p \le .001$.

TABLE 3.9 Age, Beliefs, and Alcohol Use of Women Using Different Levels of "Severe" Defensive Violence

Characteristics	1 Non- defensive 0% n = 205	2 Some Defensive 1%–49% n = 75	3 Mostly Defensive 50%–99% n =45	4 All Defensive 100% n = 31	F	SNK
	Mean					
Age	22.0	22.5	22.6	27.3	10.2***	4>1, 2, 3
Drinking alcohol with partner	2.9	3.1	2.8	2.9	1.0	
Sex role beliefs	3.8	3.8	3.9	3.9	1.5	

$*p \le .05; **p \le .01; ***p \le .001.$

TABLE 3.10 Background of Women Using Different Levels of "Severe" Defensive Violence

Background	1 Non- defensive 0% n = 205	2 Some Defensive 1%–49% n = 75	3 Mostly Defensive 50%–99% n = 45	4 All Defensive 100% n = 31	Chi-sq.
	Mean				
Lived with partner past year	23.5	36.7	48.0	37.9	11.6**
Marital status:					
never married	75.9	62.9	52.8	40.5	
married	7.2	8.6	5.0	10.5	
live with	10.5	23.1	38.6	24.5	
separated	2.8	3.6	3.6	11.7	
divorced	3.2	1.8	0.0	12.8	42.8**
Alcohol use with partner in past year, "often" or "very often":					
	27.1	31.5	17.7	30.8	

$*p \le .05; **p \le .01; ***p \le .001.$

women experience a three-phase battering cycle: (a) the tension-building phase, (b) the explosion or acute battering incident, and (c) calm, loving respite. Based on numerous interviews with battered women, she concluded that

> the battered woman occasionally does provoke a phase-two incident. When this occurs, the couple usually has been involved in battering behavior for a long period of time. The woman often senses that the period of inevitability is very close, and she cannot tolerate her terror, her anger, or anxiety any longer. She also knows from experience that the third phase of calm will follow the acute battering incident. She would prefer to get the second phase over with rather than to continue in fear of it, so she provokes the batterer into an explosion. She then has control over when and why the incident occurs, rather than being at his total mercy. (p. 60)

Other women may have hit first because of a well-founded fear of being beaten or raped by their dating partners (Hanmer & Saunders, 1984). Unfortunately, the methods used in the CNS are not able to uncover such preemptive strikes as a possible motive. It is important that such probing be included in any future studies.

These data begin to challenge the increasingly common assertion by people whom we refer to as "people without data" (Schwartz & DeKeseredy, 1994b), such as Fekete (1994), that violence in Canadian college dating is sexually symmetrical, that women are extremely violent—perhaps as violent as men. If the only measure of violence is a simple measure of prevalence, then the CNS, like most studies based on the CTS, does in fact find that women are very violent. However, in this study an investigation of motives seems to modify such a finding. Given that a great deal of women's violence is self-defensive or "fighting back," it will be important in the future to carefully parcel out just how much of women's violence can be legitimately compared with men's violence.

The hypothesis that women using defensive violence would have experienced higher rates of severe victimization, including physical and sexual assault, was supported by the CNS data presented in this chapter. There has not been extensive interview and qualitative research on dating violence on the type of severe victimization reported in these surveys, but such findings are completely consistent with research conducted on other victimized women. For example, Angela Browne (1987, pp. 96-97) found that some of the women who have killed their intimate male partners in self-defense have experienced brutal forms of sexual and

BOX 3.1.

Sexual Abusive Acts Reported by Battered Women Who Killed in Self-Defense

In many of the homicide relationships, the men required sex after beatings, and this seemed like rape to the women. At times, it was also extremely painful because of injuries sustained in the earlier assault. In one fairly typical case, the man wanted sex every day during the last two or three years the couple was together, whether or not there had been violence, and this was almost always abusive. He would choke, pinch, or bite the woman; he also forced a variety of objects into her vagina and compelled her to perform oral sex on him, holding her by the head and pulling out chunks of her hair with his hands. It seemed that he hurt her so as to become excited.

In another case, the woman reported that her partner forced some kind of sexual activity on her three or four times a week during the final year of their relationship. He would rape her with food objects and penile attachments or begin to masturbate on her face and stomach when she was sleeping. Often, she woke during the night to find him forcing anal intercourse. He was very rough with this; she bled after most incidents. Her arms and shoulders were always bruised from being held down. He seemed intent to hurt her. She would stuff the corner of a pillow in her mouth to keep from screaming. He beat her if she cried out, and she knew it terrified the children. She began getting severe stomach cramps at night and eventually developed ulcers. Several times, he also tried to force sexual activity between her and the family dog. She resisted desperately, and he would try to hold her down and still control the dog. Finally, he gave up, but she was always bruised from these attempts and sometimes received a beating afterward for resisting.

SOURCE: Browne (1987, pp. 96-97).

physical assault. Some terrifying examples of this problem can be found in Box 3.1.

There was also a nonsignificant tendency for women using defensive violence to seek medical help at a higher rate than other women and a significant tendency for them to seek other formal help, which suggests

---

BOX 3.2.

Self-Help Homicide

Consider what the world must look like to Kathleen Kaplan of New Hampshire. When she was fourteen her stepfather raped her. She ran away from home, into the arms of Morton (Jack) Kaplan, then forty-seven, who married her at fourteen and during the next ten years, beat her "often," compelled her to have an abortion, and forced her into nude dancing and prostitution. When she asked for a divorce, he threatened to cut the fingers and ears off their baby. She tried to kill herself. According to a *New York Times* report: "The police refused to intervene. When a friend offered to kill Mr. Kaplan, Ms. Kaplan thought it was a joke. But the friend called her later and said he had killed Mr. Kaplan, and she paid him." She pleaded guilty to second-degree murder and was sentenced to thirty years in prison (the hit man was acquitted). Her case hit the news again when New Hampshire Governor John Sununu, just before leaving for Washington to become President Bush's chief of staff, granted Kathleen Kaplan a conditional pardon; after fifteen months of working outside the prison, she was to be released, having served little more than eight years in prison. One condition of her pardon was that she relinquish all rights to her son. Raped as a youngster,

---

that these women are the defensive recipients of attacks rather than the instigators. It seems less likely that they would be calling the police to report their own violence.

As mentioned above, there have not been many qualitative studies of battered women who fight back against dates or boyfriends. There have been some excellent studies of such women who have been forced to the extreme of killing these men to save their own lives or to get away. In one such study, Ann Jones (1994, pp. 100-101) argues that the seemingly extreme case she outlines in Box 3.2 is not really all that extreme. Although relatively few women kill their intimate partners, a tremendous number of women (including those in dating relationships) find themselves in physical danger and without any help from friends, family, or the police. Thus, they find that their best hope of protecting themselves is to engage in violent behavior themselves.

beaten, terrorized, and sold for a decade; imprisoned for eight years and deprived of her child—Kathleen Kaplan is now expected to be grateful to the man who released her rather than keep her locked up, as the law prescribed for another twenty-two years. And many good citizens of New Hampshire opposed the early release of this "murderer."

This is not an extreme case. In fact, it's quite routine. Like Kathleen Kaplan, women in danger often seek help from police and prosecutors and judges who, as we have seen, decline to protect them. It is left to women, then, to help themselves as best they can. So it should come as no surprise that some women kill the men who abuse them. The number of women who kill has decreased steadily since battered women's shelters opened in the 1970s, indicating that women do not want to kill their assailants but to escape them. (During the same period the number of men killing wives and girlfriends has gone steadily up.) Currently, in the United States about five hundred married women and about half as many unmarried women every year commit what some legal scholars have termed "self-help homicide": in self-defense or as a last resort, they kill the men who rape and batter them.

SOURCE: Jones (1994, pp. 100-101).

Those with differing levels of defensive violence did not differ in their patriarchal beliefs or their approval of male-to-female dating violence, giving no support to the hypotheses that these would be related. We had further hypothesized that women whose violent acts were not used in self-defense would drink more alcohol with their partners. This was true for women using little or no defensive "nonsevere" violence, but there was no relationship for those who used severe violence. Therefore, this hypothesis was partly supported.

Data Limitations

The research reported in this chapter was exploratory, and thus the findings should be taken cautiously. For example, cross-sectional data cannot be used to draw conclusions about causal directions. Therefore, we can argue from our data that women's use of defensive violence was related to their partner's violence. This may mean, as we have suggested here, that the more violent the partner's violence, the more likely that women are to respond with self-defensive or "fighting back" violence. Others have suggested a different timing pattern. Feld and Straus (1990) suggest that the husband's greater violence is likely to come after the wife's minor violence. At least on the anecdotal level, we know that many women have said that if they use minor violence, even in self-defense, their partner is more likely to escalate the violent encounter with greater violence of his own (e.g., Fojtik, 1977-1978). Knowing that women's use of defensive violence is related to her partner's violence does not tell us whether she is reacting to greater violence or whether he is responding to her efforts at self-defense with greater violence.

As more older women enroll in college, those who conduct research and provide services need to be aware that the most severe dating violence may have occurred with divorced and separated women long before their arrival on campus. For example, the CNS asked about violence in dating relationships since leaving high school. It is possible that these women were abused by the same dating partner in high school, after high school, and during marriage. Like several woman interviewed by Kurz (1995), their divorce and separation may have been the result of violence. For example, one women told Kurz that she left her husband

> after a big fight where he was physically abusive. First I went to the Emergency Room. Then I went to the Police Roundhouse. The police came to the house and made him leave. . . . I got a restraining order. It lasted for a whole year.
>
> There was violence constantly for 10 years. It would usually happen on the weekends. We would fight over small things like, if he would go out on Friday, I would say I want to go out on Saturday. But slowly over the years something was clicking inside. I said to myself, "Are you going to let someone else run your life?" (p. 54)

Another reason for caution is that respondents were not asked about their behavior and possible motives one incident at a time. We do not know about the correlations using incidents as the unit of analysis. Further, a substantial number of women use violence in response to their male partners' attempts to physically, sexually, economically, or psychologically control them (Cascardi, Vivian, & Meyer, 1991). Unfortunately, the CTS used in this survey mainly conceptualized violence as a means of settling conflicts or disputes. In retrospect, we might have obtained a higher percentage of women who reported using violence in self-defense if we had asked questions about response to men's control-instigated violence or psychological abuse (Ellis, 1995).

Another limitation is that we only asked about three motives. Other researchers have found a large percentage of undergraduates reporting other motives, such as retaliation for emotional hurt or a felt need to protect themselves (e.g., Follingstad et al., 1991) as well as those reported here. While we presume these would be covered by our category of "fighting back," it is possible that they are not.

Chapter Summary

A key finding of the CNS is that differing pictures emerge of women in dating relationships when they are categorized by how much of their violence is defensive violence. At one extreme are those who say that their violence is never used defensively to respond to an assault. They tend to be younger, never married, victims of emotional abuse, and more likely to drink alcohol with their partners. They tend to use most forms of violence less often. At the other extreme are women whose violence is always used in self-defense. These women are likely to be older, to be separated or divorced, and to have suffered the highest rates of sexual and physical abuse, in combination with threats and emotional abuse. The more abuse they suffered, the more likely it was they would respond with "severe" violence.

Thus, our overall conclusion is that much of the violence by Canadian undergraduate women is in self-defense and should not be labeled "mutual combat" or "male partner abuse." Furthermore, a profile is provided of the women who are the most victimized and most likely to try to defend themselves. This discovery that there are distinctly different groups in terms of their likelihood to use self-defense can be used to guide service programs and future research.

Notes

1. See Schwartz and DeKeseredy (1993) for more information on this problem.
2. The new CTS is also referred to as the CTS2. See Straus, Hamby, Boney-McCoy, and Sugarman (1995) for more information on this instrument.

3. Specifically, 39% did not give any of these three motives for "minor" violence, and 33% did not give any of the three for "severe" violence.

4. This very complex information, which involves 10 types of victimization and four levels of use of violence, is not shown here in a table for space reasons.

5. It should be noted that a growing body of empirical literature shows that many separated women are at great risk of being physically, sexually, and psychologically abused by their estranged male partners. See Ellis and Stuckless (1996) and Kurz (1995, 1996) for some recent research on postseparation woman abuse.

4

Risk Factors and
Dating Abuse

> While research on men's violence toward women raises a number of
> complicated issues, it is sometimes forgotten that men's violence is men's
> behavior. As such, it is not surprising that the more fruitful efforts to
> explain this behavior have focused on male characteristics. What is
> surprising is the enormous effort to explain male behavior by examining
> characteristics of women. It is hoped that future research will show more
> about the factors that promote violent male behavior and that stronger
> theory will be developed to explain it. (Hotaling & Sugarman, 1986,
> p. 120)

What is to be done about curbing the alarming rates of physical,
sexual, and psychological abuse described in Chapter 2? Before we and
others committed to enhancing female dating partners' physical and
emotional safety can adequately answer this important question, it is first
necessary to identify the key sources or *risk factors* associated with the
types of male-to-female victimization uncovered by the CNS and other
dating abuse studies. Risk factors are typically defined in the social scientific woman abuse literature as attributes of a couple, victim, or perpe-
trator that are associated with an increased probability of male-to-female
victimization (Hotaling & Sugarman, 1986). They may be causes, co-
occurrences, or consequences of abuse (Smith, 1990b).

In this chapter, we present new findings generated by the CNS on
five major risk factors associated with woman abuse in Canadian post-

93

secondary school courtship: the ideology of familial patriarchy, male peer support, exposure to pornographic media, dating status, and alcohol consumption. It should be noted in passing that, like many other feminist and profeminist scholars, CNS researchers devoted little attention to identifying the characteristics of the female survivors in their sample, for a number of reasons. The first problem is perhaps more ideological. The entire tone and direction of the research make certain presumptions, at least in many persons' minds. Looking at the victims rather than the offenders can be interpreted as blaming women for their partners' abusive conduct. Research that examines how abused female dating partners differ from those who are not abused suggests that there is something "wrong" with those who are victimized by their intimate partners (Bograd, 1988). What will it tell us if we find that battered women are less intelligent or more intelligent than their partners? Do less intelligent or more intelligent women deserve to be beaten?

At any rate, it may not make any difference. Despite our distress expressed above, a great many researchers have in fact looked at these women specifically to see how they might differ from other women. Previous research on woman abuse in marital and cohabiting relationships (e.g., Smith, 1990b) and in-depth reviews of the published literature reveal that focusing on the characteristics of victims or survivors is futile. For example, Hotaling and Sugarman (1986) found only 1 variable out of 42 characteristics allegedly related to wife-victims that consistently discriminated between abused women and those who were not abused. Most researchers suggest that this finding is consistent with the argument that any woman is a possible object of violence. What differs is not the woman, but the man. If the man is a batterer, he will batter any woman with whom he is intimate.

The Ideology of Familial Patriarchy

In Canada, as in the United States and other advanced industrial nations (e.g., Japan), a substantial number of male actions, values, and beliefs are microsocial expressions of broader patriarchal forces. Simply put, this means that the problem is not one in which individual men simply all happen to suffer from the same psychopathy, or weak ego, or whatever. Rather, they all live in the same society, and the single individual man is partially a reflection of the values and beliefs that are expressed by the broader society. We are arguing that these broader forces are patriarchal. What is patriarchy? There are many different answers to this question. In fact, the definition of patriarchy is the subject of much heated debate. It is not uncommon, however, to follow scholars such as Dobash and Dobash (1979), who assert that the patriarchy is made up of two elements: a structure and an ideology. Structurally, the patriarchy is a hierarchical social organization in which males have more power and privilege than females. This is simple enough, but it does not answer a number of questions. Why do men maintain this power? Why don't they, in the spirit of fair play, simply give up enough power to equalize the power between men and women? Why don't women rebel against their inferior position? The answer is the other part of patriarchy: the ideology. This is not unique to this particular social formation, of course, but it happens to be patriarchy that we are talking about. In this case, the ideology of patriarchy provides a political and social rationale for itself. Both men and women come to believe that it is "natural" and "right" that women be in inferior positions. Men feel completely supported in excluding women, and up to a point, women feel that their exclusion is correct (DeKeseredy & Schwartz, 1993). To someone (male or female) who believes completely in the ideology of patriarchy, the entire concept of equal rights or women's liberation is a pretty difficult topic, sounding not only wrong but unnatural—literally, it goes against nature.

This sounds fairly simple, and in fact most definitions of patriarchy are fairly simple. There are, however, other types of male power systems. *Social patriarchy* is a term often used to refer to the type of male domination at the societal level, as discussed above. A subsystem of social patriarchy, often called *familial patriarchy,* refers to male control in domestic or intimate settings (Barrett, 1980; Eisenstein, 1980; Ursel, 1986). These two components really cannot be pulled too far apart; Smith (1990a) argues that one variant cannot be fully understood without reference to the other. Still, when dealing with violence within intimate relationships, a number of feminist researchers argue that the center of attention should be familial patriarchy, because that is the specific domain or setting where the violence is taking place (Martin, 1977; Millett, 1969; D. Smith, 1983; M. Smith, 1990a). This being the case, DeKeseredy and Kelly (1993b) originally examined the influence of the ideological element of familial patriarchy on the incidence (events that took place in the year before the survey) of female victimization in college and university dating relationships.

Modified versions of definitions of familial patriarchy offered by Smith (1990a) and DeKeseredy and Schwartz (1993) informed the one

BOX 4.1.

Einstein's Terms of Endearment Show Wedded Bliss Is Relative: "Wash My Clothes, Clean My Room," Scientist Told Wife

LONDON—A darker side of Albert Einstein emerged Tuesday from one of the scientist's 400 private papers to be auctioned by Christie's in New York next month.

In the letter, released for the first time, Einstein lays down a harsh charter of terms that his first wife, Mileva Maric, would have to obey if he were to continue living with her.

The letter is believed to date from April 1914, when the couple set up home in Berlin with their two sons after Einstein was appointed director of a new physics institute at Berlin University.

By then the marriage was far from happy, with Einstein dedicating all his time to research as he prepared his General Theory of Relativity for publication in 1915.

The 35-year-old scientist had also been conducting a secret two-year-long affair with his cousin Elsa, who he would marry on Valentine's Day, 1919.

In the letter to Mileva, Einstein dictates these terms:

employed in the CNS: *a discourse that supports the abuse of women who violate the ideals of male power and control over women in intimate relationships.* Relevant themes of this ideology are an insistence on women's obedience, respect, loyalty, dependency, sexual access, and sexual fidelity (Barrett & McIntosh, 1982; Dobash & Dobash, 1979; Pateman, 1988). Some examples of some of these themes are provided in Box 4.1.

These themes were operationalized with two indices used by Smith (1990a). One index measures patriarchal beliefs, and the other measures patriarchal attitudes. Cronbach's alpha coefficients (.79 for beliefs and .76 for attitudes) show that these indicators are reliable and consistent with Smith's (1990a) item factor analysis of female responses (.79 and .71, respectively). Tables 4.1 and 4.2 present the responses to these items, and as anticipated, most of the respondents do not report espousing a

A. You will see to it:
   1) that my clothes and linen are kept in order;
   2) that I am served three regular meals a day in my room;
   3) that my bedroom and study are always kept in good order and that my desk is not touched by anyone other than me.
B. You will renounce all personal relations with me, except when these are required to keep up social appearances. In particular, you will not request:
   1) that I sit with you at home;
   2) that I go out with you or travel with you.
C. You will promise explicitly to observe the following points in any contact with me:
   1) You will expect no affection from me and you will not reproach me for this;
   2) You must answer me at once when I speak to you;
   3) You must leave my bedroom or study at once without protesting when I ask you to go;
   4) You will promise not to denigrate me in the eyes of the children, either by word or by deed.

A few months after receiving this missive, Mileva took her sons, Hans, Albert and Eduard, back to Zurich, supposedly for a holiday. In fact, it was the beginning of the end of the marriage. She was never to return to her husband's side.

SOURCE: Roger Highfield, *Ottawa Citizen* (October 30, 1996, p. A2).

set of beliefs and attitudes supportive of patriarchy in intimate male-female relationships.

However, when these beliefs are correlated with whether the men actually engaged in physical, social, or sexual abuse, the results come out as predicted. The results presented in Table 4.3 demonstrate that men who espouse patriarchal beliefs and attitudes are more likely to engage in sexual, physical, and psychological abuse. All of the correlations reported in this table are significant at the .05 level. The correlation between sexual abuse and the patriarchal forces described in Table 4.3 is consistent with data showing that American men who sexually assault their dating partners tend to hold sexist or traditional beliefs.[1]

However, the data in Table 4.3 do not answer an important question of central concern to DeKeseredy and Kelly (1993b, p. 28) and the late

TABLE 4.1 Percentage of Respondents With Patriarchal Beliefs
            (N = 1,307)

Beliefs	Strongly Agree	Agree	Disagree	Strongly Disagree
A man has the right to decide whether or not his wife/partner should go out in the evening with her friends	2.3	7.2	49.6	41.0
A man has the right to decide whether or not his wife/partner should work outside the home	1.7	4.4	41.5	52.3
Sometimes it is important for a man to show his wife/partner that he is the head of the house	3.8	14.3	35.8	46.1
A man has the right to have sex with his wife/partner when he wants, even though she may not want to	0.9	1.5	35.5	62.1

SOURCE: Adapted from DeKeseredy and Kelly (1993b, p. 33).

TABLE 4.2 Percentage of Respondents Who Approve of a Man
            Slapping His Dating Partner or Girlfriend (N = 1,307)

Attitudes	Yes	Depends	No	Don't Know
She won't do what he tells her to do	1.5	2.9	95.2	0.5
She insults him when they are home alone	1.0	5.3	92.5	1.2
She insults him in public	1.5	8.0	88.9	1.5
She comes home drunk	1.3	5.7	91.3	1.6
She is sobbing hysterically	1.3	9.6	86.7	2.4
She won't have sex with him	0.9	1.9	96.4	0.8
He learns that she is dating another man	6.2	15.2	72.8	5.7
She hits him first when they are having an argument	7.1	22.4	66.4	4.0

Michael D. Smith (1990a): "Which group of men are prone to an ideology that perpetuates and legitimates woman abuse in university and college dating relationships?" Informed by DeKeseredy and Schwartz's (1993) male peer support model, DeKeseredy and Kelly (1993b) hypothesized that men who receive proabuse male peer support are most likely to adhere to the ideology of familial patriarchy, and it is to this risk factor that we now turn.

TABLE 4.3 Correlation Matrix, Means, and Standard Deviations of Sexual, Physical, and Psychological Abuse (N = 755)

Variables	1	2	3	4	5	6	7	8	9	10	$\bar{x}$	S
1. Physical abuse	1.00	.47	.48	.21	.36	.23	.22	.01	.28	.01	.05	2.3
2. Psychological abuse		1.00	.33	.21	.23	.34	.27	.09	.24	.16	4.6	4.9
3. Sexual abuse			1.00	.25	.31	.22	.28	<u>.04</u>	.23	<u>.04</u>	2.0	0.5
4. Respondents' patriarchal beliefs				1.00	.30	.14	.21	.11	.31	.10	13.7	2.1
5. Respondents' patriarchal attitudes					1.00	.20	.23	.11	.70	.12	22.9	1.9

SOURCE: Adapted from DeKeseredy and Kelly (1993b, p. 43).
NOTE: Given the large size of the sample, all bivariate correlations, except those that are underlined, meet or exceed the criterion level of statistical significance.

Male Peer Support

In recent years, one of the most popular attempts to explain the physical, sexual, and psychological victimization of women in college courtship is the argument that male peer support groups encourage, create, and justify such abuse. Male peer support, in this context, refers to "the attachments to male peers and the resources that these men provide which encourage and legitimate woman abuse" (DeKeseredy, 1990, p. 130). The ways in which all-male social networks contribute to their members' abusive actions are briefly described below.[2]

Male friends play an important role in the college careers of many men. Peer groups often provide members with resources such as social companionship, academic guidance, financial assistance, and emotional support (Cohen & Hoberman, 1983; Farr, 1988; Gwartney-Gibbs & Stockard, 1989; Levine & Perkins, 1980). Further, these all-male alliances directly and indirectly supply men with a repertoire of norms, values, and behaviors that shape their relations with women in dating relationships. For example, in contrast to popular myths about the highly romantic and erotic nature of North American courtship, many men instead find these interactions heavily marked by conflict and stress (DeKeseredy, 1988), and some men experience considerable stress when their partners reject or fail to live up to the ideals of familial patriarchy (DeKeseredy & Schwartz, 1993; Schwartz & DeKeseredy, 1997).

However, these women are regarded as appropriate targets of abuse by some male friends. They tell their friends to sexually, physically, and psychologically mistreat dating partners who challenge their patriarchal authority and/or who refuse to provide them with sexual gratification (Schwartz & DeKeseredy, 1997). Researchers in several studies (e.g., Kanin, 1985) have documented the existence of male social networks that approve of sexual assaults on certain dating partners, such as women who do not want to engage in sexual intercourse but have been defined by the men as highly sexually active: "teasers," "economic exploiters," or "pick-ups." Still, the problem remains for these men that they are committing rape. How can these generally law-abiding men convince themselves that they are still upstanding citizens while committing felony rape? One of many answers is that their peer support groups provide them with a "vocabulary of adjustment." By learning, and gaining support for, the idea that what they are doing is normal behavior (e.g., the women asked for it), they are able to engage in violent behavior that does not alter their conceptions of themselves as normal, respectable men (Kanin, 1967b).

This same phenomenon has been advanced as an explanation for wife beating. Both Bowker (1983) and Smith (1991) have argued that married men have peer groups that provide them with emotional and verbal support for upholding the tenets of familial patriarchy in a violent manner. The problem with these formulations is that they had not been systematically tested using national representative samples of male respondents. Using CNS data, DeKeseredy and Kelly (1993b) attempted to fill this research gap.

Woman abuse is, of course, multidimensional in nature (DeKeseredy & Hinch, 1991). There is no question that proabuse male peer support is similarly multidimensional (DeKeseredy, 1990; Schwartz & DeKeseredy, 1997). In other words, there are a variety of ways in which male college peers perpetuate and legitimate female victimization. Still, one set of researchers cannot study everything. Time and financial limitations restricted the CNS survey to a focus on the following five variants of male peer support.

(1) Routine activities. This first type of male peer support was operationalized by constructing a seven-item index (Cronbach's alpha = .73) that measures the frequency of participation in the following activities with other men (in an all-male environment) in a typical month in the past year:

- worked on school assignments,
- exercised or played sports,
- attended sports events as a spectator,
- went to bars or nightclubs,
- went to movies or plays,
- went out for dinner or lunch,
- worked for wages (e.g., a part- or full-time job or summer job).

(2) Informational support. This variable refers to the guidance and advice that influences men to sexually, physically, and psychologically abuse their dating partners. To measure this variable, DeKeseredy and Kelly (1993b) created an index (Cronbach's alpha = .70) by adding male respondents' scores on seven items developed by DeKeseredy (1988). For each of the following questions, respondents were asked to circle either yes or no:

Did any of your male friends tell you that . . .

- you should respond to your dates' or girlfriends' challenges to your authority by using physical force, such as hitting or slapping?
- it is alright for a man to hit his date or girlfriend in certain situations?
- your dates or girlfriends should have sex with you when you want?
- if a man spends money on a date, she should have sex with him in return?
- you should respond to your dates' or girlfriends' challenges to your authority by insulting them or putting them down?
- you should respond to your dates' or girlfriends' sexual rejections by employing physical force to obtain sex?
- it is alright for a man to physically force a woman to have sex with him under certain conditions?

(3) Attachments to abusive male peers. To measure this variable, another index was constructed. This index, which included the items below, had Cronbach's alpha = .65.[3]

To the best of your knowledge, how many of your male friends . . .

- have ever made physically forceful attempts at sexual activity with women they were dating which were disagreeable and

offensive enough that the woman responded in an offended
manner such as crying, fighting, screaming, or pleading?

- have ever used physical force, such as hitting or beating, to
resolve conflicts with their girlfriends and/or dating partners to
make them fulfill some demand?

- insulted their dating partners and/or girlfriends, sworn at them,
and/or withheld affection?

The response categories were none, 1 or 2, 3 to 5, 6 to 10, more than
10, and don't know.

(4) Peers' patriarchal attitudes. This variant of male peer support was
measured using an index (Cronbach's alpha = .80) consisting of the eight
items found in the patriarchal attitude index presented in Table 4.2. The
response categories for these items are "yes," "depends," "no," and
"don't know." The items were introduced with the following preamble:

> Now we would like to ask you some more questions about your current
> male friends. Some people think it is alright for a man to slap his dating
> partner or girlfriend in certain situations. Other people think it is not
> alright. For each of the following situations, please tell us if your male
> friends would approve of a man slapping his dating partner or girlfriend.
> Would they approve if *(circle the number which best represents your
> answer)* . . .

(5) Peer pressure to have sex. To measure this variable, respondents
were asked "How much pressure did your friends place on you to have
sex with your dating partners and/or girlfriends?" The response categories were "a great deal," "considerable," "moderate," "little," and "none."

Data Analysis

Correlation analysis was used by DeKeseredy and Kelly (1993b) to
measure the strength of association between the patriarchal ideology,
male peer support, and woman abuse variables. The resulting matrix
showing all of the variables together is shown in Table 4.4. Each of the
three woman abuse variables (physical, sexual, and psychological) was
then regressed on the patriarchal ideology and male peer support variables to determine their independent and part contribution to the three
forms of abuse. Squaring the part correlations yields the unique propor-

tion of variation in the abuse variables that is explained by each of the predictor variables.

In the information that follows, both correlation and regression analyses will be presented. These types of analyses can be used to answer different questions. The simple question for correlational analysis is the strength of the relationship between any two variables. Multiple regression, however, is used to show the effect when a series of predictor variables are taken into account at the same time. For example, it is commonly found that a variable is strongly correlated with a dependent variable, but when it is entered into a multiple regression formula, it does not provide any help in explanation at all.

Woman Abuse in Canadian Postsecondary School Courtship: The Contribution of Familial Patriarchy and Male Peer Support

Table 4.4 shows the following:

- Attachment to abusive peers and informational support are the male peer support variables most strongly associated with psychological abuse.
- Men who hold patriarchal attitudes are the most likely to physically assault their dating partners.
- Respondents' patriarchal attitudes and informational support are associated, albeit not very strongly, with all three forms of woman abuse.
- Respondents who espouse patriarchal beliefs are more likely to have friends who hold patriarchal attitudes (.31), while those who hold patriarchal attitudes are much more likely to associate with peers who possess similar attitudes (.70).
- All of the associations reported here are statistically significant.

Thus, in terms of the discussions here, there does seem to be some relationship between the holding of patriarchal attitudes and abuse. Certainly, there seems to be a definite tendency for men to see their friends as peer support groups: Those with patriarchal attitudes report that their friends have similar attitudes.

The results of DeKeseredy and Kelly's (1993b) multivariate analysis are presented in Tables 4.5, 4.6, and 4.7. Table 4.5 shows the following:

- Taken together, the patriarchal ideology and male peer support variables explain 21% of the variation in the incidence of sexual abuse.
- Respondents' patriarchal attitudes constitute the most important determinant of sexual abuse, followed by informational support, respondents'

TABLE 4.4 Correlation Matrix, Means, and Standard Deviations of Sexual, Physical, and Psychological Abuse ($N = 755$)

Variables	1	2	3	4	5	6	7	8	9	10	x̄	S
1. Physical abuse	1.00	.47	.48	.21	.36	.23	.22	.01	.28	.01	.05	2.3
2. Psychological abuse		1.00	.33	.21	.23	.34	.27	.09	.24	.16	4.6	4.9
3. Sexual abuse			1.00	.25	.31	.22	.28	.04	.23	.04	2.0	0.5
4. Respondents' patriarchal beliefs				1.00	.30	.14	.21	.11	.31	.10	13.7	2.1
5. Respondents' patriarchal attitudes					1.00	.20	.23	.11	.70	.12	22.9	1.9
6. Attachment to abusive peers						1.00	.42	.20	.39	.17	4.2	1.5
7. Informational support							1.00	.23	.52	.09	13.4	1.4
8. Pressure to have sex								1.00	.19	.11	1.5	0.5
9. Peers' patriarchal attitudes									1.00	.12	22.3	2.5
10. Routine activities										1.00	17.6	7.8

SOURCE: Adapted from DeKeseredy and Kelly (1993b, p. 43).
NOTE: Given the large size of the sample, all bivariate correlations, except those that are underlined, meet or exceed the criterion level of statistical significance.

TABLE 4.5 Ordinary Least Squares Estimates of the Effects of Male Peer Support on Sexual Abuse ($N = 586; R = .46; R^2 = .21; F = 22.1; p < .001$)

Predictor Variable	b	Beta	Standard Error of b	F
Pressure to have sex	−.09	−.06	.06	2.15
Respondents' patriarchal attitudes	.12	.301*	.02	30.92
Routine activities	−.002	−.02	.01	0.42
Attachment to abusive peers	.03	.06	.02	2.16
Respondent's patriarchal beliefs	.07	.20*	.01	24.08
Informational support	.15	.23*	.03	24.30
Peers' patriarchal attitudes	−.04	13**	.02	4.58

SOURCE: Adapted from DeKeseredy and Kelly (1993b, p. 44).
*$p < .001$; **$p < .01$; constant 15.1.

TABLE 4.6 Ordinary Least Squares Estimates of the Effects of Male Peer Support on Physical Abuse ($N = 577$; $R = .47$; $R^2 = .22$; $F = 23.5$; $p < .001$)

Predictor Variable	b	Beta	Standard Error of b	F
Pressure to have sex	−.36	−.09	.15	5.81
Respondents' patriarchal attitudes	.44	.42*	.05	60.84
Routine activities	−.01	−.04	.01	1.24
Attachment to abusive peers	.10	.08	.05	3.58
Respondents' patriarchal beliefs	−.10	.12**	.03	8.77
Informational support	-.30	.18*	.07	14.84
Peers' patriarchal attitudes	−.11	−14**	.05	4.98

SOURCE: Adapted from DeKeseredy and Kelly (1993b, p. 44).
*$p < .001$; **$p < .01$; constant 12.8.

patriarchal beliefs, and the familial patriarchal attitudes of peers. All four are statistically significant predictors of sexual abuse with the first three variables being highly statistically significant *($p < .001$)*

- None of the other three variables had significant independent effects on sexual abuse.

Table 4.6 presents the results of the analysis in which physical abuse is regressed on the same set of predictor variables. DeKeseredy and Kelly found that, taken together, these variables explain 22% of the variation in the incidence of this type of female victimization. Table 4.6 also shows the following:

- Respondents' patriarchal attitudes are clearly the most important determinant of male assaults on their dating partners. In fact, this variable is almost two and one half times as strong a predictor as informational support, which is the next most important variable. Both of these predictors are statistically significant at the .001 level.
- Patriarchal attitudes of peers and respondents' patriarchal beliefs are both statistically significant predictors, but only at the .05 level.

The results of these two analyses are fairly clear. In terms of both sexual assault and physical assault on dating partners, the most important explanatory variable in this research is the patriarchal attitude of the man himself, with the man's patriarchal beliefs also statistically significant. There is no question that the level of adherence to familial patriarchy (at

TABLE 4.7 Ordinary Least Squares Estimates of the Effects of Male
              Peer Support on Psychological Abuse ($N = 572$; $R = .45$;
              $R^2 = .20$; $F = 20.3$; $p < .001$)

Predictor Variable	b	Beta	Standard Error of b	F
Pressure to have sex	−.17	−.02	.38	.20
Respondents' patriarchal attitudes	.36	.141**	.14	6.47
Routine activities	.06	.09	.02	5.58
Attachment to abusive peers	.90	.27*	.14	39.75
Respondents' patriarchal beliefs	.28	.12**	.09	8.89
Informational support	.78	.18*	.20	14.96
Peers' patriarchal attitudes	−.23	−.11**	.13	3.11

SOURCE: Adapted from DeKeseredy and Kelly (1993b, p. 46).
$*p < .001$; $**p < .01$; constant 16.7.

least as measured by the instruments here) is an important factor in the
level of sexual and physical violence committed by these men.

However, the informational support provided by their peers is also
important. These men report that they have been told by their friends
that it is acceptable or even required behavior for them to hit or slap
their dates or girlfriends or to physically force them into sexual behavior,
at least under certain conditions.

The incidence scores for psychological abuse were regressed using
the same set of variables included in Table 4.6. Table 4.7 shows the
following:

- Taken together, the seven predictor variables explain 20% of the variation
  in psychological abuse.
- Attachment to abusive peers is the most important predictor.
- In the order of their relative importance, informational support, respondents' patriarchal attitudes, and respondents' patriarchal beliefs also had
  significant independent effects on psychological abuse.
- All four variables were statistically significant predictors, with peers'
  attitudes significant at the $p = .001$ level.

Of interest, when dealing with psychological or emotional abuse, the
same factors that are important in physical and sexual abuse are also
important here: patriarchal beliefs and attitudes, and informational
support. However, here, for the first time, what is called "attachment to
abusive peers" is the most predictive variable. This suggests that men who

TABLE 4.8 Unique Variance in the Incidence of Sexual, Physical, and Psychological Abuse Explained by Statistically Significant Predictor Variables

Predictor Variable	Percentage of Variance Explained		
	Sexual Abuse	*Physical Abuse*	*Psychological Abuse*
Respondents' patriarchal attitudes	5.2	5.0	3.0
Informational support	3.7	4.2	3.7
Peers' patriarchal attitudes	2.8	2.6	—
Respondents' patriarchal beliefs	3.0	4.2	3.0
Attachment to abusive peers	—	—	5.0
Total	14.7	16.0	15.0
r^2	21.0	22.0	20.0

SOURCE: Adapted from DeKeseredy and Kelly (1993b, p. 46).

have friends who physically, sexually, and emotionally abuse their woman friends are also prone to the same behavior.

Another way to look at the relative contribution of the various important predictor variables is to compute part correlations and then to square them. Table 4.8 shows, when all of these variables are acting at the same time, the contribution of the men's patriarchal beliefs, their attitudes, and the three male peer support variables to the variance explained within each of the three types of woman abuse. This is a good review of the material we have covered in the earlier tables.

- Patriarchal attitudes account for the largest amount of variance (5.2%) explained in sexual and physical abuse.
- A male peer support variable, attachment to abusive peers, explains the largest amount of variance in psychological abuse (5%).
- When they are combined, two male peer support variables, informational support and attachment to abusive peers, explain more of the variation in psychological abuse (8.7%) than do respondents' patriarchal beliefs and attitudes (6%).
- The above pattern is reversed, however, for sexual abuse (8.2% versus 6.5%, respectively) and physical abuse (9.2% versus 6.8%, respectively).
- Taken together, the four statistically significant predictor variables explain 70% of the total variance explained in sexual abuse, 75% of the total variance explained in psychological abuse, and 73% of the total variance explained in physical abuse.

Summary of CNS Data Analysis

DeKeseredy and Kelly's (1993b) analysis of CNS data shows that Canadian men who report abusing their girlfriends and dating partners are more likely than those who do not report abusive behavior to endorse an ideology of familial patriarchy. If they are supported by male peers, these men are even more likely to abuse their partners. The initial question here, whether male peer support contributes to female victimization in Canadian college courtship, has been confirmed.

However, male peer support does not seem to take the same form in all cases of woman abuse (Schwartz & DeKeseredy, 1997). One of the findings in this chapter has been that different forms of male peer support are relatively more or less important for different types of female victimization. For example, informational support and peers' patriarchal attitudes are related to all three types of woman abuse examined in this book: physical, sexual, and psychological abuse. Routine activities do not seem to be related to any of the three, and peers' patriarchal attitudes only predict psychological abuse. Thus, how important for woman abuse might be the specific elements of male peer support, respondents' patriarchal beliefs, and respondents' patriarchal attitudes on woman abuse in Canadian college and university dating relationships varies with the type of victimization.

There is one important statistical warning to make here, however. All of the work above points out that the combined effect of all of the male peer support variables and the attitude and belief variables explains only about 21% of the variance in woman abuse in courtship. Obviously, then, a great deal remains to be explained. In other words, there are variables missing from this analysis that are important to locate before we can reach a fuller understanding.

Part of the problem is measurement error. The way in which respondents were forced to answer certain questions may have reduced the amount of explanatory power of several of the variables. As we have pointed out earlier in this book, many researchers worry that there is measurement error inherent in asking respondents to recall events that may have taken place more than a year previously. But there are other factors not measured here that could have changed the amount of the variance that was explained. For example, there were few variables that measured differences in the respondent himself. (Is he prone to violence? Is he low on self-control? Does he have little concern for the feelings of others or the consequences of his behavior?) There are situational variables that many feel are important: Were one or both parties drinking? Did these events take place in the context of a date or just between friends? Another factor that many have felt important (Schwartz & DeKeseredy, 1997) has been the type of male peer support available: Did the respondent feel the mild pressure of some guys at a bar he goes to or the steady pressure of fraternity or sports team brothers?

For example, according to DeKeseredy and Kelly (1993b), two variables that might be significantly associated with all types of abuse are a "past history of violence" on the part of the man and a history of learning about male dominance. The past history, they suggest, does not only mean a history of violence toward former girlfriends or dates but could include violence toward anyone, such as sisters, friends, or relatives. Past violence, many theorists have argued, is one of the best predictors of present or future violence (Monahan, 1981). As to male dominance, simply growing up in a family marked by parental familial patriarchal values and norms may be an enabling factor that allows a man to engage in woman abuse as he grows up (Bowker, 1983).

Pornography

Several theorists have argued that the contribution of pornography to woman abuse in dating is related to male peer support. For example, some men learn to sexually objectify women through their exposure to pornographic media (Jensen, 1995), and they often learn these lessons in groups, such as pornographic film showings at fraternity houses. Fraternity "brothers" also typically go to pornographic theaters in groups. For example, some of the brothers interviewed by Sanday (1990) stated that

> seeing pornography is something to do before their parties start. They want to learn what it's like to "have a two foot dick" and to have a good time together. They never go alone, always together. They go together in order to have a good time, laugh, and make jokes during the movie. They dissociate themselves from the men who go alone to porno movies downtown and sit in seats "with coats and newspapers spread out over their laps" and "jerk off" during the movie. They believe this is sick, but they don't think "getting off" while reading *Playboy* privately or enacting a porno fantasy in their house is necessarily sick. (p. 129)

Some studies (e.g., Bergen, 1996; Harmon & Check, 1989; Itzin & Sweet, 1992; Russell, 1990) demonstrate at least some link between the victimization of currently or formerly married or cohabiting women and the consumption of pornography. However, to the best of our knowledge, prior to the CNS, there have been no large-scale empirical attempts to examine whether exposure to pornography is related to physical and sexual abuse in North American college dating relationships. Using CNS data gathered from all male and female respondents who answered the quantitative question on pornography (see Chapter 1) and the questions on the prevalence (since leaving high school) of sexual and physical victimization (see Chapter 2), we wanted to fill this research gap by determining the extent to which pornography is related to these two types of victimization.

Of the 1,638 women in our sample who both dated and answered the quantitative question on pornography, 137 (8.4%) stated that they were upset by their dating partners trying to get them to do what they had seen in pornographic media. This is very similar to the 10% figure that Russell (1990) reports for her similar question, although it should be pointed out that, for the most part, Russell interviewed women significantly older than the women here. What may be most important to our research on the contribution of pornography is that Table 4.9 shows there is a significant relationship between being upset by men's attempts to imitate pornographic scenes and sexual victimization. Of those who were sexually abused, 22.3% had also been upset by attempts to get them to imitate pornographic scenarios. Only 5.8% of the women who were not victimized reported being upset by pornography. These figures compare well with Itzin and Sweet's (1992) report of the British Cosmopolitan Survey, although their crude methodology and cruder style of reporting the results make any real comparison impossible. We had some worry that the large number of married women here would affect these relationships, but tables based on women who were never married, or never married but living with a male partner, look virtually identical to the full Table 4.9.

Of interest, similar questions were asked of the men in this survey, although the men were asked about their role as offenders. Here, fully 6.8% of the men admitted that they had upset their dating partners by trying to get them to imitate pornography. Further, the men were more likely to admit being forcible sexual victimizers if they also admitted to upsetting a woman in this way. Almost four times as many upsetters (9.3%) as nonupsetters (2.4%) also admitted to committing a forcible

TABLE 4.9 College Sexual Victimization by Pornography
(*N* = 1,638 Women)

		Have you been made upset by being asked to act out pornography?		
		Yes	No	Total
Forced into sexual acts since high school	Yes	57 22.3% 41.6%	199 77.7% 13.3%	256 100.0%
	No	80 5.8% 58.4%	1,302 94.2% 86.7%	1,382 100.0%
		137	1,501	1,638

NOTE: Chi-square = 76.51; *df* = 1; *p* = .0000; phi = .216.

sexual victimization after high school. This relationship is statistically significant (*p* = .000), although weak (phi = .104).

The relationship shown for sexual violence in Table 4.9 also seems to hold for physical violence. Table 4.10 shows that, like some of the survivors of wife rape included in Bergen's (1996) sample, women who indicated that they were physically assaulted at least once since leaving high school were also much more likely to have been upset by being asked to do what their dating partners had seen in pornographic pictures, movies, and so on. Consider the brutal acts described below by one of the wife rape survivors interviewed by Bergen (1996):

> He was really into watching porno movies, and he tried to make me do all sorts of things. And I [didn't] like it. He hurt my stomach so bad because I was pregnant, and he was making me do these things. I think he's a sadist—he pulls my hair and punches me and slaps me and makes me pass out. (p. 18)

Of the female CNS respondents who reported being physically abused in a dating relationship, 15.4% also reported being upset by pornography. Only 4.5% of those who were not physically victimized reported being upset. Although the relationships in Tables 4.9 and 4.10 are not extremely strong, they are statistically significant (*p* = .000). The

TABLE 4.10 College Physical Victimization by Pornography
              (*N* = 1,653 Women)

		Have you been made upset by being asked to act out pornography?		
		Yes	No	Total
Physical victimization	Yes	90	500	590
since high school		15.3%	84.7%	100.0%
		65.2%	33.0%	
	No	48	1,015	1,063
		4.5%	95.5%	100.0%
		34.8%	67.0%	
		138	1,515	1,653

NOTE: Chi-square = 57.183; *df* = 1; *p* = .0000; phi = .186.

same relationship noted above for men holds true for physical violence
also. One third of all of those who admitted to upsetting a woman with
requests to imitate pornography also admitted to physically abusing a
woman after high school. Of those who did not admit to upsetting a
woman, 17.2% admitted to physical abuse. Although it is not uncommon
to point to fraternity houses as a source of pornography influences (e.g.,
Sanday, 1990), CNS data show that there was no difference between
fraternity members and other men in the rates at which they admit to
upsetting a woman by trying to get her to imitate pornography.

   No doubt, as with any highly sensitive topic, these findings are quite
conservative in that many women will not disclose incidents on a survey
such as the CNS. In general, paper-and-pencil surveys uncover fewer
incidents than would much more costly face-to-face measures (National
Research Council, 1996). Further, as Harmon and Check (1989) point
out, one might suspect underreporting in that women could be upset by
what their partners are asking or demanding but still be completely unaware that pornography was related to their partners' actions. Finally, a
more comprehensive study limited to this single issue might investigate
the differing and changing nature of messages in pornography as well as
the effect that this might have (Brosius, Weaver, & Staab, 1993; Cowan
& Dunn, 1994).

The most important limitation of these data is that the correlational approach taken in this study does not allow any confidence that the same people who committed the physical and sexual abuse are also making these women uncomfortable with pornography. Of course, the data from the men suggest that there is a relationship here to investigate. Still, future researchers with a more narrow focus (and thus the ability to ask deeper questions) should consider ways to discover whether the same men are abusers and pornography "upsetters."

Pornography Summary

The CNS data presented here help us to tentatively conclude that pornography plays a major role in the sexual and physical abuse of Canadian women in college and university dating relationships. These findings mirror the abuse reported by married and formerly married women (Bergen, 1996; Harmon & Check, 1989). It may be worthwhile to note that this survey did not cover situations in which women welcomed the opportunity to act out pornography. Just as sexual abuse questions only ask about unwanted sex, the pornography question here only asks about attempts to imitate pornography that caused distress.

Does pornography cause woman abuse? Certainly this question cannot be answered from correlational data. The problem is that it might very well be that the same factors that cause a man to abuse women might also cause him to purchase pornography (Jensen, 1996). In other words, eliminating pornography might not have an effect on the amount of woman abuse. However, the relationship discovered in the CNS shows that male attempts to get women to imitate scenes in pornographic media are a component of the problem of woman abuse in university dating.

Dating Status

Previous North American dating violence studies show that the length and intimacy level of heterosexual relationships are strongly associated with physical, sexual, and psychological abuse.[4] Following these studies and the theoretical work done by Ellis and DeKeseredy (1989), a major objective of the CNS was to test the following hypothesis: *The more serious the dating relationship, the more likely men are to physically and sexually abuse their dating partners.*

Three questions were used to measure dating status. For each of the following, respondents were asked to circle either yes or no. Of course, female participants were asked about their relationships with men.

Just in the past 12 months alone . . .

- have you engaged in casual dating with women (e.g., a good time with no future commitment or obligation on the part of you and your dating partner)?
- have you had any serious dating relationships with women (e.g., involving a great deal of commitment and intimacy)?
- have you ever moved in with or lived regularly with a girlfriend?

Consistent with previous research, the data presented in Table 4.11 support our hypothesis,[5] as can be seen in the following examples:

- Cohabiting men are more sexually and physically abusive, and cohabiting women are more likely to be abused in a one-year period, than those involved in serious and casual dating relationships.
- Male offenders and female survivors in serious dating relationships report higher incidence rates of physical and sexual abuse than those in casual relationships. The relationship is not as clear here, probably because the idea of a "serious" relationship covers so much ground in the minds of students. Nevertheless, the comparison between serious and casual relationships is statistically significant.

What accounts for the data presented in Table 4.11? According to Ellis and DeKeseredy (1989), the DAD model offers a promising explanation for why those in more serious relationships are at greater risk of experiencing physical and sexual abuse. The DAD model contends that woman abuse varies with dependency, availability, and deterrence. In other words, dating status groups characterized by high dependency, high availability, and low deterrence will produce a disproportionate number of abusers and survivors. It is to a more detailed description of the DAD model that we now turn.

The Dependency, Availability, Deterrence (DAD) Model

In woman abuse research, *dependency* has been used extensively to explain why abused women remain in violent relationships (e.g., Gelles, 1976; Kalmuss & Straus, 1982). More specifically, women who are more

TABLE 4.11 Female Victimization, and Male Admitted Victimizing,
by Dating Status

	Cohabiting	Serious	Casual	Total
Female victimization:[a]				
any abuse	103	238	43	384
	34.9%	26.8%	17.7%	26.9%
no abuse	192	649	200	1,041
	65.1%	73.2%	82.3%	73.1%
	295	887	243	1,425
	20.7%	62.2%	17.1%	100%
Male admitted victimizing:[b]				
any abuse	51	137	40	228
	34.9%	22.6%	16.4%	22.9%
no abuse	95	470	204	769
	65.1%	77.4%	83.6%	77.1%
	146	607	244	997
	14.6%	60.9%	24.5%	100%

a. Chi-square = 20.09; df = 2; p = .0000; Cramer's V = .12.
b. Chi-square = 17.87; df = 2; p = .0001; Cramer's V = .13.

economically and emotionally dependent on their spouses or cohabiting
partners are more likely to remain in abusive relationships, even when
abuse is frequent and serious (Barnett & LaViolette, 1993). Although
dependency is both useful and relevant to help explain why women stay
in abusive relationships, dependency is also an important factor in explaining the behavior of men. When the focus shifts from female victims
to the dependency of male offenders, we may discover that dependency,
and therefore woman abuse, varies with dating status (Barnett et al.,
1997; Ellis & DeKeseredy, 1989).

The CNS found that the more serious the dating relationship, the
more likely men are to physically and sexually abuse their girlfriends or
dating partners. Men in dating relationships that involve a high degree
of intimacy may be more emotionally dependent on their partners than
men in casual dating relationships. We know that in many marriage relationships, men are sometimes extremely jealous, which when combined
with dependency can cause battering designed to force the woman to
remain under the control of the man. These are men who already have
the interdependency symbolized by a marriage license. In a dating

context, a man without this tie might abuse a woman in an attempt to establish or maintain the dependence or commitment of the woman on him (DeKeseredy, 1989). Abuse may be perceived as a way of increasing the level of emotional commitment among female dating partners (Billingham, 1987), and there is empirical support for this contention in the dating violence literature.

For example, Makepeace (1981) found that 44.7% of the dating relationships that had experienced violence remained intact, and 29% became more involved. Of the 53% of women who were still dating abusive partners in Cate, Henton, Koval, Christopher, and Lloyd's (1982) study, 37% indicated that their relationships had improved. Similarly, Henton et al. (1983) found that of the 41% of their respondents who were dating violent partners, 36% reported that their relationships had improved. Finally, 30% of Roscoe and Benaske's (1985) female respondents eventually married the men who beat them during courtship.

Turning next to the relevance of *availability,* the second factor in the DAD model, Cohen, Kluegel, and Land (1981) found that time at risk was related to abuse rates. For example, men involved in dating relationships that are characterized by a high degree of intimacy, such as cohabitors, may have higher abuse rates than males in casual dating relationships because they spend much more time with their partners than do men in less intimate relationships (Billingham, 1987; Laner & Thompson, 1982). Indeed, frequent contact with women provides men with more opportunities to abuse them.

There are many ways to explain deviant behavior. Many theorists look at deviance itself, but social control theorists (e.g., Hirschi, 1969) take deviant or criminal behavior for granted and attempt to explain why people vary in their conformity to legal and social norms. This point of view is important in looking at the effect of *deterrence,* the final factor in the DAD model. To social control theorists, variations in conformity are a function of a person's bond to society, and one important element of the bond to society is investments or a stake in conformity (Hirschi, 1969; Toby, 1957). Applied to woman abuse, this theory explains variations in conformity to criminal law and social norms proscribing woman abuse by pointing to the losses that would be incurred if this behavior were discovered, publicized, and punished (Ellis & DeKeseredy, 1996). Men with the most to lose, with the greatest stake in conformity, are most likely to be deterred by the threat of legal and/or social punishment. Those with least to lose are least likely to be deterred by formal or informal sanctions (DeKeseredy & MacLeod, 1997).

Another way of stating this might be to focus on just what does stop a man from abusing women. We have not seen much evidence that arrests, convictions, or prison terms by themselves can have much of an effect. On the other hand, informal controls seem to have an effect (National Research Council, 1996). Williams and Hawkins (1989) found that if a person was worried about being thought of poorly by those important to him, or by those he is socially attached to, he is more likely to refrain from committing physical assault on intimate partners. Let's take as an example the social fraternity on the college campus. Suppose that the fraternity discovered that one of its brothers had forced a woman into sexual acts or had taken advantage of a vulnerability (such as drunkenness) to have sex with her when she was not a willing partner. If every time this happened, the brother was expelled or suspended from the fraternity, and it was made very plain by the other brothers that a serious wrong had been committed, certainly not all but much coercive sexual behavior would end by at least those men who value their fraternity membership.

Cohabiting men may be more violent than men involved in less serious relationships because they have a lower stake in conforming with social and legal norms proscribing woman abuse (Ellis & DeKeseredy, 1989). For example, many cohabiting couples are more socially isolated in their communities (Stets & Straus, 1990). Socially isolated men tend to be less concerned with loss of reputation as a sanction (Ellis & DeKeseredy, 1996). Moreover, police may provide cohabiting women with little assistance because they may be viewed as involved in immoral relationships. Female cohabitors may be viewed as less deserving of legal support, and thus, their male partners are not likely to be deterred by the threat of legal sanctions (Yllö & Straus, 1981).

In addition to males with a low stake in conformity, men with a past history of woman abuse, with greater aggressive habit strength, are also likely to be overrepresented among cohabiting couples. Some wife abuse researchers and aggression theorists, such as Megargee (1982), argue that aggressive habit strength, a function of the individual's past history of violence, is one of the best predictors of future violence (Fagan, Stewart, & Hanson, 1983; Monahan, 1981). Other things being equal, the greater the male's aggressive habit strength, the less likely he is to be deterred by either formal or informal sanctions made contingent on his violent behavior.

In sum, the DAD model contributes to a sociological understanding of the relationship between dating status and woman abuse reported in this chapter. Nevertheless, future studies should test this perspective and other attempts to explain why woman abuse varies with marital and dating status (e.g., Ellis, 1989) with more rigorous empirical evaluation.

Alcohol Consumption

Heavy drinking is common on North American college campuses (Levine & Kanin, 1986; Margolis, 1992; Schwartz & DeKeseredy, 1997), and many researchers have tried to find a causal link between alcohol use and woman abuse in college dating relationships. Although none has been able to uncover a direct cause-and-effect relationship, some argue that the actual physiological effects of alcohol increase the likelihood that men will victimize their dating partners (e.g., Bohmer & Parrot, 1993). Those who argue in this way might suggest that lowered inhibitions, just to pick one example, could lead a man to start a fight he might not engage in when sober.

There are others, however, who see the same behavior but do not think that it is the pharmacological effects of alcohol that are causing this behavior. Rather, they believe that it is more likely that men's expectations about the effects of alcohol can be used to justify their abusive behavior, especially sexual violence (Abbey, 1991). In many parts of our society, you are "allowed" to be violent or nonrational when drunk, so it makes a convenient excuse to claim that you were drunk. For example, Rae (1995) interviewed a youth at a treatment center who responded to a question about what he would do if he were insulted in a bar:

> Depends on how drunk you are. If you're drunk, and he calls you a name, start beatin' the shit out of him. If you aren't drunk, you should probably just laugh at him, cause he's probably just drunk and runnin' off at the mouth. If you're drunk though, you don't have no choice. You just jump up and hit him. (pp. 107-108)

In a meta-analysis of a variety of studies, Hull and Bond (1986) report that this expected effect of alcohol increases sexual arousal more strongly than the real effect. In fact, men who think they have drunk alcohol (but haven't) seem to be more aggressive than men who think they have not. Whatever the relationship, Ward, Chapman, Cohn, White, and Williams (1991) argue that at the very minimum, "alcohol is an important part of the student lifestyle and . . . unwanted sexual experiences are a product of that lifestyle" (p. 68).

Of course, both men and women drink. Substantial research has shown that both the offender and the victim commonly had been drinking at the time of a sexual assault (Muehlenhard & Linton, 1987; Shotland, 1992), but researchers have not made much of this finding in the literature. Koss (1988) reported that 55% of the rape victims in her survey were intoxicated at the time of the assault, but few observers have compared the drinking behavior of (at least) self-identified victims of sexual assault with those who have not been victimized. Although we have done so, as will be explained below, it is still difficult to understand what to make of these findings. We generally believe that women who are drunk or high on drugs make easier victims than sober women.

Still, it is commonly argued that men who drink more often and more heavily are more likely to be sexual and physical assault offenders and that women who drink more heavily are more likely to be assaulted (Barnes et al., 1991; Schwartz & Pitts, 1995). To investigate this relationship in our data, then, we hypothesized the following:

- Men who drink more often than other men are more likely to physically and sexually assault their dating partners.
- Men who drink with their dating partners and/or girlfriends more often than other men are more likely to engage in physical and sexual abuse.
- Women who drink more often than other women are more likely to be targets of physical and sexual abuse in dating.
- Women who drink with their dating partners and/or boyfriends more often than other women are more likely to be targets of physical and sexual abuse.

Some progressive or feminist readers may ask, "What is the meaning of hypotheses stating that women who have been victimized drink more often than many other women?" (Schwartz & Pitts, 1995, p. 14). Indeed, these hypotheses seem to contradict our statement at the beginning of this chapter on the futility of trying to identify the characteristics of victims. However, as explained in Schwartz and Pitts (1995), the analysis we tested does not suggest that women engage in unsafe behavior and therefore wish or deserve to be victimized by male intimates. Rather, we are arguing that motivated male offenders are searching for women who might do something unsafe—something that gives the offender an edge or the ability to take the upper hand in victimization. Moreover, the research reported here is heavily influenced by Schwartz and Pitts's (1995) feminist routine activities theory, one that integrates three concepts: routine activities, place, and lifestyle. Before we describe our alcohol consumption measures and our findings, it is first necessary to describe this theoretical perspective.

Schwartz and Pitts's Feminist Routine Activities Theory

Schwartz and Pitts's starting point is the alarmingly high number of sexual assaults on North American college campuses. One of the more popular mainstream criminological theories of the 1990s is routine activities theory, which has its roots in the original argument made by Cohen and Felson (1979). These theorists would argue that the reason for the high number of sexual assaults can be seen as the result of three factors: There are male students motivated to assault women; there are available suitable targets; and there is an absence of capable guardians willing to intervene. However, Schwartz and Pitts argue that feminist theory is strongest exactly where mainstream routine activity theories such as Cohen and Felson's (1979) are weakest: explaining why there are motivated offenders on college campuses. Most routine activities theories simply take it for granted that there are a number of motivated offenders in the world and do not seek to explain their presence or prevalence. Feminist theory, on the other hand, would suggest that part of the reason is the presence of male peer groups that encourage and legitimate the sexual exploitation of women, particularly intoxicated women (DeKeseredy & Schwartz, 1993; Sanday, 1990; Schwartz & DeKeseredy, 1997). Men who belong to these social networks are more likely than nonmembers to be motivated to sexually assault women (DeKeseredy & Kelly, 1993b, 1995). For example, several studies show that men who report having friends who support getting women drunk specifically so that they cannot resist sexual advances are themselves likely to report using similar strategies (Boeringer, 1996; Schwartz & Nogrady, 1996).

Schwartz and Pitts contend that two lifestyle factors increase women's "suitability" (in the words of Cohen and Felson's theory) as targets of sexual assault. Although no lifestyle offers protection against rape, for campus-oriented acquaintance rapes, two contexts increase vulnerability: (a) drinking to the point of being unable to resist forceful sexual advances and (b) engaging in social activities with sexually predatory men.

So far, we have motivated offenders and vulnerable victims. Their copresence on campuses provides men with opportunities to engage in predatory sexual assault. Nevertheless, opportunities for assaulting women do not necessarily translate into action. An essential element of routine activities theory is that the presence or absence of capable guardians will help determine whether these events take place. Unfortunately, many campuses are "effective-guardian-absent" contexts. For example, many campuses do not seriously punish those who sexually abuse women, even if they engage in extremely brutal behavior, such as gang rape (Bohmer & Parrot, 1993; DeKeseredy, 1996b; McMillen, 1990; Schwartz, 1991; Schwartz & DeKeseredy, 1997). Even criminal justice personnel often disregard acquaintance and/or date rapes (Warshaw, 1988).

Alcohol Consumption Measures

The three following questions on alcohol consumption were included in the CNS. Different, appropriate wording was used for male and female respondents (e.g., "boyfriend" rather than "girlfriend"). The first question simply asks people to report whether they drank alcohol in the past 12 months. Those who answered yes were then asked to respond to the second alcohol question: If yes, how often on average did you drink alcoholic beverages in the past 12 months? Then, respondents were asked to report how often they drank with their dating partners or boyfriends (girlfriends) in the past 12 months. Further, the identical questions were asked about drug use.

Results

Because the question on alcohol use only asks about the past 12 months, we only used the incidence of abuse (past 12 months) data. Simply put, the data strongly confirm the hypotheses above. The more men and women drink, and the more they drink with their partners, the more likely it is that they report giving or receiving abuse in the past 12 months. The pattern of abuse and drug use was identical.

In all of the tables, with physical abuse and sexual abuse combined, the amount of abuse dramatically increases from those who drink little to those who drink more heavily. As with most studies, we found that well under 10% of all students claimed to drink less than once per month,

TABLE 4.12 How Often Do Women (by Victimization) and Men (by Admitted Victimizing) Drink?

	1-2 Times a Month	Once a Week	2-3 Times a Week	4-7 Times a Week	Total
How often women drink:[a]					
any abuse	265	160	128	13	566
	37.7%	48.6%	55.4%	61.9%	44.1%
no abuse	438	169	103	8	718
	62.3%	51.4%	44.6%	38.1%	55.9%
How often men drink:[b]					
any abuse	48	51	98	23	220
	15.2%	19%	29.1%	31.5%	22.2%
no abuse	267	217	239	50	773
	84.8%	81%	70.9%	68.5%	77.8%

a. Chi-square = 29.130; df = 3; p = .0000; Cramer's V = .151.
b. Chi-square = 23.329; df = 3; p = .0000; Cramer's V = .153.

so the comparisons we made were for those students who drank at least once or twice a month and those who drank up to four to seven times a week. Among the men, as can be seen in Table 4.12, 15.2% of the light drinkers, but 31.5% of those who drink four or more times a week, claimed to be physical or sexual abusers. Among the women, 37.7% of the light drinkers and 61.9% of the heavier drinkers were victimized in some manner. Both relationships are statistically significant. The tables are very similar when the question is how often you drink with your girlfriends (boyfriends) or dating partners. In fact, the tables are just as similar when the question is whether the student has taken drugs in the past 12 months or how often he or she regularly takes drugs with a partner. The more often drugs are taken, and the more often with a dating partner, the more abuse is admitted to by the men and the more victimization is claimed by the women. For example, among the men, roughly 20% of those who do not use drugs admit to any abuse, while over 50% of those who "often" use drugs admit to at least one victimization. For women, 37.2% of those who never use drugs but more than 75% of those who used drugs often or very often claimed at least one victimization.

Clearly, then, although we cannot shed any light on the exact causal nature of the relationship between alcohol and drug use and physical and sexual victimization of college and university women, we can show that there is a relationship. Where one occurs, the other is more likely to occur. The analysis here clearly shows, in line with Schwartz and Pitts (1995), that it would be a reasonable presumption that college-level programming designed to reduce alcohol and drug abuse would be an important method of reducing the physical and sexual abuse of women.

Chapter Summary

Obviously, not all Canadian men abuse their college and university dating partners and/or girlfriends. Indeed, the CNS data reported here show that some men are much more likely to do so than others. Those who are more likely to do so are those who (a) adhere to the ideology of familial patriarchy, (b) have friends who perpetuate and legitimate woman abuse, (c) are exposed to pornographic media, (d) are in more serious relationships, and (e) drink (or use drugs) often and do so frequently with their dating partners. Moreover, women who drink (or use drugs) often and who do so frequently with their dating partners are at greater risk of being abused.

Several theoretical perspectives help explain some of the key findings presented in this chapter, such as the male peer support models developed by DeKeseredy (1988) and Schwartz and DeKeseredy (1997), Ellis and DeKeseredy's (1989) DAD model, and Schwartz and Pitts's (1995) feminist routine activities theory. However, a review of the social scientific literature on male-to-female victimization in college courtship shows that much more theory construction and theory testing is necessary (Sugarman & Hotaling, 1989). Certainly we are no nearer than before to developing a causal model or even reaching agreement on exactly why it is that alcohol and drug use increases physical and sexual assault. We hope that future North American studies will take this concern much more seriously.

In the meantime, however, the women who are currently being physically, sexually, and psychologically abused cannot afford to sit back and hope that researchers and theorists develop greater insight into the reasons their dating partners victimize them. Something must be done now to help curb the alarming rates of abuse described in Chapter 2. As Currie (1995) correctly points out in an article presenting the results of her study on women's safety on campus, "Research alone, does not result in social change. Social transformation is the consequence of a number of inter-related activities which often require lobbying, the development of policy initiatives, consultation, etc." (p. 44). Thus, in Chapter 5, we suggest several progressive ways of preventing and controlling woman abuse in postsecondary school dating relationships.

Notes

1. See Cate and Lloyd (1992) for a review of these U.S. findings. It may be important to note that these findings do not necessarily apply to rape myths generally (see Schwartz & Nogrady, 1996).

2. See DeKeseredy and Schwartz (1993), Schwartz and DeKeseredy (1997), and the special issue of *Violence Against Women* (Vol. 2, No. 2, 1996) for more detailed information on the relationship between male peer support and woman abuse on college campuses and in postsecondary school courtship.

3. This alpha coefficient may be somewhat depressed because of the low number of items used in the computation (Jackson, 1988). However, it is adequate to support the level of interpretation presented in this chapter.

4. See Cate and Lloyd (1992), DeKeseredy (1988), and DeKeseredy and Hinch (1991) for comprehensive reviews of these studies.

5. The data presented here include only the abusive experiences of those who either dated or lived with an intimate partner in the 12 months prior to the survey (incidence).

5

Progressive Policy Proposals

> There are real dangers inherent in taking a unidimensional approach to as complex a real-life issue as violence: simplistic solutions to complex problems are not only ineffective, they can escalate the problem. It is *our* responsibility—as individual scholars and as members of the communities affected by violence—to ensure that the web of violence is interrupted safely, justly, and humanely. It is the responsibility of our institutions and our professional associations to acknowledge the gravity of the situation, to acknowledge the role that they may be playing in condoning violence—as well as the role that they *must* play in facilitating attempts to address the issues. (Stark-Adamec, 1996a, p. 143, emphasis in original)

Too many university and community college administrators trivialize or ignore woman abuse on campuses and their immediate surroundings (Currie & MacLean, 1993). Moreover, some campus administrations and faculty (e.g., Fekete, 1994) indirectly or directly endorse the antifeminist backlash against strategies to raise awareness about date rape and other forms of male-to-female victimization in postsecondary school courtship. Consider the 1989 "Queen's University scandal" described by Ron Thorne-Finch in Box 5.1. An important lesson to be learned from this event is that, similar to what has recently occurred in the United States, as Canadian women began to gain on achieving their goals of getting universities, communities, the general public, and the government to take woman abuse seriously, a "backlash" movement arose with the aim of stopping and reversing any gains these women might have made (Faludi, 1991).

BOX 5.1.

The Queen's University Anti-Rape Campaign

In the fall of 1989, a committee of the student union at Queen's University in Kingston, Ontario, launched a campaign against date rape in order to raise awareness of the issue, dispel many of the myths, and reduce its frequency. A major component of the program was a "No Means No" slogan intended to challenge one of the most common rape myths that women are always ready for, and wanting, sex but often play coy and pretend otherwise in order to test the sexual desirability of the male partner; a "real man" will not accept no for an answer. The posters were displayed around campus.

By the first week of October, several signs mocking the anti-rape campaign had appeared in windows of the Gordon House men's residence. Their aggressive wording betrayed the fear that many women know often lies beneath male bravado. "No Means Yes," "No Means More Beer," and "No Means Kick Her in the Teeth" reflect the tone of the response among these men. On 11 October 1989, a group of women organized, painted "No Means No" on the side of Gordon House, and sent letters to the parents of students with signs in their windows, informing them their sons were engaging in misogynist activities. The next day, after more signs appeared in the windows of Gordon House and other campus residences, the dean of women ordered the signs removed by 2:00 p.m. the following day.

On October 13th, the signs indeed disappeared; the issue, however, was by no means resolved. An open struggle continued for the next few weeks. The dons in Gordon House held a gender awareness week, providing seminars on sexual assault, rape, and the effect of the signs. On October 26th, the Alma Mater Society assembly discussed the issue but chose not to take any action because the Main Campus Residence Council (MCRC) was to examine the issue on the same day. While the MCRC did hold an open meeting, they chose not to punish the offenders. Instead, they advocated a gender awareness week for all the residences. On November 2nd, the issue began to draw national attention, with the media giving the story top billing.

It is telling that during all this time, there had been no formal response from the university administration. At 9:00 a.m., on November 9th—well over a month after the men's signs appeared—

thirty women staged a sit-in at Queen's principal David Smith's office, demanding an apology for the administration's inaction, the retention of the dean of women, and the institution of a sexual assault awareness campaign by the administration for the entire campus. Only then did the administration finally respond. Within a day, it called for a joint open meeting in January 1990 of the Gender Issues Board, the Alumni Weekend Board, and the Orientation Review Board (ORB). The administration also requested the ORB to establish an annual open meeting in September to deal with misogynist activities during "Frosh week," an initiation period for new students. On the afternoon of November 10th, the thirty women left the principal's office noting they had succeeded in raising the awareness of sexual assault issues at Queen's University. Yet because of their brave and admirable efforts—and their victory—these women were confronted by men on the street and received harassing phone calls.

The Queen's scandal indicated that despite gains made by feminists since the 1970s, not much has changed in our society. . . . There was no need to wait until thirty women took direct action. Would the administration have continued to ignore the issue if the sit-in had not occurred? While this will never be known, their month-long delay is an appalling and frightening sign. By choosing not to respond—and inaction is a conscious choice—until they were coerced, the administration in effect provided support and encouragement to the Gordon House offenders. If university administrations, at Queen's and elsewhere, really want to reduce date rape—which has been termed a "campus epidemic"—there are numerous proactive steps that could be implemented. Mandatory gender awareness seminars, permanent anti-rape campaigns directed at changing male—as opposed to female—behaviour, improved lighting and escort services on campus to enable women to walk around safely at night, and established policies to promptly respond to misogynist material or activities are just a few of the possible options. Unfortunately, the Queen's scandal verifies that such programs—and thus the safety of all women—receive a low priority indeed.

What happened at Queen's is just another example of how men have responded negatively to demands for an end to male violence against women.

SOURCE: Ron Thorne-Finch (1992, pp. 214-216); reprinted by permission.

Unfortunately, at the time of writing this chapter, the whole woman abuse discourse is "characterized by a general atmosphere of mistrust and a well-organized backlash against feminism" (Levan, 1996, p. 350). An excellent example of how many men feel is the letter to the editor we have reproduced in Box 5.2. Some feminist and profeminist men and women, such as the woman who wrote the response also included in Box 5.2, consider the male letter-writer to be a "reinforcer of the *status quo*." According to Thorne-Finch (1992):

> Reinforcers of the *status quo* go to great lengths to ensure that the traditional social order is maintained. They see little wrong with the existing divisions between men and women, and strive to protect them. While not all reinforcers may directly practice violence towards women, their theories and values help legitimize the violence of men in general. In the struggle to end male violence against women, reinforcers are one of the most difficult obstacles, though certainly not the only one. Men who simply avoid the issue of male violence are also an impediment. (pp. 216-217)

Virtually anyone who studies violence against women and supports feminist conclusions has stories to tell about being attacked by "reinforcers of the status quo." A growing number of conservatives have begun to mobilize to deny that there is a problem with physical and sexual abuse against women in society (see, e.g., Fekete, 1994) and to strongly oppose any strategies or struggles to end woman abuse in postsecondary school dating (and, of course, other key symptoms of gender inequality). Of course, the Canadian National Survey described in this book is no exception. One example of many might be the move by University of Alberta philosopher Ferrel Christensen, who on January 12, 1996, sent a letter to Health Canada, the federal agency that funded the CNS. He enclosed a petition and an unpublished article claiming that Walter DeKeseredy and Katharine Kelly had violated ethical principles and presented CNS data that intentionally distorted the perception of truth. It should be noted in passing that only six other people signed this petition, and the Canadian Sociology and Anthropology Association did not find DeKeseredy and Kelly guilty of violating ethical principles. Of course, this is not surprising because these researchers had obtained approval to administer their questionnaires from 44 different ethical review committees situated at each of the institutions included in the CNS.

BOX 5.2.

Letters to the Editor

Letter One:
He's Tired of Men Being Treated as Second Class

I applaud the courage and conviction of Barbara Amiel, in her Dec. 8 column, "Canadian media cower under orthodoxy's reign of terror," in going against what has been a mainstream conviction of modern society. Men are not all pigs, nor are they women-beating monsters. But that is not what is portrayed by the popular media.

Much is said about the plight of women and children battered by men. It is in style to complain that men, on average, still make more than women. But little is said about the problems and issues men face in today's society. The roles are reversed.

I can't count the jobs I won't even bother applying for because I am a white male. When I called the RCMP (Royal Canadian Mounted Police) to enquire about their training programs, they laughed at me. It seems unless you are female or belong to a visible minority, you have no chance getting a job in any federal organization.

Women's issues today have been elevated to gospel. In the news there are countless spots on dead-beat dads who won't pay their child-support bills. We hear not a peep about mothers who will not let fathers see their children because of some slight or grudge. The popular consensus seems to be that mothers are more important to a child anyhow, so the access of a father is secondary to the rights of a mother.

Sexism has not disappeared. It has not even declined. It has just reversed itself. Fifty years ago, women were considered second-class citizens. Now men are.

I am tired of being treated as a potential rapist, child beater, or deadbeat dad. I am tired of having it assumed that because I am male, I am capable of atrocities, and because someone is female, she is not. It is time for society to grow up, and the rights warriors start campaigning for equal rights, not just revenge.

Letter Two:
We Just Want Things More Equitable

John Smith (pseudonym) says in his Dec. 17 letter that he is tired of men being treated as second class. He might perhaps consider a hypothetical letter written by Mary: "Tired of women being treated as second class, I can't count the jobs I won't even bother applying for because I am a black female. When I called the RCMP (Royal Canadian Mounted Police) to enquire about their training programs, they laughed at me. It seems that unless you are male and white you have no chance of getting a job in any federal organization. I am tired of being treated as a potential sex object, child bearer or stay-at-home mom."

I do not believe there is a spirit of revenge against men abroad, it is simply a matter of attempting to make things more equitable.

SOURCE: These letters appeared in the December 17, 1996 (p. A14) and December 28, 1996 (p. B7) issues of the *Ottawa Citizen*. The authors' names are not presented here to protect their anonymity.

As in the United States, the Canadian backlash was led by conservative male academics who have no background in social science research, have never conducted a victimization or self-report survey on woman abuse, and have never revealed any comprehensive knowledge of this complex field. Yet these are all people who have the confidence to report that sexual and physical abuse of women is not a problem.

However, it isn't only Ph.D.s who attacked these surveys. For example, Walter DeKeseredy received hate mail and harassing phone calls from anonymous "men's rights" advocates. Furthermore, shortly after DeKeseredy and Kelly released the first report on their CNS data to the press in February 1993, the all-female support staff at Carleton University's Department of Sociology and Anthropology received so many harassing phone calls that a male student was hired to answer phone calls in the department's main office over the next week or so.

In sum, the data presented throughout this book were not, to say the least, warmly received by a substantial number of North Americans, especially by males who hold patriarchal attitudes and beliefs similar to those described in Chapter 4. Thus, it is fair to assume that a large number of North Americans will not support the policy initiatives advanced in this chapter. Indeed, many obstacles remain in the struggle to stop woman abuse in university and college dating and in other intimate contexts (e.g., marriage, cohabitation). We can expect the following (Vanier Institute of the Family, 1995, p. 7):

- the active resistance of those who are threatened by change;
- funding and resource shortages as governments cut spending;
- institutional barriers that perpetuate historical inequities;
- social attitudes and traditions that are resistant to change; and
- territoriality, institutionalization, and other problems within the various movements, campuses, and agencies that are created to help curb woman abuse.

This does not mean, however, that those committed to stopping the abusive behaviors described in this book should give up or take what some criminologists have begun calling an "idealist" position. Idealists generally feel that it is a waste of time to struggle for short-term goals, that woman abuse in university and college dating will not end until there is radical social change in the structure of postsecondary schools and society as a whole. It is our contention that new short-term strategies must be developed to deal with the kind of obstacles we can anticipate in the future. As women involved in university and college-based struggles for gender equality have recognized for years, people seeking an end to all forms of woman abuse must recognize that "it will be a long haul" and that it is necessary to establish long-term goals and celebrate victories where you can find them (Thorne-Finch, 1992, p. 259).

Moreover, it is important to recognize that there are no simple solutions to the problems examined in this book. Thus, as suggested by Stark-Adamec (1996a) and other progressives involved in the movement to end all forms of violence and abuse on campus, we must work toward developing a "multiagency" approach (Jones et al., 1986). This strategy calls for actions that are interdisciplinary, collaborative, and focused on the "attitudinal, physical, financial and systemic barriers to access, equity, and safety for students in our post-secondary education system" (Stark-Adamec, 1996a, p. 145).

What, specifically, is to be done about the types of male-to-female victimization examined in this book? It is far beyond the scope of this chapter to describe the profusion of progressive policies advanced by North American academics, campus administrators, and student organizations. In fact, several books on this topic are available, and we urge readers to peruse them for more detailed discussions on how to make unsafe learning environments safer. Both Thorne-Finch (1992) and Bohmer and Parrot (1993) have a wide variety of suggestions to make on this subject. Rather than provide a superficial overview of the strategies described in these and other sources, we will narrow our focus here to recommendations that are consistent with the CNS data described throughout this book. It is to "breaking the silence" (Kelly, 1988) that we turn to first.

Naming the Problem

Less than 10% of Canadian university and college women who are abused by their dating partners report their experiences to someone in authority at their school (Currie, 1995). When they do report them, too often they are not taken seriously by campus officials, police officers, and other agents of social control (Bernstein, 1996). Consider the ways in which the following University of British Columbia female students who had the courage to report their victimization were treated by people in authority at their campus (Currie, 1995):

> They [campus security] showed up, implied I was overreacting, and left. (22-year-old female, who reported being verbally harassed and followed)

> Student Counseling is a joke. A man just sat there watching me cry. I never went back. (21-year-old female, who reported being raped by a male acquaintance) (p. 82)

When these things happen to women, there are many possible reactions, particularly for those women who have made the decision not to go public with their experience. Some organizations, such as sororities, serve as places for some women to vent their pain (Schwartz & DeKeseredy, 1997). Other women have other types of support groups. One newer type of reaction for such women that is now occurring in many universities is to write graffiti in public washrooms to vent their anger, shame, and pain. A story about this newer phenomenon, as it took place at Carleton University in Ottawa, appears in Box 5.3. Other women drop out of school, transfer to other universities or colleges, and, only in the rarest or bravest cases, sue the school where their abuse took place

(text continued on p. 137)

BOX 5.3.

The Writing on the Wall

The stall in the women's bathroom at Mike's Place on the second floor of the Unicentre was covered in black, blue and pink graffiti.

The discourse on rape began when someone used a permanent black marker to write the Rape Crisis Centre's phone number on the stall door.

It isn't unusual to find graffiti of this nature in campus washrooms. At the University of Manitoba, a program was started last year to help people get answers to their questions about safe sex. People wrote questions about sex on boards installed in the washrooms and the answers were later posted.

The numbers for the Rape Crisis Centre and campus security are written on the inside of many women's washroom stall doors at Carleton. Morag Anderson, the co-ordinator of the Women's Centre, says it may have been a group of women or one woman who started it. Then it may have caught on and others started spreading the word.

This time, however, someone responded to the graffiti.

> *To whoever wrote this (the Rape Crisis Centre number), a large percentage of women who have been raped at some point. They DO NOT want to be reminded by this. Please do NOT write on the stalls. I have been raped. AND I DO NOT want to be reminded of it. Thank you. Please consider this when you make a comment.*

Jane Keeler, human rights educator with the Office of the Status of Women at Carleton, says the graffiti show women have very strong feelings about danger.

Also, their approaches to dealing with the danger they feel differ. Some women feel public information is the way to deconstruct their fears. Others don't want to be constantly aware of the threat of physical and sexual violence.

But both groups, and the variations in between, desire to protect themselves.

This is a resource all women and men should be aware of whether or not you agree with it or choose to use it. Education leads to progress and change.

The existence of the Rape Crisis Centre is not meant to remind us of the price of RAPE but as a step towards HEALING. It is your choice not to access the Rape Crisis Centre for your rape, that is respected. But allow those women who want the choice to call this centre the opportunity to access the telephone number.

Gada Mahrouse, the public education co-ordinator for the Rape Crisis Centre, says while she doesn't condone the writing on the wall, she's glad to hear someone felt strongly enough to share the phone number with other women.

She notes the bathroom graffiti are a safe way for women to find out about the Rape Crisis Centre and to write the number down. A bathroom stall is a more private environment than, for instance, picking up a pamphlet in a public place.

Mahrouse says the issue of rape is often controversial because many people think a woman shouldn't dwell on the past, that she should just get on with her life. But Mahrouse says the centre workers find women need a safe environment to talk about assault.

All women are different and take their own time to work through things, she says, but most often when a sexual violation is not dealt with it translates into other problems later on. And that's why the centre makes services for rape victims available.

Honey, stop living in fear! Put some justice in your life and call this number. There is sisterhood out there for a reason. We CARE!

If you haven't dealt with it, acknowledged it wasn't your fault and are "hiding" it as a secret shame, then you "don't want to be reminded." It's not your shame, deal with it and let others, and realize the wrong needs to be addressed—to erase the shame sister. It doesn't happen to "bad" people it happens to most women . . . And I'm not bad!

> *Then why do I see posters and such screaming a woman is raped every 30 seconds, a man beats a woman every. . . . We do not want to be made afraid of going outside. Thank you.*

> *Because this is TRUE—and you're not afraid, you're stupid.*

Over time the wall incurred additions.

Someone corrected, in bright pink marker, the Rape Crisis Centre number when it changed a year ago and added its focus as a resource for information and non-judgmental counselling. This person also accentuated the graffiti about providing choices with a pink check mark to show she agreed with women being provided with choices.

Bathroom graffiti allow anonymity, providing a comfortable space for individuals to vent their private feelings and opinions.

Carleton professor of sociology Walter DeKeseredy says "it could be a sign people are concerned about issues . . . I don't know for sure, but the people writing on the wall may be uncomfortable about talking about such things."

He says he thinks it is good dialogue is happening and adds if people take offence to the defacing of school property a comment board for students could be set up either in the bathrooms or in other spots around school.

> *Every dame wants to be raped.*

> *To whomever wrote this appalling note: Is this supposed to be amusing? Are you absolutely out of your mind? I guess some people never get out of the Dark Ages. So just to set the record straight, no one and I mean absolutely no one wants to get raped! To state anything otherwise is not only stupid, but also insensitive and rude. And to write such a statement on this wall, when there is an already heated, as well as emotional, argument/discussion going on, exposes you as the low form of life that you really are. Your form of power trip doesn't cut it here.*

As in many debates, the appearance of offensive material is the point at which the debate degenerates.

And that's exactly what happened to the wall.

It was good while the debate was respectful, says Mahrouse. But the last point threw the debate into an Internet-like flame war.

Mike's Place manager Andrew Prime started getting complaints the debate was getting out of hand. So now the wall is painted over. Building operations painted over the wall on the weekend of Sept. 14-15.

Prime says they wouldn't have painted the wall if someone hadn't put up offensive material. He says someone may put the Rape Crisis Centre's phone number on the newly painted wall, sparking the debate again.

Keeler says it is good for public places like Mike's Place to allow the graffiti to remain, but understands why they painted over the debate. The flame represented a change in tone in the debate, Keeler says, agreeing the flame was similar to those experienced by groups on the Internet.

Harassment can occur through graffiti and some women may have felt threatened by the flame, she adds, interpreting the "dame" statement as a rape threat.

"It goes over the edge," she says. She agrees the debate may start again.

But at the Women's Centre, Anderson says she wishes Mike's Place hadn't painted over the graffiti.

"I think they should just wash off the flame," she says. "Once again (women) are being silenced."

Keeler says our society must allow people to take different positions. None of the viewpoints is perfectly right, nor more valid than others.

And that, she says, is why debate and dialogue like the bathroom discourse on rape are so important.

SOURCE: This box includes excerpts of an article published by Fraser and Kar (1996, pp. 20-21); reprinted by permission.

(Bohmer & Parrot, 1993; Currie & MacLean, 1993). These are all the actions of women who do not believe that the university's structures of support have been put in place to help them in their time of need. Rather, these actions indicate that many abused women "come to feel that the university does not belong to them" (Currie, 1995, p. 91).

How can universities and colleges overcome or minimize these problems? Obviously, effective campus-based prevention, control, and counseling strategies must be developed immediately throughout North America. However, to do so, administrators must first develop the *will* to take action against woman abuse in postsecondary school dating. In other words, they need to publicly acknowledge that various types of male-to-female victimization occur on their campuses and that they fully intend to develop a set of norms and goals that establish the unacceptability of woman abuse (Bohmer & Parrot, 1993; Calkin, 1996). Administrators seem to be grudgingly willing to admit to stranger assaults and to fund such items as escort patrol vehicles, emergency telephones with blue lights, complex security systems and lobby guards, and extensive path and parking lot lights. Unfortunately, few campuses have put similar money and expertise into dealing with the much more common forms of woman abuse discussed in this book.

A public statement of the will to take action is, of course, only the first step. If there is anything that student activists have learned, it is the slogan that "talk alone is cheap." It will do little, if anything, to overcome the lack of confidence among students that their campus administrators care about their well-being (Currie, 1995). For many female students, especially those who have been sexually, physically, and psychologically abused by male dating partners, action speaks louder than words. Campus administrators must begin to formulate and implement specific and direct policies to curb woman abuse.

Elementary and High School-Based Education and Awareness Programs

Both of us give lectures to undergraduate classes, which include discussions of woman abuse in various educational contexts and some brief policy recommendations. It is not unusual to have student comments, particularly from more mature students, along the following lines:

> You tell us that many men who abuse their university and college dating partners engaged in this behavior before they came to postsecondary schools. So why should we wait until they come to university or college before we start taking steps to curb male-to-female abuse in dating? I mean, isn't this approach similar to closing the barn doors after the horses have left?

This point is well taken and warrants considerable attention here and by the broader North American educational community. It is not unusual, at least on college campuses, to forget that an extremely high number of high school dating relationships are violent (Bergman, 1992; Peterson & Olday, 1992) and that student learning can be badly, and negatively, affected by violence that takes place outside the school (Bruckerhoff & Popkewitz, 1991).

How can we prevent young boys from becoming abusive in adolescent and adult heterosexual, intimate relationships? Elementary and high school-based educational and awareness programs, such as videos, workshops, presentations, plays, and classroom discussions, are relevant and potentially effective prevention strategies. These programs help provide an atmosphere in which students show more respect for each other (Bohmer & Parrot, 1993) and can change attitudes, increase knowledge, and change behavioral intention (Jaffe et al., 1992). Many abused female teenagers want school educational programs and strongly believe that these initiatives would have helped prevent them from entering violent relationships (Fitzpatrick & Halliday, 1992). Furthermore, if these programs are not provided, students typically will receive a biased education from either gossip or the uninformed sensational media (Bohmer & Parrot, 1993).

Part of the problem of programs that have not worked in the past is that they have operated on a "haphazard, one-classroom-at-a-time approach" (Jaffe et al., 1992, p. 131). The difficulty is that while any single teacher may do an excellent job, it is very difficult to counteract the broad variety of influences that these students are encountering. If only a single teacher, or a few teachers, are engaged in programming against woman abuse, then the influence of the students in the other classes, when combined with parents, the mass media, and other broader societal influences, will no doubt make these programs a very doubtful enterprise. Only when all of the teachers, counselors, and administrators at the school are in complete agreement, providing a consistent and regular message over a long period of time, supported by the parents and other members of the family, is there a hope that many of the students will begin to seriously engage these issues.

Specifically, school-based prevention programs throughout Canada and the United States should attempt to

- increase knowledge about woman abuse;
- address the patriarchal forces that perpetuate and legitimate woman abuse;
- promote early warning signs of abusive patterns in intimate relationships;
- expand definitions of abuse to include verbal, emotional, physical, and sexual victimization;
- provide information on community-based social support services; and
- develop an ongoing, systemwide commitment to preventing woman abuse and all violence in relationships (Jaffe et al., 1992).

Evaluation research suggests that North American high schools should consider implementing a primary prevention program. Examples of U.S. secondary school prevention programs that might be considered are the Minnesota School Curriculum Project (see Jones, 1991) and the model developed by the Rape Treatment Center (RTC) of Santa Monica Hospital Medical Center, Santa Monica, California (see Roden, 1991). Two of the larger programs have been implemented in Canada. Box 5.4 briefly describes the program undertaken in London, Ontario, by the Family Court Clinic and the Board of Education for the City of London. The student intervention component of this program resulted in positive changes in high school students' dating violence attitudes, knowledge about woman abuse and family violence, and behavioral intentions with regard to dating violence intervention. Another interesting intervention is in Manitoba (Manitoba Department of Education and Training, 1993), where schools implemented recommendations from a study commissioned by Manitoba Justice. Here, a 13-lesson health curriculum was devised for grades 5 through 8, designed to reduce violence both in everyday life and also in intimate relationships.

Men Working to End Woman Abuse in University and College Dating

It is becoming more and more common for women who work to end woman abuse in a variety of intimate and public contexts to stress the

BOX 5.4.

A Canadian Example of a Successful Secondary School Primary Prevention Program on Violence in Intimate Relationships

The target audience was students in grades 9 to 13 in a large public board of education. The Board of Education for the City of London is a large school system in a middle-sized city and has over 45,000 students in 80 secondary and elementary schools. Four high schools participated in the evaluation, as they were the first to undergo the intervention. In each school, a school-based committee planned and implemented a large group auditorium presentation component and a classroom discussion component, facilitated jointly by knowledgeable community professionals and teachers. Speakers from community agencies concerned with wife assault and treatment of batterers; speakers from the Police Department and Board of Education; videos on wife assault and its effects on child witnesses; student plays; a professional theater company; and a talk by a survivor of abuse were used by the schools. Myths and facts about wife assault were addressed at each school's auditorium presentation. Classroom discussion facilitators included professionals from counseling centers for women, children and men, the police, women's shelters, etc. Each facilitator attended a half-day training workshop.

Two schools employed a half-day intervention, with approximately one-and-one-half hours for the auditorium presentation and one hour for classroom discussion. Two schools employed a full-day intervention. The full-day intervention allowed the students to go beyond basic knowledge and awareness of the issues into the development of action plans. For example, each classroom was asked by facilitators to formulate a school action plan to address the problem of family violence over the coming year. Classrooms generated ideas such as student plays on violence, organization of violence awareness weeks and fundraising activities for local services for abused women.

SOURCE: Jaffe et al. (1992, p. 132).

importance of men becoming part of the solution (DeKeseredy & MacLeod, 1997). For example, the authors of the *Final Report of the Canadian Panel on Violence Against Women* contend that

> we need all men in Canada to make a clear commitment to women's equality and to ending all forms of violence against women. We deserve a Canadian society that will no longer tolerate the daily acts of violence against women. Is this an impossible dream or can it be a future Canadian reality? Can all men accept the challenge to examine their behaviour as individuals and as members of a community? We believe they can. Many are doing so already. (Canadian Panel on Violence Against Women, 1993, p. 102)

While many male university students support their peers' abusive conduct (see Chapter 4), the good news is that a growing number of men on campus strongly disapprove of the brutal ways in which men treat their dating partners and female students in general. Consider the following men's statements made to University of British Columbia researcher Dawn Currie (1995):

> Several times I have witnessed male students riding around campus in a van shouting abusive remarks at pedestrians, including myself (which leaves me feeling embarrassed to be associated with them by gender and university). (33-year-old male)

> I'm tired of a few male assholes creating a bad image for the male population. (24-year-old male)

> Somehow I feel that the majority of violence against women and homosexuals is largely attributable to "jocks"—the men's man. My general impression is that the "typical" males—"booze, broads and baseball"— seem the least tolerant and the least informed. (34-year-old male)

> But I think this is a product of years and years of male dominance in all aspects of society. I believe that this will only change over a long period of time if education is employed to change the attitudes of men and women. Men need to learn to control and deal with their inferiority complexes. Harassing women, in any way, is the way men physically assert their "supposed" dominance over the opposite sex. Wrong, wrong, wrong. (22-year-old male) (p. 180)

On college campuses across North America, men are working in such programs as Man to Man About Rape (Ring & Kilmartin, 1992) and the Fraternity Violence Education Project (Mahlstedt, Falcone, &

Rice-Spring, 1993) to reduce the amount of violent behavior on campus. After careful consideration of the alternatives, many men have concluded that the best way to run prevention programming for male college students is to base the material on feminist interpretations (Haggard, 1991). Unfortunately, the number of men on North American campuses who adhere to feminist values and beliefs and who are strongly committed to ending woman abuse pales in comparison with their patriarchal counterparts (DeKeseredy, 1996b). Indeed, many men are uncomfortable giving up their patriarchal power and are much more attracted to antifeminist backlash arguments about political correctness, academic freedom, and individual rights (Hornosty, 1996). Other men sharply disapprove of sexism and woman abuse but have not participated in the struggle to eliminate these problems for one or perhaps more of the following reasons:

- They don't know how to respond.
- They don't feel there is a place for them in the movement to stop woman abuse.
- They experience feelings of guilt and shame.
- They don't know other men who are working to end woman abuse and thus they feel fearful, isolated, and afraid of doing the wrong thing (Funk, 1993, p. 81).

Much more work needs to be done to recruit men to engage in profeminist efforts to end woman abuse on campuses and their immediate surroundings. A useful goal would be to hasten the day when most male students actively and publicly struggle to make unsafe learning environments safer. In the meantime, however, the small number of men who have overcome the above and other barriers to responding to woman abuse should seriously consider taking the following individual and collective steps, slightly modified from those outlined by Funk (1993, pp. 105-128):

- Ensuring that survivor service organizations have the funding to stay open
- Actively and caringly supporting survivors of woman abuse
- Participating equally in the cleaning and maintenance of residences
- Respecting women's space
- Not viewing pornography
- Not interrupting women
- Talking with other men about woman abuse

- Confronting expressions of sexism
- Exposing the connections between sexism, racism, heterosexism, and other expressions of oppression in the ways they all support a culture of woman abuse
- Actively listening to women and reading literature on their issues, problems, concerns, and so on
- Building, sustaining, and maintaining men against woman abuse groups
- Developing a commitment to nonviolence
- Doing anti-woman abuse education

It should also be noted that a central component of becoming involved in the profeminist men's movement to end woman abuse involves finding out much more about what prevents men from becoming antisexist. According to Ghez (in press), focus group sessions with a variety of men, including former abusers, provide a useful way of achieving this goal.

An additional concern, as several men have pointed out (e.g., Funk, 1993; Thorne-Finch, 1992), is becoming aware of how doing profeminist work affects men personally. For example, like female activists, many antisexist males experience "burnout," and feelings of vulnerability, fear, anger, and disgust are common for people who start taking steps to curb male-to-female victimization. Despite these problems, it is essential for activist men to maintain their commitment and never give up because their work can make a difference, as the following examples illustrate.

- Research shows that campaigns that encourage men to hold other men accountable for their abuse are likely to be effective, while those that indiscriminately blame all men are not.
- Male friends and relatives of woman abusers can have a major impact on their behavior by addressing the abuse directly and defining it as unacceptable.
- Communicating with men about the importance of condemning abuse and providing them with some advice on how to directly confront abusers in a way that does not jeopardize their female partners will eventually create an environment in which woman abuse becomes socially unacceptable (Ghez, in press).

In sum, there are a variety of ways in which men can take part in the struggle to end woman abuse in postsecondary school courtship and other contexts, and the strategies identified here constitute just the tip of the iceberg. As we have suggested, entire books have been written on the subject and should be consulted (e.g., Funk, 1993; Thorne-Finch, 1992). Although there are hundreds of initiatives that might be put into a list of useful strategies in which to engage, perhaps Thorne-Finch (1992) lays out the most important point of all:

> Men can no longer excuse themselves and pretend it does not happen. They are all responsible in some way—even if only indirectly. Distancing themselves from this issue will not accomplish anything; only active involvement will bring about the needed changes. The time has come. The longer men procrastinate, the more they jeopardize the emotional and physical well-being of millions of women. (p. xviii)

Responding to Pornography

As shown in Chapter 4 and other publications (e.g., Sanday, 1990, 1996), proabuse male peer support and the negative effects of exposure to pornography are related. In addition to facilitating sexist male bonding on campus, pornography can

- help shape a male-dominant or patriarchal view of sexuality,
- contribute to a user's difficulty in separating sexual fantasy and reality,
- be used to initiate victims and break down resistance to sex, and
- provide a training manual for the types of woman abuse addressed in this book (Jensen, 1995, p. 32).

It is not our intention to advocate censorship on campus. However, a starting point for a number of interesting discussions can be Sanday's description in Box 5.5 of a screening of *Deep Throat* at the University of Pennsylvania. Implicitly, it asks the following question: What is the value of allowing students to show and watch pornographic media on campus? In response to this question, some students who claim to be concerned about the financial well-being of student organizations, athletic teams, and other campus-based organizations contend that pornographic movies generate a substantial amount of money for these groups. For example, according to Sanday (1996), in 1984 the University of Pennsylvania student organization that showed pornographic movies made $3,000—more than it gleaned from any other business venture. Is this a legitimate argument: that such films should be allowed because they are profitable? What else might be allowed solely on the grounds that it is profitable?

BOX 5.5.

The Showing of *Deep Throat* at the University of Pennsylvania

Before the showing of *Deep Throat*, Linda Lovelace, its star, was brought by Penn's Women's Center to speak. Nearly two thousand people attended her talk. She spoke about her imprisonment during the making of the film, the beatings she suffered, and pointed out that the film shows the bruises on her body.

Two days later protesters, mostly female, and moviegoers, mostly male, showed up to see the film. The atmosphere was rowdy, and although it was against university rules, many males came carrying beer cans. Throughout the screening the voices of the film were drowned out by the constant din created by males chanting, "Bruises, bruises."

While waiting for the film to start, mindful of the protesters out-side, men in the audience yelled, "We can have our fun," and "Hey, we're here to see Linda. We're gonna love her bruises." A chant went up, *"Deep Throat, Deep Throat,* let's go Quakers, let's go." Men excitedly pointed to one another in the audience, yelling names and strutting around. "Hey Smith, hey, Jones, what are you doing here?" "Psi Omega's here!!"

One man stood up and shouted, "Hey, you girls out there," refer-ring to the protesters, "watch out for the popcorn trick," referring to a movie in which a man sticks his erect penis in a popcorn box and offers popcorn to the woman next to him.

Once the movie started, the audience cheered and shouted, "Bruises, bruises," as Linda appeared on the screen in a short dress. Deep husky voices shouted, "Blow job, blow job," "Black leather," "Jerk off, jerk off!!" The "bruises" refrain was especially deafening in those scenes where they were clearly visible. At one point, a man shouted, "Ugly bitch," and another added, "She's really ugly all over, including her bruises."

The audience cheered whenever Linda did a "deep throat" blow job. One man yelled, "Why can't my girlfriend do that?" During another blow job, a man screamed, "I'm *horny!!"* "Fuck her," another voice chimed in.

Almost all of the women present as spectators left the theater before the end of the film. The scene played out their worst fears of what getting caught in a locker room after a particularly nasty game and becoming the object of male wrath might be like.

After it was over, some of the protesters interviewed males as they left. The reaction they encountered was mixed. Some expressed little enthusiasm for the movie and admitted they wouldn't go to another porn film. One was disgusted by the whole scene, yet he felt that it should be shown on campus. Another was bored saying, "It makes sex very mechanical." Another male, a freshman, came up to the protesters and said in a coaxing tone, "Come on, she must have enjoyed some of that," referring to Linda Lovelace. "Look at her facial expressions. She never looked like she was upset. She had only one bruise on her thigh." He concluded, "I'd go to another porn film. It really looked like she was getting into it."

SOURCE: Sanday (1996, pp. 203-205).

Certainly drugs and gambling are highly profitable. Should student organizations be allowed to sell drugs as part of university-sanctioned activities? Or is this a bad example because drugs are illegal?

Of interest, there are many types of films that cannot be found on campus, mostly because they do not exist. Rather than outright censorship, North Americans have managed to express their outright disgust and dismay at even the slightest hint of harm to animals in motion pictures. Where the plot line requires an animal to be fictionally harmed (say, a horse and rider in a Western gallop over a cliff), Hollywood producers find it essential to report in the credits that their set was inspected and monitored by animal rights organizations. Even then, however, there are virtually no movies that show animals burned, dismembered, stabbed or shot to death, electrocuted, beaten or kicked, or raped. We save these images for stories about women and men.

Similarly, there are no movies available showing approvingly the mass execution of Jews, gypsies, and the mentally ill by the German Nazis in World War II. There are no proslavery pictures showing approvingly how whites needed to beat, starve, and torture African slaves to get them to behave "properly." Why is this the case? Essentially, it is because people in North America have shown a very high intolerance for pictures of this nature being shown in places like college campuses. Why is it that we have very firm reactions against seeing a sheep raped and then burned to death but find it appropriate, or at least a free speech issue, to allow films approvingly showing women being beaten, raped, and then burned to death?[1] As we said, we are not arguing here for censorship, because neither of us is in favor of censorship. We are, however, arguing that in a better society, it would be considered morally reprehensible to show or attend certain types of films, just as it is now for nondocumentary films about animal torture, proslavery violence, or Nazi killings (Schwartz, 1987).

It is important to point out that there is no single feminist position on pornography. Rather, a variety of positions flourishes. For example, Catharine A. MacKinnon (1993) has become the best known proponent of the position that pornography is an important source, if not the only source, of women's inequality in modern society. A variant of this position comes from Helen Longino (1995), who argues that the wrong of pornography is the lie it tells about the necessity of women's sexual and political subordination to men. Although we are very clear about the limitations of the CNS in examining this question, the material we presented in Chapter 4 (summarized in Table 4.10) makes it clear that there is reason to be concerned about the possibility of a strong connection between men viewing pornography and violence against women.

However, although many writers seem to think that this position exhausts the limits of feminist analysis (see, e.g., Linz & Malamuth, 1993, and most media descriptions of the feminist position on rape), in fact there is a lively feminist anticensorship position (e.g., Rubin, 1993; Segal & McIntosh, 1993). Essentially, these authors believe that the evils to women of pornography are overstated and that there are many areas of struggle necessary for feminists.

Actually, for a more extreme position, feminists informed by the writings of Anna Gronau (1985) contend that pornography, even its violent forms, should be freely available on campus and other public places (e.g., stores, theaters) because it is *functional* for women. According to Gronau, pornography reminds women of the patriarchal forces that victimize and exploit them. If it is banned, then it is much more difficult for women to struggle against hidden patriarchy than it is to fight against the blatant and extreme forms of sexism found in pornography. Thus far, no one has taken up the challenge to study these contentions empirically.

It should be clear here that our own position is that pornography is purposely designed, for the most part, to be humiliating and degrading to women and that efforts to make it socially unacceptable would be useful and important. We do follow the path taken by Gloria Steinem (1993) and others, however, in suggesting that pornography consists of those media images that combine sexual imagery with violence or degradation. We are hardly advocating the elimination of all sexually explicit media. We would much rather advocate the elimination of all violently explicit media (Schwartz, 1987).

One cautionary note, however, is that one must be very careful when attempting to use pornography to make the points above. We actually have shown pornographic images in some of our courses (a course on violence against women sponsored by the women's studies program) and understand its use as an educational tool in the right environment. Women, in particular, as Gronau suggests, often have not been exposed to pornography and are unaware of the level of antiwoman hatred embedded in many of the best-selling videos and magazines. However, even when pornography is used in classrooms, lecture halls, and so on to generate "honest talk and careful hearing" (Jensen, 1995, p. 52), there is a chance that such events can turn into "celebrations of male sexual power" similar to one described in Box 5.5. Sanday's description reminds us that members of campus communities intent on demonstrating the devastating consequences of pornography should be prepared to deal with hostile, sexist, male reactions. Unfortunately, despite the fact that a growing number of male students are either joining antisexist collectives or taking individual stands against patriarchy and woman abuse, there are still many men who, regardless of where they view pornography, cheer the actions of men who brutalize women on screen, in magazines, and in other media (Jensen, 1995; Stoller, 1991). The continuing power of gender role stereotypes and various forms of sexism indicates how far campuses and other formal institutions still have to go (Sanday, 1996).

Alcohol Policies

Like many U.S. studies on the "dark side of courtship" (Lloyd, 1991), the CNS found that alcohol is related to woman abuse in postsecondary school dating. Elsewhere (Schwartz & DeKeseredy, 1997), we have comprehensively reviewed the U.S. social scientific literature on the relationship between alcohol consumption and sexual abuse on campus.

What we found was a clear relationship, even if the direct path that the relationship took was not as clear. Most researchers in the field are certain that alcohol plays a role in violence against women on college and university campuses. For example, the CNS found a relationship between the number of times a week that men went out drinking and the likelihood that they would be admitted physical or sexual abusers of women on campus. Schwartz and Nogrady (1996) found a statistically significant difference between admitted sexual aggressors and those who claimed not to be sexual aggressors based on the number of drinks they claimed to have had each time they went out drinking.

Here we take on the related issue: What is to be done about this problem? As we have noted above, the first step is not to work with college students but to begin working with elementary and high school students. There is growing community support for elementary and high school-based interventions, and many North American schools have developed such strategies. The one perhaps most commonly used is resistance skills training (RST). In the 1970s, research began to point out the limits of knowledge-based educational efforts, and the mood shifted toward programs designed to give students specific skills to allow them to resist pressures to engage in drinking. Unfortunately, there is no reason to believe that these programs or other comprehensive school curriculums are any more effective than the earlier knowledge-based programs in reducing drinking among elementary and high school students (Gorman, 1995; Stevens, 1996).

Part of the problem is that alcohol abuse is tied to a wide variety of high-risk behaviors (Harvey, 1995), but school programs are rarely targeted in a way to be relevant specifically to high-risk students (Cohen & Linton, 1995; Elmquist, 1995). If the main causes of alcohol abuse are outside the school, such as peer support or family dynamics, then a simple educational program provided by the school will not have very much effect on the students' behavior (Kline & Canter, 1994).

In this book, we have speculated on the need to start work with youths long before they come to college or university and long before they develop a fairly hardened set of attitudes that facilitate woman abuse. In the field of alcohol abuse, there is no question that there is a need to start early—long before the youths begin drinking—to deal with their expectations of alcohol, reasons for drinking, and other issues (James, Moore, & Gregersen, 1996). In fact, one set of researchers recommends that interventions to prevent alcohol misuse begin no later than third grade (Vega, Gil, & Zimmerman, 1993).

This is not to suggest that there are no solutions that work. Much of the problem comes from programs that are haphazard, partial, or unsupported by the entire school administration structure or that do not bring parents into the program (Hahn, 1996). Botvin, Baker, Dusenbury, Botvin, and Diaz (1995) report that, at least in a middle-class white population, a properly implemented junior high school program that includes both general life skills and social resistance skills and that includes at least two years of booster sessions may reduce alcohol use. Harris and Ludwin (1996) suggest that social norms can be changed to discourage drug and alcohol use by high school students, although it is unclear whether these norms are definitely related to actual drug use. In discussing woman abuse programs above, we pointed out that programs that are put together by only one teacher, or a group of teachers, are bound to fail over the long haul. In the same way, alcohol and drug abuse programs must be supported by an entire school administration, and supported regularly and consistently.

Unfortunately, there must also be a great deal more work in assessment. A great deal of the literature describes programs and speculates that people will or won't like taking them, but there is much less literature carefully measuring whether or not the behavior of alcohol- and drug-using youths is affected (Ellickson & Bell, 1992). For example, DeWit, Timney, and Silverman (1996) outline a popular drug education training package called Teacher Training in Preparation (TTIP) for elementary and high school teachers to work in teaching drug education. Their research suggests that teachers like the program. The next step is to find out if it changes the drug-taking behavior of students.

At the college and university level, it is naive to assume that campus officials can dramatically reduce the rates of victimization described in this book by simply closing down campus bars and banning alcohol from residences, campus dances, and other social functions. Indeed, there is no empirical evidence showing that women on alcohol-free campuses are safer than those where alcohol is not restricted (Schwartz & DeKeseredy, 1997). In fact, many women are sexually assaulted by their dating partners off campus, where they can often drink freely.

Still, we cannot deny the fact that alcohol abuse is part of a lifestyle, especially for men, that also seems to foster woman abuse in college dating. We also know that alcohol abuse seriously affects many students' academic performance as well as their physical and psychological health (DeKeseredy & Schwartz, 1996). In fact, we know that the activities of heavy drinkers affect non-heavy drinkers adversely also (Wechsler, Moeykens, Davenport, Castillo, & Hansen, 1995). Thus, campus-based alcohol awareness programs and seminars are necessary. Furthermore, more colleges need to hold woman abuse seminars that make alcohol and drug abuse awareness a major part of their programming (Abbey, Ross, McDuffie, & McAuslan, 1996).

The first problem almost always is to get the attention of the administration. For example, Gianini and Nicholson (1994) suggest that administrators on campus should attempt to gain support for alcohol abuse prevention programs by convincing the campus president that it is part of an overall plan to improve the college image. It may sound a bit cynical to argue that we should not ever assume that college administrations would like to improve the life of students but, instead, that we should arrange things so that the president can use feature stories and photo opportunities to gain positive press. Yet this is exactly the suggestion made in an important student personnel journal. Another source of pressure on campus top administrators comes from campus legal officers, who are becoming aware that, at least in the United States, courts are becoming more and more willing to hold institutions responsible when a serious event like a rape actually takes place, if they have failed in the past to have prevention programs in place (Fossley & Smith, 1995).

When a university is ready to start programming, there are model programs available (Grossman, Canterbury, Lloyd, & McDowell, 1994). The problem is that we cannot be sure yet which programs are most effective. Programs that involve skills training seem to reduce overall drinking but do not seem to stop occasional heavy drinking (Kivlahan, Marlatt, Fromme, Coppel, & Williams, 1990). A great deal of work remains to be done to develop and test effective programs for use on the college and university campus.

Unfortunately, however, as we pointed out elsewhere (Schwartz & DeKeseredy, 1997), the problem is more complex than simply cutting back on drinking: Many sober men abuse their dating partners also. Simply eliminating alcohol from campus will do little, if anything, to address the other risk factors identified by the CNS. For example, a man may stop drinking, but this does not mean he will stop associating with sexist male peers and refrain from consuming pornography. Thus, alcohol policies should be used only in conjunction with other strategies advanced in this chapter as well as in other sources (e.g., Bohmer & Parrot, 1993).

Chapter Summary

The primary objective of this chapter was to review several prevention and control strategies informed by CNS risk factor data. Will these
initiatives make a difference? This is an empirical question, one that can
only be answered by first developing a collective will to (a) recognize that
woman abuse in postsecondary school dating is a major problem and (b)
implement these progressive policies (Calkin, 1996).

Because Canadian research on the types of male-to-female victimization examined in this book is in its infancy, Calkin (1996) is correct to
point out that faculty, administrators, students, and other members of
the academic community still have much to learn about preventing and
responding to these behaviors. No doubt, mistakes will be made and
there will be considerable resistance to change from "reinforcers of the
status quo." Nevertheless, one of the most important points to consider
here is to avoid oversimplified solutions (Mahlstedt et al., 1993). Often,
they do more harm than good and fail to address the many and complex
sources of woman abuse in university and college dating (Stark-Adamec,
1996a). Indeed, what is required is a multiagency approach, one that
involves the joint efforts of students, faculty, administrators, campus
security, and many other members of the campus community. Woman
abuse in college dating as well as other major symptoms of gender
inequality cannot be stopped unless institutions of higher learning develop a *collective* responsibility for achieving this goal (Stark-Adamec,
1996b).

Note

1. We are not talking here about so-called snuff movies, where the claim is made that
the woman in the movie is actually murdered. We are just talking about day-to-day R-rated
movies that you can see on TV. If the rape-murder isn't shown in graphic detail, the movie
will probably be open to children.

The Methodology of the CNS

The purpose of this appendix is to answer some of the more technical questions that some readers might have about how the Canadian National Survey was administered. The Institute for Social Research (ISR) at York University was contracted to develop the sample design and carry out the activities necessary to create the final data set. Much of the information below depends on Pollard (1993). The final questionnaires were written by the principal investigators, Walter DeKeseredy and Katharine Kelly, and administered in both French and English, in both male and female versions.

First, the ISR divided the country into several geographic strata to allow the number of universities and colleges selected to take part in the survey to more accurately represent the distribution of Canadian students. One additional strata consisted of English language institutions in primarily French-speaking areas as well as French language institutions in primarily English-speaking areas. At this point, a list of all colleges with more than 100 students and all universities with more than 500 students was prepared. The universities list included four-year and graduate institutions, while the community colleges list included both two-year schools and colleges that offered a trade or vocational orientation.

The sample selection procedure then called for a random number system to be used to select the institutions that would take part, with a goal of 27 universities and 21 colleges, plus backup schools to replace any that might refuse to participate. The random system with replacement allowed for a school to be selected more than once, and in fact this did happen four times. Thus, the 48 chosen institutions actually consisted of 44 institutions, plus four that were counted twice.

To provide for the possibility that students at different levels of study might respond differently, in each school two classes were chosen: one for incoming students and one for more advanced students. The latter were third-year students, except in the case of two-year colleges, in which case second-year students were used.

Another part of the sampling frame was to list all programs of study in each institution. A main program of study was selected for each institution using random numbers, with the chances of being chosen being weighted by the percentage of students enrolled. Once a larger field was selected (arts, engineering), then all subjects taught in this field were listed and the process was repeated to select a specific subject.

At this point, chairs of the 96 departments randomly selected were approached by telephone in an attempt to gain approval for the principal investigators to travel to the site and administer the questionnaire. After written approval was received, the chair and the investigators worked together to determine the exact date and time and the class to be used. Of course, as might be expected in a sensitive area such as the one being studied by the CNS, some professors chose not to participate. Other selected classes did not meet a final selection criterion of at least 35 enrolled students in a university class and 20 students in a college class. By these criteria, 21 classes were ruled ineligible and had to be replaced, while 17 professors refused to participate. Of the 48 original institutions, 2 chose not to participate at all. All were replaced by the system explained above.

In addition to the approval of the Ethics Committees of both Carleton University and York University, ethics review committees at the colleges and universities where the questionnaires were being administered typically required that the CNS submit to ethics review. Our review requests were approved by every school requiring such approval, except for one that determined that the study could go forward without specific approval from that committee.

Before the close of the data collection phase of the project, the research team was able to visit 95 of the 96 classes selected for participation. The approval for the last class came after the data collection phase was shut down.

A member of the research team traveled to each data collection class and conducted the actual data collection. All students were carefully told that participation was completely voluntary and that they were free to stop taking the survey at any time. After the class completed the surveys, a member of the research team "debriefed" the class, explaining the purpose of the survey and the nature of the problem of abusive relationships. A list of local agencies that offered help, shelter, and counseling to people in abusive relationships was made available to each class.

Female Version:
Male-Female Dating
Relationships Questionnaire

This is the first national Canadian survey on problems in male-female dating relationships. It is sponsored by Health and Welfare Canada and is being conducted by Carleton University Professors Walter DeKeseredy and Katharine Kelly. Please read the instructions for each section carefully and answer each question as honestly as you can. Please note that any information you provide will be kept completely confidential. Participation in this study is strictly voluntary. We think that you will find this questionnaire interesting.

It will take different people different lengths of time to fill in the survey. Some will not take too long to complete it; others will take longer. But all of your answers are important to us, so take your time and be as honest as possible. When you have completed the questionnaire, a researcher will pick it up from you.

The results of this survey will be made widely available and hopefully used to improve relations between male and female dating partners. If you have any questions, please contact Walter DeKeseredy or Katharine Kelly at the phone number provided.

Thank you for taking the time to complete this questionnaire.

IF YOU HAVE FILLED OUT THIS QUESTIONNAIRE IN ANOTHER CLASS, DO NOT COMPLETE THIS ONE. PLEASE RETURN IT IMMEDIATELY TO THE RESEARCHER.

First we would like to ask some general questions about your dating patterns. Please circle the number which best represents your answer.

1. Have you been involved in a dating relationship with a male at any point in your life, no matter how short-term or casual, or long-term and serious?
      Yes
      No

IF NO, PLEASE GO TO QUESTION 11. IF YOU ARE CURRENTLY MARRIED AND HAVE NOT DATED IN THE LAST 12 MONTHS, PLEASE GO TO QUES-TION 10.

2. **Just in the past 12 months alone,** have you engaged in casual dating with men (i.e., a good time with no future commitment or obligation on the part of you and your dating partner)?
      Yes
      No

(i) If yes, please estimate how many different persons you have had such casual (not serious) dates with in the last 12 months?

_____

3. **Just in the past 12 months alone,** have you had any serious dating relation-ships with men (i.e., involving a great deal of commitment and intimacy)?
      Yes
      No

(i) If yes, please estimate how many different persons you have had such serious (not casual) dates with in the last 12 months?

_____

4. **Just in the past 12 months alone,** have you ever moved in with or lived regularly with a boyfriend?
      Yes
      No

5. **Just in the past 12 months alone,** have you ever been engaged to a boy-friend?
      Yes
      No

6. **Just in the past 12 months alone,** have you engaged in casual dating with men who do not share your ethnic background?

Yes

No

7. **Just in the past 12 months alone,** have you had any serious dating relationships with men who do not share your ethnic background?

Yes

No

8. **Just in the past 12 months alone,** have you ever moved in with or lived regularly with a boyfriend who does not share your ethnic background?

Yes

No

9. **Just in the past 12 months alone,** have you ever been engaged to a boyfriend who does not share your ethnic background?

Yes

No

10. We have been asking about the past 12 months only. **Since leaving or graduating from high school,** however, have you had dating partners or boyfriends?

Yes

No

11. What does the term dating mean to you? Please answer in the space below.

_____

_____

_____

_____

12. Now, we would like to ask you some general background questions. This information will allow us to compare your responses to other Canadian students. Please circle **only one** number which best represents your answer. Where there are blanks, please write out the answer. Please note your responses will be kept completely confidential.

a. How old are you? _____

b. What year did you leave or graduate from high school? _____

c. Please list the courses (e.g., history, sociology) and course level (e.g., first year) you are taking this term.

_____

_____

_____

d. What is your year of study?
   1. First year
   2. Second year
   3. Third year
   4. Fourth year
   5. Other (i.e., special student)

e. What year did you begin college/university? _____

f. What subject or program are you majoring in, or do you expect to major in?

_____

g. Do you identify yourself as an Aboriginal (e.g., Metis, status/nonstatus Indian) person?
   Yes
   No

h. Which ethnic or cultural group do you identify with? Please circle the number which best represents your answer.
   1. Central American (El Salvador, Honduras, etc.)
   2. Scandinavian (Denmark, Sweden, Norway)
   3. French Canadian
   4. English Canadian
   5. British (Scotland, Wales, England, N. Ireland)
   6. W. European (France, Germany, Holland, etc.)
   7. E. European (Russia, Poland, Baltic States, Hungary, etc.)
   8. S. European (Italy, Spain, Portugal, Greece, etc.)
   9. Far Eastern (Japan, China, India, Hong Kong, etc.)
   10. African (specify if North, Central, or South) _____
   11. Caribbean
   12. Middle Eastern (Israel, Lebanon, Iran, Iraq, etc.)
   13. Latin American
   14. Other (please specify) _____

i. What is your marital status?
   1. Never married and not living with a male partner
   2. Married and living with your spouse
   3. Living with a male partner
   4. Separated and not living with a male partner
   5. Divorced and not living with a male partner
   6. Widowed and not living with a male partner

j. What country were you born in? _____

k. Are you a recent (i.e., within the last five years) immigrant to Canada?
   Yes
   No

l. Are you a refugee from another country?
   Yes
   No

m. Are you a foreign student?
   Yes
   No

13. Do you currently belong to a sorority?
    Yes
    No

IF YES PLEASE GO TO QUESTION 15.

14. Have you ever belonged to a university or college sorority?
    Yes
    No

15. The next questions are about how safe you generally feel in public places these days. For each of the following situations please tell us if you would feel: very safe, reasonably safe, neither safe nor unsafe, somewhat unsafe, or very unsafe. Please circle the NUMBER which best represents your answer. How safe do you feel or would you feel?

	Very Safe	Reasonably Safe	Neither Safe nor Unsafe	Somewhat Unsafe	Very Unsafe
a. walking alone after dark	1	2	3	4	5
b. riding a bus or street-car alone after dark	1	2	3	4	5
c. riding a subway alone after dark	1	2	3	4	5
d. walking alone to your car in a parking lot after dark	1	2	3	4	5
e. waiting for public transportation alone after dark	1	2	3	4	5

f. walking past men you
   don't know, while
   alone after dark   1   2   3   4   5

g. being alone in your own
   home after dark   · 1   2   3   4   5

IF YOU HAVE NEVER BEEN INVOLVED IN A DATING RELATIONSHIP,
PLEASE GO TO QUESTION 24.

16. Sexual relations are common in dating relationships. The next questions are
    about your sexual experiences with dating partners and/or boyfriends.
    Below is a list of things that might have happened to you in the last 12
    months and/or since you left high school. Please answer either YES or NO
    to both sections of each question. IF YOU ARE OR HAVE BEEN MAR-
    RIED, PLEASE NOTE THESE QUESTIONS REFER ONLY TO DATING
    RELATIONSHIPS.

	IN THE LAST 12 MONTHS	*SINCE LEAVING HIGH SCHOOL* *(including the last 12 months)*

	YES	NO		YES	NO

a. Have you given in to sex play (fondling, kissing, or petting but not intercourse) when you didn't want to because you were overwhelmed by a man's
   continual arguments and pressure?

	1	2		1	2

b. Have you engaged in sex play (fondling, kissing, or petting but not intercourse) when you didn't want to because a man used his position of authority (boss, professor, supervisor, etc.) to make you?

	1	2		1	2

c. Have you had sex play (fondling, kissing, or petting but not intercourse)
   when you didn't want to because a man threatened or used some degree of
   physical force (twisting your arm, holding you down, etc.) to make you?

	1	2		1	2

d. Has a man attempted sexual intercourse (getting on top of you, attempting
   to insert his penis) when you didn't want to by threatening or using some
   degree of physical force (twisting your arm, holding you down, etc.), but
   intercourse did not occur?

	1	2		1	2

e. Has a man attempted sexual intercourse (getting on top of you, attempting
   to insert his penis) when you didn't want to because you were drunk or
   high, but intercourse did not occur?

	1	2		1	2

	IN THE LAST 12 MONTHS		SINCE LEAVING HIGH SCHOOL *(including the last 12 months)*	
	YES	NO	YES	NO

f. Have you given in to sexual intercourse when you didn't want to because you were overwhelmed by a man's continual arguments and pressure?

	1	2	1	2

g. Have you had sexual intercourse when you didn't want to because a man used his position of authority (boss, professor, supervisor) to make you?

	1	2	1	2

h. Have you had sexual intercourse when you didn't want to because you were drunk or high?

	1	2	1	2

i. Have you had sexual intercourse when you didn't want to because a man threatened or used some degree of physical force (twisting your arm, holding you down, etc.) to make you?

	1	2	1	2

j. Have you engaged in sex acts (anal or oral intercourse or penetration by objects other than the penis) when you didn't want to because a man threatened or used some degree of physical force (twisting your arm, holding you down, etc.) to make you?

	1	2	1	2

17. We are particularly interested in learning more about your dating relationships. No matter how well a dating couple gets along, there are times when they disagree, get annoyed with the other person, or just have spats or fights because they're in a bad mood or tired or for some other reason. They also use many different ways to settle their differences. Below is a list of some things that might have been done to you by your boyfriends and/or dating partners in these circumstances. Please circle the number which best represents your answer in each of the following situations. Please note the items are repeated twice. The first set is for the past twelve months; the second set covers all of your experiences since you left high school. IF YOU ARE OR HAVE BEEN MARRIED, PLEASE NOTE THESE QUESTIONS REFER <u>ONLY TO DATING RELATIONSHIPS.</u>

IN THE LAST 12 MONTHS

	Once	Twice	3-5 Times	6-10 Times	More Than 10 Times	Never
a. Insulted or swore at you	1	2	3	4	5	6
b. Put you down in front of friends or family	1	2	3	4	5	6

c. Accused you of having affairs or flirting with other men	1	2	3	4	5	6
d. Did or said something to spite you	1	2	3	4	5	6
e. Threatened to hit or throw something at you	1	2	3	4	5	6
f. Threw, smashed, or kicked something	1	2	3	4	5	6
g. Threw something at you	1	2	3	4	5	6
h. Pushed, grabbed, or shoved you	1	2	3	4	5	6
i. Slapped you	1	2	3	4	5	6
j. Kicked, bit, or hit you with his fist	1	2	3	4	5	6
k. Hit or tried to hit you with something	1	2	3	4	5	6
l. Beat you up	1	2	3	4	5	6
m. Choked you	1	2	3	4	5	6
n. Threatened you with a knife or a gun	1	2	3	4	5	6
o. Used a knife or gun on you	1	2	3	4	5	6

SINCE LEAVING HIGH SCHOOL
(including the last 12 months)

	Once	Twice	3-5 Times	6-10 Times	More Than 10 Times	Never
a. Insulted or swore at you	1	2	3	4	5	6
b. Put you down in front of friends or family	1	2	3	4	5	6
c. Accused you of having affairs or flirting with other men	1	2	3	4	5	6
d. Did or said something to spite you	1	2	3	4	5	6
e. Threatened to hit or throw something at you	1	2	3	4	5	6

f. Threw, smashed, or kicked something	1	2	3	4	5	6
g. Threw something at you	1	2	3	4	5	6
h. Pushed, grabbed, or shoved you	1	2	3	4	5	6
i. Slapped you	1	2	3	4	5	6
j. Kicked, bit, or hit you with his fist	1	2	3	4	5	6
k. Hit or tried to hit you with something	1	2	3	4	5	6
l. Beat you up	1	2	3	4	5	6
m. Choked you	1	2	3	4	5	6
n. Threatened you with a knife or a gun	1	2	3	4	5	6
o. Used a knife or gun on you	1	2	3	4	5	6

18. We realize that it may be difficult to discuss some of your dating experiences, but if we may, we would like to ask you a few questions about the most recent incident in which you were physically, sexually, or emotionally hurt by a boyfriend or dating partner. Please circle the letter or number which best represents your answer. IF YOU HAVE NOT BEEN HURT BY A BOY-FRIEND OR MALE DATING PARTNER, PLEASE GO TO QUESTION 19.

    a. Please indicate whether the last incident was:

        a) physical abuse

        b) sexual abuse

        c) emotional abuse

        d) both a and b

        e) both a and c

        f) both b and c

        g) a, b, and c

    b. Did you ever turn to anyone for help?
        Yes
        No

(IF NO, PLEASE GO TO QUESTION 19)

    c. Did you turn to at least one friend for help?
        Yes
        No

(IF NO, PLEASE GO TO ITEM d)

(1) How satisfied were you with the help you received from this/these friend(s)?
      1. Very satisfied
      2. Satisfied
      3. Not satisfied

    d. Did you turn to the police (not campus security) for help?
      Yes
      No

(IF NO, PLEASE GO TO ITEM e)

(1) How satisfied were you with the help you received from the police?
      1. Very satisfied
      2. Satisfied
      3. Not satisfied

    e. Did you turn to at least one family member for help?
      Yes
      No

(IF NO, PLEASE GO TO ITEM f)

(1) How satisfied were you with the help you received from this/these family member(s)?
      1. Very satisfied
      2. Satisfied
      3. Not satisfied

    f. Did you turn to a religious leader for help?
      Yes
      No

(IF NO, PLEASE GO TO ITEM g)

(1) How satisfied were you with the help you received from this person?
      1. Very satisfied
      2. Satisfied
      3. Not satisfied

    g. Did you turn to a medical professional for help (e.g., doctor, nurse, etc.) for help?
      Yes
      No

(IF NO, PLEASE GO TO ITEM h)

(1) How satisfied were you with the help you received from the medical professional?
- 1. Very satisfied
- 2. Satisfied
- 3. Not satisfied

h. Did you turn to a campus counselling service for help?
Yes
No

(IF NO, PLEASE GO TO ITEM i)

(1) How satisfied were you with the help you received from the counselling
service?
- 1. Very satisfied
- 2. Satisfied
- 3. Not satisfied

i. Did you turn to a women's group or women's centre for help?
Yes
No

(IF NO, PLEASE GO TO ITEM j)

(1) How satisfied were you with the help you received from the women's group
or women's centre?
- 1. Very satisfied
- 2. Satisfied
- 3. Not satisfied

j. Did you turn to campus security for help?
Yes
No

(IF NO, PLEASE GO TO ITEM k)

(1) How satisfied were you with the help you received from campus security?
- 1. Very satisfied
- 2. Satisfied
- 3. Not satisfied

k. Did you turn to a crisis centre or crisis hot-line for help?
Yes
No

(IF NO, PLEASE GO TO ITEM l)

(1) How satisfied were you with the help you received from the crisis centre or crisis hot-line?

    1. Very satisfied
    2. Satisfied
    3. Not satisfied

l. Did you turn to the campus administration for help?

    Yes
    No

(IF NO, PLEASE GO TO ITEM m)

(1) How satisfied were you with the help you received from the campus administration?

    1. Very satisfied
    2. Satisfied
    3. Not satisfied

m. Did you turn to anyone else for help?

If so, please indicate below who you turned to. IF NOT, PLEASE GO TO QUESTION 19.

_____

_____

_____

_____

19. Now, we would like to ask you some more questions about your dating relationships. Please indicate if YOU HAVE EVER used the following methods to settle disputes with your boyfriends and/or dates SINCE LEAVING HIGH SCHOOL (including the last 12 months). Please circle the number which best represents your answer. IF YOU ARE OR HAVE BEEN MARRIED, PLEASE NOTE THESE QUESTIONS REFER ONLY TO DATING RELATIONSHIPS.

	Once	Twice	3-5 Times	6-10 Times	More Than 10 Times	Never
a. Threw something at him	1	2	3	4	5	6
b. Pushed, grabbed, or shoved him	1	2	3	4	5	6
c. Slapped him	1	2	3	4	5	6

IF YOU ANSWERED NEVER TO ALL OF THE ABOVE THREE ITEMS, DO NOT ANSWER THE NEXT THREE QUESTIONS (i.e., on items a, b, and c).

PLEASE GO TO THE SECTION THAT IMMEDIATELY FOLLOWS THESE QUESTIONS. IT IS MARKED WITH AN ASTERISK (*).

On items a, b, and c, what percentage of these times overall do you estimate that in doing these actions you were primarily motivated by acting in self-defence, that is, protecting yourself from immediate physical harm? Circle the number which best represents your answer.

0%....10%....20%....30%....40%....50%....60%....70%....80%....90%....100%

On items a, b, and c, what percentage of these times overall do you estimate that in doing these actions you were trying to fight back in a situation where you were not the first to use these or similar tactics? Circle the number which best represents your answer.

0%....10%....20%....30%....40%....50%....60%....70%....80%....90%....100%

On items a, b, and c, what percentage of these times overall do you estimate that you used these actions on your boyfriends or dates before they actually attacked you or threatened to attack you? Circle the number which best represents your answer.

0%....10%....20%....30%....40%....50%....60%....70%....80%....90%....100%

*Again, please indicate if YOU HAVE EVER used any of the following methods to settle disputes with your boyfriends or dates since you left high school. Please circle the number which best represents your answer.

		Once	Twice	3-5 Times	6-10 Times	More Than 10 Times	Never
d.	Kicked, bit, or hit him with your fist	1	2	3	4	5	6
e.	Hit or tried to hit him with something	1	2	3	4	5	6
f.	Beat him up	1	2	3	4	5	6
g.	Choked him	1	2	3	4	5	6
h.	Threatened him with a knife or a gun	1	2	3	4	5	6
i.	Used a knife or gun on him	1	2	3	4	5	6

IF YOU ANSWERED NEVER TO ALL OF ITEMS d to i, GO TO QUESTION 20.

On items d to i, what percentage of these times overall do you estimate that in doing these actions you were primarily motivated by acting in self-defence, that is, protecting yourself from immediate physical harm? Circle the number which best represents your answer.

0%....10%....20%....30%....40%....50%....60%....70%....80%....90%....100%

On items d to i, what percentage of these times overall do you estimate that in doing these actions you were trying to fight back in a situation where you were not the first to use these or similar tactics? Circle the number which best represents your answer.

0%....10%....20%....30%....40%....50%....60%....70%....80%....90%....100%

On items d to i, what percentage of these times overall do you estimate that you used these actions on your boyfriends or dates before they actually attacked you or threatened to attack you? Circle the number which best represents your answer.

0%....10%....20%....30%....40%....50%....60%....70%....80%....90%....100%

20. NOW WE WOULD LIKE TO ASK YOU A FEW QUESTIONS ABOUT YOUR HIGH SCHOOL (i.e., GRADES 9-13) <u>DATING RELATIONSHIPS</u>. PLEASE CIRCLE THE WORD WHICH BEST REPRESENTS YOUR ANSWER.

    a. Did you date boys when you were in high school?
        Yes
        No

(IF NO, PLEASE GO TO QUESTION 21)

    b. In high school, did a male dating partner and/or boyfriend ever <u>threaten to use physical force</u> to make you engage in sexual activities?
        Yes
        No

    c. In high school, did a male dating partner and/or boyfriend ever <u>use physical force</u> in an attempt to make you engage in sexual activities, whether this attempt was successful or not?
        Yes
        No

    d. In high school, did a male dating partner and/or boyfriend ever <u>intentionally emotionally hurt</u> (i.e., insult, say something to spite you) you?
        Yes
        No

    e. In high school, did a male dating partner and/or boyfriend ever <u>intentionally physically hurt</u> you?

        Yes

        No

21. THE NEXT QUESTIONS ARE ABOUT YOUR <u>ELEMENTARY SCHOOL</u> (i.e., GRADES 1-8) <u>DATING RELATIONSHIPS</u>. PLEASE CIRCLE THE WORD WHICH BEST REPRESENTS YOUR ANSWER.

    a. Did you date boys when you were in elementary school?

        Yes

        No

(IF NO, PLEASE GO TO QUESTION 22)

    b. In elementary school, did a male dating partner and/or boyfriend ever <u>threaten to use physical force</u> to make you engage in sexual activities?

        Yes

        No

    c. In elementary school, did a male dating partner and/or boyfriend ever <u>use physical force</u> in an attempt to make you engage in sexual activities, whether this attempt was successful or not?

        Yes

        No

    d. In elementary school, did a male dating partner and/or boyfriend ever <u>intentionally emotionally hurt</u> (i.e., insult, say something to spite you) you?

        Yes

        No

    e. In elementary school, did a male dating partner and/or boyfriend ever <u>intentionally physically hurt</u> you?

        Yes

        No

22. **The next questions are about your use of alcohol and drugs in the last 12 months. Please circle the number which best represents your answer.**

    a. Did you drink alcoholic beverages in the last 12 months?

        1. Yes

        2. No

(IF NO, PLEASE GO TO ITEM d)

    b. If yes, how often on average did you drink alcoholic beverages in the last 12 months?

      1. Once a week
      2. 2-3 times a week
      3. 4-6 times a week
      4. Every day
      5. Once or twice a month
      6. Don't know

c. How often did you drink with your boyfriends and/or dating partners in the last 12 months?

      1. Never
      2. Very seldom
      3. Occasionally
      4. Often
      5. Very often

d. In the last 12 months, did you use recreational drugs (e.g., hash, marijuana, cocaine, speed, LSD, heroin)?

      1. Never
      2. Very seldom
      3. Occasionally
      4. Often
      5. Very often

e. How often have you used recreational drugs (e.g., hash, marijuana, cocaine, speed, LSD, heroin) with your boyfriends and/or dating partners in the last 12 months?

      1. Never
      2. Very seldom
      3. Occasionally
      4. Often
      5. Very often

23. Thinking about your entire university and/or college career, have you ever been upset by dating partners and/or boyfriends trying to get you to do what they had seen in pornographic pictures, movies, or books?

      1. Yes
      2. No

(IF NO, PLEASE GO TO QUESTION 24)

(1) If you were upset, can you tell us what happened? Please provide this information in the space below.

_____

_____

_____

_____

24. **Have you EVER BEEN:**

   a) Raped and/or sexually assaulted by someone OTHER THAN A DATING PARTNER.
      Yes
      No

   i) If yes, was this person a stranger?
      Yes
      No

   b) Physically assaulted by someone OTHER THAN A DATING PARTNER.
      Yes
      No

   i) If yes, was this person a stranger?
      Yes
      No

   c) Sexually harassed by someone OTHER THAN A DATING PARTNER.
      Yes
      No

   i) If yes, was this person a stranger?
      Yes
      No

25. The next questions are about your beliefs. For each of the following statements, please tell us if you <u>strongly agree, agree, disagree</u>, or <u>strongly disagree</u>. Circle the number which best represents your answer.

	Strongly Agree	Agree	Disagree	Strongly Agree	Don't Know
a. A man and his wife/ partner should have equal say in deciding how to spend the family income	1	2	3	4	5

b. A man and his wife/
partner should share
the household chores if
they are both working
outside the home   1   2   3   4   5

c. A man has the right to
decide whether or not
his wife/partner should
go out in the evening
with her friends   1   2   3   4   5

d. A man has the right to
decide whether or not
his wife/partner should
work outside the home   1   2   3   4   5

e. Sometimes it is impor-
tant for a man to show
his wife/partner that he
is the head of the house   1   2   3   4   5

f. Any woman who is
raped is at least partly
to blame   1   2   3   4   5

g. A man has the right to
have sex with his wife/
partner when he wants,
even though she may
not want to   1   2   3   4   5

h. If a man hits his wife/
partner, it's because
he's lost his temper and
gone out of control   1   2   3   4   5

26. Now we would like to ask you a few questions about your attitudes for each of the following situations. Please tell us if you would approve of a man slapping his dating partner or girlfriend. Would you approve if (circle the number which best represents your answers) . . .

	Yes	Depends	No	Don't Know
a. she won't do what he tells her to do	1	2	3	4
b. she insults him when they are home alone	1	2	3	4
c. she insults him in public	1	2	3	4
d. she comes home drunk	1	2	3	4

e.	she is sobbing hysterically	1	2	3	4
f.	she won't have sex with him	1	2	3	4
g.	he learns that she is dating another man	1	2	3	4
h.	she hits him first when they are having an argument	1	2	3	4

27. We really appreciate the time you have taken to complete this survey. And we'd like to assure you that everything you have told us will remain <u>strictly confidential.</u>

We realize that the topics covered in this survey are sensitive and that many women are reluctant to talk about their dating experiences. But we're also a bit worried that we haven't asked the right questions.

So now that you have had a chance to think about the topics, have you had any (any other) experiences in which you were physically and/or sexually harmed by your dating partners and/or boyfriends while you attended college or university? Please provide this information in the space below.

_____

_____

_____

Appendix C

Male Version: Male-Female Dating Relationships Questionnaire

This is the first national Canadian survey on problems in male-female dating relationships. It is sponsored by Health and Welfare Canada and is being conducted by Carleton University Professors Walter DeKeseredy and Katharine Kelly. Please read the instructions for each section carefully and answer each question as honestly as you can. Please note that any information you provide will be kept completely confidential. Participation in this study is strictly voluntary. We think that you will find this questionnaire interesting.

It will take different people different lengths of time to fill in the survey. Some will not take too long to complete it; others will take longer. But all of your answers are important to us, so take your time and be as honest as possible. When you have completed the questionnaire, a researcher will pick it up from you.

The results of this survey will be made widely available and hopefully used to improve relations between male and female dating partners. If you have any questions, please contact Walter DeKeseredy or Katharine Kelly at the telephone number provided.

Thank you for taking the time to complete this questionnaire.

IF YOU HAVE FILLED OUT THIS QUESTIONNAIRE IN ANOTHER CLASS, DO NOT COMPLETE THIS ONE. PLEASE RETURN IT IMMEDIATELY TO THE RESEARCHER.

First we would like to ask some general questions about your dating patterns. Please circle the number which best represents your answer.

1. Have you been involved in a dating relationship with a woman at any point in your life, no matter how short-term or casual, or long-term and serious?

    Yes

    No

IF NO, PLEASE GO TO QUESTION 11. IF YOU ARE CURRENTLY MARRIED AND HAVE NOT DATED IN THE LAST 12 MONTHS; PLEASE GO TO QUESTION 10.

2. Just in the past 12 months alone, have you engaged in casual dating with women (e.g., a good time with no future commitment or obligation on the part of you and your dating partner)?

    Yes

    No

(i) If yes, please estimate how many different persons you have had such casual (not serious) dates with in the past 12 months? _____

3. Just in the past 12 months alone, have you had any serious dating relationships with women (e.g., involving a great deal of commitment and intimacy)?

    Yes

    No

(i) If yes, please estimate how many different persons you have had such serious (not casual) dates with in the past 12 months? _____

4. Just in the past 12 months alone, have you ever moved in with or lived regularly with a girlfriend?

    Yes

    No

5. Just in the past 12 months alone, have you ever been engaged to a girlfriend?

    Yes

    No

6. Just in the past 12 months alone, have you engaged in casual dating with women who do not share your ethnic background?

    Yes

    No

7. Just in the past 12 months alone, have you had any serious dating relationships with women who do not share your ethnic background?

    Yes

    No

8. Just in the past 12 months alone, have you ever moved in with or lived regularly with a girlfriend who does not share your ethnic background?

    Yes

    No

9. Just in the past 12 months alone, have you ever been engaged to a girlfriend who does not share your ethnic background?

    Yes

    No

10. We have been asking about the past 12 months only. Since leaving or graduating from high school, however, have you had dating partners or girlfriends?

    Yes

    No

11. What does the term dating mean to you? Please answer in the space below.

    _____

    _____

    _____

    _____

12. Now, we would like to ask you some general background questions. This information will allow us to compare your responses to other Canadian students. Please circle <u>only one</u> number which best represents your answer. Where there are blanks, please write out the answer. Please note that your responses will be kept completely confidential.

    a. How old are you? _____

    b. What year did you leave or graduate from high school? _____

    c. Please list the courses (e.g., history, sociology) and course level (e.g., first year) you are taking this term.

    _____

    _____

    _____

    _____

d. What is your year of study?
  1. First year
  2. Second year
  3. Third year
  4. Fourth year
  5. Other (i.e., special student)

e. What year did you begin college/university? _____

f. What subject or program are you majoring in, or do you expect to major in?

---

g. Do you identify yourself as an Aboriginal (e.g., Metis, Status/Nonstatus Indian) person?
  Yes
  No

h. Which ethnic or cultural group do you identify with? Please circle the number which best represents your answer.

  1. Central American (El Salvador, Honduras, etc.)

  2. Scandinavian (Denmark, Sweden, Norway)

  3. French Canadian

  4. English Canadian

  5. British (Scotland, Wales, England, N. Ireland)

  6. W. European (France, Germany, Holland, etc.)

  7. E. European (Russia, Poland, Baltic States, Hungary, etc.)

  8. S. European (Italy, Spain, Portugal, Greece, etc.)

  9. Far Eastern (Japan, China, India, Hong Kong, etc.)

  10. African (specify if North, Central, or South)_____

  11. Caribbean

  12. Middle Eastern (Israel, Lebanon, Iran, Iraq, etc.)

  13. Latin American

    14. Other (please specify) _____

  i. What is your marital status?

    1. Never married and not living with a male partner

    2. Married and living with your spouse

    3. Living with a male partner

    4. Separated and not living with a male partner

    5. Divorced and not living with a male partner

    6. Widowed and not living with a male partner

  j. What country were you born in? _____

  k. Are you a recent (i.e., within the last five years) immigrant to Canada?
     Yes
     No

  l. Are you a refugee from another country?
     Yes
     No

  m. Are you a foreign student?
     Yes
     No

13. The next questions are about your participation in various recreational, school, or work activities with other men. How many times IN A TYPICAL MONTH <u>in the past year</u> have you engaged in each activity with other men? Only include those events which were all-male.

	Once	Twice	3-5 Times	6-10 Times	More Than 10 Times	Never
a. Worked on school assignments	1	2	3	4	5	6
b. Exercised or played sports	1	2	3	4	5	6
c. Attended sports events as a spectator	1	2	3	4	5	6
d. Went to bars or nightclubs	1	2	3	4	5	6
e. Went to movies or plays	1	2	3	4	5	6
f. Went out for dinner or lunch	1	2	3	4	5	6
g. Worked for wages (e.g., a part-time or full-time job, summer job)	1	2	3	4	5	6

14. Do you belong to any social clubs or community organizations that allow only male members?

     Yes

     No

15. Do you currently belong to a fraternity?

     Yes

     No

16. Have you ever belonged to a fraternity?

     Yes

     No

17. The next questions are about your current male friends' dating relationships. For each of the following questions please circle the number which best represents your answer.

    a. To the best of your knowledge, how many of your male friends have ever made physically forceful attempts at sexual activity with women they were dating which were disagreeable and offensive enough that the woman responded in an offended manner such as crying, fighting, screaming, or pleading?

       1. None

       2. One or two

       3. Three to five

       4. Six to ten

       5. More than ten

       6. Don't know

    b. To the best of your knowledge, how many of your male friends have ever used physical force, such as hitting or beating, to resolve conflicts with their girlfriends and/or dating partners to make them fulfil some demand?

       1. None

       2. One or two

       3. Three to five

       4. Six to ten

       5. More than ten

       6. Don't know

    c. To the best of your knowledge, how many of your friends insult their dating partners and/or girlfriends, swear at them, and/or withhold affection?

       1. None

       2. One or two

       3. Three to five

       4. Six to ten

5. More than ten

6. Don't know

18. The next questions are about the information your current male friends may have given you concerning how to deal with problems in male-female dating relationships.

   a. Did any of your male friends ever tell you that you should respond to your dates' or girlfriends' challenges to your authority by using physical force, such as hitting or slapping?

      Yes

      No

   b. Did any of your male friends ever tell you that it is alright for a man to hit his date or girlfriend in certain situations?

      Yes

      No

   c. Did any of your male friends ever tell you that your dates or girlfriends should have sex with you when you want?

      Yes

      No

   d. Did any of your male friends ever tell you that if a man spends money on a date, she should have sex with him in return?

      Yes

      No

   e. Did any of your male friends ever tell you that you should respond to your dates' or girlfriends' challenges to your authority by insulting them or putting them down?

      Yes

      No

   f. Did any of your male friends ever tell you to respond to your dates' or girlfriends' sexual rejections by employing physical force to obtain sex?

      Yes

      No

   g. Did any of your male friends ever tell you that it is alright for a man to physically force a woman to have sex with him under certain conditions?

      Yes

      No

   h. How much pressure did your friends place on you to have sex with your dating partners and/or girlfriends?

      1. A great deal

      2. Considerable

      3. Moderate

4. Little

5. None

19. Now we would like to ask you some more questions about your current male friends. Some people think it is alright for a man to slap his dating partner or girlfriend in certain situations. Other people think it is not alright. For each of the following situations, please tell us if your male friends would approve of a man slapping his dating partner or girlfriend. Would they approve if *(circle the number which best represents your answer . . .)*

	Yes	Depends	No	Don't Know
a. she won't do what he tells her to do	1	2	3	4
b. she insults him when they are home alone	1	2	3	4
c. she insults him in public	1	2	3	4
d. she comes home drunk	1	2	3	4
e. she is sobbing hysterically	1	2	3	4
f. she won't have sex with him	1	2	3	4
g. he learns that she is dating another man	1	2	3	4
h. she hits him first when they are having an argument	1	2	3	4

20. The next questions are about your beliefs. For each of the following statements, please tell us if you strongly agree, agree, disagree, or strongly disagree. Circle the number which best represents your answer.

	Strongly Agree	Agree	Disagree	Strongly Agree	Don't Know
a. A man and his wife/ partner should have equal say in deciding how to spend the family income	1	2	3	4	5
b. A man and his wife/ partner should share the household chores if they are both working outside the home	1	2	3	4	5

c. A man has the right to decide whether or not his wife/partner should go out in the evening with her friends   1   2   3   4   5

d. A man has the right to decide whether or not his wife/partner should work outside the home   1   2   3   4   5

e. Sometimes it is important for a man to show his wife/partner that he is the headof the house   1   2   3   4   5

f. Any woman who is raped is at least partly to blame   1   2   3   4   5

g. A man has the right to have sex with his wife/partner when he wants, even though she may not want to   1   2   3   4   5

h. If a man hits his wife/partner, it's because he's lost his temper and gone out of control   1   2   3   4   5

21. In a previous question we asked you about the attitudes of your friends. Now we would like to ask you a few questions about *your attitudes*. For each of the following situations, please tell us if YOU would approve of a man slapping his dating partner or girlfriend. Would you approve if *(circle the number which best represents your answer)* . . .

	Yes	Depends	No	Don't Know
a. she won't do what he tells her to do	1	2	3	4
b. she insults him when they are home alone	1	2	3	4
c. she insults him in public	1	2	3	4
d. she comes home drunk	1	2	3	4
e. she is sobbing hysterically	1	2	3	4
f. she won't have sex with him	1	2	3	4

g. he learns that she is dating
    another man   1   2   3   4

h. she hits him first when they
    are having an argument   1   2   3   4

IF YOU HAVE NEVER BEEN INVOLVED IN A DATING RELATIONSHIP,
PLEASE GO TO QUESTION 28.

22. Sexual relations are common in dating relationships. The next questions
     are about your sexual experiences with dating partners and/or girlfriends.
     Below is a list of things you might have done in the last 12 months and/or
     since you left high school. Please answer either YES or NO to both sections
     of each question. IF YOU ARE OR HAVE BEEN MARRIED, PLEASE
     NOTE THESE QUESTIONS REFER ONLY TO DATING RELATION-
     SHIPS.

	IN THE LAST 12 MONTHS		SINCE LEAVING HIGH SCHOOL *(including the last 12 months)*	
	YES	NO	YES	NO

a. Have you engaged in sex play (fondling, kissing, or petting but not inter-
    course) with a woman when she didn't want to by overwhelming her with
    continual arguments and pressure?

	1	2	1	2

b. Have you engaged in sex play (fondling, kissing, or petting but not inter-
    course) with a woman when she didn't want to by using your position of
    authority (boss, professor, supervisor, etc.)?

	1	2	1	2

c. Have you engaged in sex play (fondling, kissing, or petting but not inter-
    course) with a woman when she didn't want to by threatening or using
    some degree of physical force (twisting her arm, holding her down, etc.)?

	1	2	1	2

d. Have you attempted sexual intercourse (getting on top of her, attempting to
    insert penis) with a woman when she didn't want it by threatening or using
    some degree of physical force (twisting her arm, holding her down, etc.),
    but intercourse did not occur?

	1	2	1	2

e. Have you attempted sexual intercourse (getting on top of her, attempting to
    insert penis) with a woman when she didn't want it because she was drunk
    or high, but intercourse did not occur?

	1	2	1	2

f. Have you engaged in sexual intercourse with a woman when she didn't want
    to by overwhelming her with continual arguments and pressure?

	1	2	1	2

g. Have you engaged in sexual intercourse with a woman when she didn't want to by using your position of authority (boss, professor, supervisor, etc.)?

| 1 | 2 | 1 | 2 |

h. Have you engaged in sexual intercourse when she didn't want to because she was drunk or high?

| 1 | 2 | 1 | 2 |

i. Have you engaged in sexual intercourse with a woman when she didn't want by threatening or using some degree of physical force (twisting her arm, holding her down, etc.)?

| 1 | 2 | 1 | 2 |

j. Have you engaged in sex acts (anal or oral intercourse or penetration by objects other than the penis) with a woman when she didn't want to by threatening or using some degree of physical force (twisting her arm, holding her down, etc.)?

| 1 | 2 | 1 | 2 |

23. We are particularly interested in learning more about your dating relationships. No matter how well a dating couple gets along, there are times when they disagree, get annoyed with the other person, or just have spats or fights because they're in a bad mood or tired or for some other reason. They also use many different ways to settle their differences. Below is a list of some things that you might have done to your girlfriends and/or dating partners in these circumstances. Please circle the number which best represents your answer in each of the following situations. Please note the items are repeated twice. The first set is for the past twelve months; the second set covers all of your experiences since you left high school. IF YOU ARE OR HAVE BEEN MARRIED, PLEASE NOTE THESE QUESTIONS REFER <u>ONLY TO DATING RELATIONSHIPS</u>.

IN THE LAST 12 MONTHS

		Once	Twice	3-5 Times	6-10 Times	More Than 10 Times	Never
a.	Insulted or swore at her	1	2	3	4	5	6
b.	Put her down in front of friends or family	1	2	3	4	5	6
c.	Accused her of having affairs or flirting with other men	1	2	3	4	5	6
d.	Did or said something to spite her	1	2	3	4	5	6
e.	Threatened to hit or throw something at her	1	2	3	4	5	6

f.	Threw, smashed, or kicked something	1	2	3	4	5	6
g.	Threw something at her	1	2	3	4	5	6
h.	Pushed, grabbed, or shoved her	1	2	3	4	5	6
i.	Slapped her	1	2	3	4	5	6
j.	Kicked, bit, or hit her with your fist	1	2	3	4	5	6
k.	Hit or tried to hit her with something	1	2	3	4	5	6
l.	Beat her up	1	2	3	4	5	6
m.	Choked her	1	2	3	4	5	6
n.	Threatened her with a knife or a gun	1	2	3	4	5	6
o.	Used a knife or gun on her	1	2	3	4	5	6

SINCE LEAVING HIGH SCHOOL
(including the last 12 months)

		Once	Twice	3-5 Times	6-10 Times	More Than 10 Times	Never
a.	Insulted or swore at her	1	2	3	4	5	6
b.	Put her down in front of friends or family	1	2	3	4	5	6
c.	Accused her of having affairs or flirting with other men	1	2	3	4	5	6
d.	Did or said something to spite her	1	2	3	4	5	6
e.	Threatened to hit or throw something at her	1	2	3	4	5	6
f.	Threw, smashed, or kicked something	1	2	3	4	5	6
g.	Threw something at her	1	2	3	4	5	6
h.	Pushed, grabbed, or shoved her	1	2	3	4	5	6
i.	Slapped her	1	2	3	4	5	6

IF YOU ANSWERED NEVER TO ALL OF THE LAST THREE ITEMS (g, h, and i), DO NOT ANSWER THE NEXT THREE QUESTIONS (on items g, h, and i). PLEASE GO TO THE SECTION THAT IMMEDIATELY FOLLOWS THESE QUESTIONS. IT IS MARKED WITH AN ASTERISK (*).

On items g, h, and i, what percentage of these times overall do you estimate that in doing these actions you were primarily motivated by acting in self-defence, that is, protecting yourself from immediate physical harm? Circle the number which best represents your answer.

0%....10%....20%....30%....40%....50%....60%....70%....80%....90%....100%

On items g, h, and i, what percentage of these times overall do you estimate that in doing these actions you were trying to fight back in a situation where you were not the first to use these or similar tactics? Circle the number which best represents your answer.

0%....10%....20%....30%....40%....50%....60%....70%....80%....90%....100%

On items g, h, and i, what percentage of these times overall do you estimate that you used these actions on your girlfriends or dates before they actually attacked you or threatened to attack you? Circle the number which best represents your answer.

0%....10%....20%....30%....40%....50%....60%....70%....80%....90%....100%

*Again, we would like to know how many times you used the following methods to settle disputes since you left high school. Please circle the number which best represents your answer in each of the following situations. IF YOU ARE OR HAVE BEEN MARRIED PLEASE NOTE THESE QUESTIONS <u>REFER ONLY TO DAT-ING RELATIONSHIPS</u>.

SINCE YOU LEFT HIGH SCHOOL
(including the last 12 months)

		Once	Twice	3-5 Times	6-10 Times	More Than 10 Times	Never
j.	Kicked, bit, or hit her with your fist	1	2	3	4	5	6
k.	Hit or tried to hit her with something	1	2	3	4	5	6
l.	Beat her up	1	2	3	4	5	6
m.	Choked her	1	2	3	4	5	6

n. Threatened her with a knife
    or a gun   1   2   3   4   5   6
o. Used a knife or gun on her 1   2   3   4   5   6

IF YOU ANSWERED NEVER TO ALL OF THE ABOVE ITEMS, GO TO QUESTION 24.

On items j to o, what percentage of these times overall do you estimate that in doing these actions you were primarily motivated by acting in self-defence, that is, protecting yourself from immediate physical harm? Circle the number which best represents your answer.

0%....10%....20%....30%....40%....50%....60%....70%....80%....90%....100%

On items j to o, what percentage of these times overall do you estimate that in doing these actions you were trying to fight back in a situation where you were not the first to use these or similar tactics? Circle the number which best represents your answer.

0%....10%....20%....30%....40%....50%....60%....70%....80%....90%....100%

On items j to o, what percentage of these times overall do you estimate that you used these actions on your girlfriends or dates before they actually attacked you or threatened to attack you? Circle the number which best represents your answer.

0%....10%....20%....30%....40%....50%....60%....70%....80%....90%....100%

24. NOW WE WOULD LIKE TO ASK YOU A FEW QUESTIONS ABOUT YOUR HIGH SCHOOL (i.e., GRADES 9-13) <u>DATING RELATIONSHIPS</u>.

    a. Did you date girls when you were in high school?
       Yes
       No

(IF NO, PLEASE GO TO QUESTION 25)

    b. In high school, did you ever <u>threaten to use physical force</u> to make a girlfriend and/or dating partner engage in sexual activities with you?
       Yes
       No

    c. In high school, did you ever <u>use physical force</u> to make a dating partner and/or girlfriend engage in sexual activities with you, whether this attempt was successful or not?
       Yes
       No

    d. In high school, did you ever <u>intentionally emotionally hurt</u> (e.g., insult, say something to spite her) your girlfriends and/or dating partners?

        Yes

        No

    e. In high school, did you ever <u>intentionally physically hurt</u> your girlfriends and/or dating partners?

        Yes

        No

25. THE NEXT QUESTIONS ARE ABOUT YOUR ELEMENTARY SCHOOL (i.e., GRADES 1-8) DATING RELATIONSHIPS.

    a. Did you date girls when you were in elementary school?

        Yes

        No

(IF NO, PLEASE GO TO QUESTION 26)

    b. In elementary school, did you ever <u>threaten to use physical force</u> to make a dating partner and/or girlfriend engage in sexual activities with you?

        Yes

        No

    c. In elementary school, did you ever <u>use physical force</u> to make a dating partner and/or girlfriend engage in sexual activities with you, whether this attempt was successful or not?

        Yes

        No

    d. In elementary school, did you ever <u>intentionally emotionally hurt</u> (e.g., insult, say something to spite her) your girlfriends and/or dating partners?

        Yes

        No

    e. In elementary school, did you ever <u>intentionally physically hurt</u> your girlfriends and/or dating partners?

        Yes

        No

26. The next questions are about your use of alcohol and drugs in the last 12 months.

    a. Did you drink alcoholic beverages in the last 12 months?

        Yes

        No

(IF NO, PLEASE GO TO ITEM d)

b. If yes, how often on average did you drink alcoholic beverages in the last 12 months?
    1. Once a week
    2. 2-3 times a week
    3. 4-6 times a week
    4. Every day
    5. Once or twice a month
    6. Don't know

c. How often did you drink with your girlfriends and/or dating partners in the last 12 months?
    1. Never
    2. Very seldom
    3. Occasionally
    4. Often
    5. Very often

d. In the last 12 months, did you use recreational drugs (e.g., hash, marijuana, cocaine, speed, LSD, heroin)?
    1. Never
    2. Very seldom
    3. Occasionally
    4. Often
    5. Very often

e. How often have you used recreational drugs (e.g., hash, marijuana, cocaine, speed, LSD, heroin) with your girlfriends and/or dating partners in the last 12 months?
    1. Never
    2. Very seldom
    3. Occasionally
    4. Often
    5. Very often

27. Thinking about your entire university and/or college career, have you ever upset dating partners and/or girlfriends by trying to get them to do what you had seen in pornographic pictures, movies, or books?

(IF NO, PLEASE GO TO QUESTION 28)

(i) If they were upset, can you tell us what happened? Please provide this information in the space below.

_____

_____

_____

_____

28. We really appreciate the time you have taken to complete this survey. And we'd like to assure you that everything you have told us will remain <u>strictly confidential</u>.

We realize that the topics covered in this survey are sensitive and that many men are reluctant to talk about their own dating experiences. But we're also a bit worried that we haven't asked the right questions.

So now that you have had a chance to think about the topics, have you had any (any other) experiences in which you physically and/or sexually harmed your dating partners and/or girlfriends while you attended college or university? Please provide this information in the spaces below.

_____

_____

_____

_____

29. Again, now that you have had a chance to think about the topics, have you had any (any other) experiences in which YOU WERE PHYSICALLY AND/OR SEXUALLY HARMED BY YOUR DATING PARTNERS AND/OR GIRLFRIENDS while you attended college or university? Please provide this information in the spaces below.

_____

_____

_____

_____

_____

_____

References

Abbey, A. (1991). Acquaintance rape and alcohol consumption on college campuses: How are they related? *Journal of American College Health, 39,* 165-169.

Abbey, A., Ross, L., McDuffie, D., & McAuslan, P. (1996). Alcohol and dating risk factors for sexual assault among college women. *Psychology of Women Quarterly, 20,* 147-169.

Adler, Z. (1987). *Rape on trial.* New York: Routledge & Kegan Paul.

Arias, I., & Beach, S. (1987). Validity of self-reports of marital violence. *Journal of Family Violence, 2,* 139-149.

Babbie, E. (1973). *Survey research methods.* Belmont, CA: Wadsworth.

Barnes, G., Greenwood, L., & Sommer, R. (1991). Courtship violence in a Canadian sample of male college students. *Family Relations, 40,* 37-44.

Barnett, O., & LaViolette, A. (1993). *It could happen to anyone: Why battered women stay.* Newbury Park, CA: Sage.

Barnett, O., Miller-Perrin, C., & Perrin, R. (1997). *Family violence across the lifespan.* Thousand Oaks, CA: Sage.

Barrett, M. (1980). *Women's oppression today: Problems in Marxist feminist analysis.* London: Thetford.

Barrett, M., & McIntosh, M. (1982). *The anti-social family.* London: Verso.

Bart, P., Miller, P., Moran, E., & Stanko, E. (1989). Guest editors' introduction. *Gender & Society, 3,* 431-436.

Bergen, R. (1996). *Wife rape: Understanding the response of survivors and service providers.* Thousand Oaks, CA: Sage.

Bergman, L. (1992). Dating violence among high school students. *Social Work, 37,* 21-27.

Bernstein, N. (1996, May 6). Behind some fraternity walls, brothers in crime. *New York Times,* pp. A1, B8.

Billingham, R. (1987). Courtship violence: The patterns of conflict resolution strategies across seven levels of emotional commitment. *Family Relations, 36,* 283-289.

Blumberg, M., & Lester, D. (1991). High school and college students' attitudes toward rape. *Adolescence, 26,* 721-729.

Boeringer, S. (1996). Influences of fraternity membership, athletics, and male living arrangements on sexual aggression. *Violence Against Women, 2,* 134-147.

Bograd, M. (1988). Feminist perspectives on wife abuse: An introduction. In K. Yllö & M. Bograd (Eds.), *Feminist perspectives on wife abuse* (pp. 11-26). Newbury Park, CA: Sage.

Bohmer, C., & Parrot, A. (1993). *Sexual assault on campus: The problem and the solution.* Toronto: Maxwell Macmillan.

Bohrnstedt, G. (1983). Measurement. In P. Rossi, J. Wright, & A. Anderson (Eds.), *Handbook of survey research* (pp. 70-121). New York: Academic Press.

Bookwala, J., Frieze, I., Smith, C., & Ryan, K. (1992). Predictors of dating violence: A multivariate analysis. *Violence and Victims, 7,* 297-311.

Botvin, G., Baker, E., Dusenbury, L., Botvin, E., & Diaz, T. (1995). Long-term follow-up results of a randomized drug abuse prevention trial in a white middle-class population. *The Journal of the American Medical Association, 273,* 1106-1112.

Bowker, L. (1983). *Beating wife-beating.* Lexington, MA: Lexington.

Bradburn, N. (1983). Response effects. In P. Rossi, J. Wright, & A. Anderson (Eds.), *Handbook of survey research* (pp. 289-328). New York: Academic Press.

Breines, W., & Gordon, L. (1983). The new scholarship on family violence. *Signs: Journal of Women in Culture and Society, 8,* 490-531.

Brosius, H., Weaver, J., & Staab, J. (1993). Exploring the social and sexual "reality" of contemporary pornography. *Journal of Sex Research, 30,* 161-170.

Browne, A. (1987). *When battered women kill.* New York: Free Press.

Bruckerhoff, C., & Popkewitz, T. (1991). An urban collaborative in critical perspective. *Education & Urban Society, 23,* 313-325.

Calkin, J. (1996). Action against violence in the academy: The will and the ways. In C. Stark-Adamec (Ed.), *Violence: A collective responsibility* (pp. 95-103). Ottawa: Social Science Federation of Canada.

Canadian Panel on Violence Against Women. (1993). *The final report of the Canadian Panel on Violence Against Women.* Ottawa: Minister of Supply and Services Canada.

Cascardi, M., Vivian, D., & Meyer, S. (1991). *Context and attributions for marital violence in discordant couples.* Paper presented at the meeting of the Association for the Advancement of Behavior Therapy, New York.

Cate, R., Henton, J., Koval, J., Christopher, F., & Lloyd, S. (1982). Premarital abuse: A social psychological perspective. *Journal of Family Issues, 3,* 79-80.

Cate, R., & Lloyd, S. (1992). *Courtship.* Newbury Park, CA: Sage.

Chang, V. (1996). *I just lost myself: Psychological abuse of women in marriage.* Westport, CT: Praeger.

Christensen, F. (1995). *A serious case of distorted science in Canada.* Unpublished manuscript, Department of Philosophy, University of Alberta, Edmonton, Alberta.

Cohen, D., & Linton, K. (1995). Parent participation in an adolescent drug abuse prevention program. *Journal of Drug Education, 25,* 159-169.

Cohen, L., & Felson, M. (1979). Social changes and crime rate trends: A routine activities approach. *American Sociological Review, 44,* 588-608.

Cohen, L., Kluegel, J., & Land, K. (1981). Social inequality and predatory criminal victimization: An exposition and test of a formal theory. *American Sociological Review, 46,* 505-534.

Cohen, S., & Hoberman, H. (1983). Positive events and social support as buffers of life change stress. *Journal of Applied Social Psychology, 13,* 95-125.

Connell, R. (1995). *Masculinities.* Berkeley: University of California Press.

Cowan, G., & Dunn, K. (1994). What themes in pornography lead to perceptions of the degradation of women? *Journal of Sex Research, 31,* 11-21.

Curran, D., & Renzetti, C. (1996). *Social problems: Society in crisis* (4th ed.). Boston: Allyn & Bacon.

Currie, D. (1994). Women's safety on campus: Challenging the university as gendered space. *Humanity & Society, 18,* 24-48.

Currie, D. (1995). *Student safety at the University of British Columbia: Preliminary findings of a study of student safety.* Vancouver: University of British Columbia.

Currie, D., & MacLean, B. (1993). Woman abuse in dating relationships: Rethinking women's safety on campus. *Journal of Human Justice, 4,* 1-24.

Davis, T., Peck, G., & Storment, J. (1993). Acquaintance rape and the high school student. *Journal of Adolescent Health, 14,* 220-224.

DeKeseredy, W. (1988). *Woman abuse in dating relationships: The role of male peer support.* Toronto: Canadian Scholars' Press.

DeKeseredy, W. (1989). Woman abuse in dating relationships: An exploratory study. *Atlantis: A Women's Study Journal, 14,* 55-62.

DeKeseredy, W. (1990). Male peer support and woman abuse: The current state of knowledge. *Sociological Focus, 23,* 129-139.

DeKeseredy, W. (1993). *Four variations of family violence: A review of sociological research.* Ottawa: Health Canada.

DeKeseredy, W. (1994). Addressing the complexities of woman abuse in dating: A response to Gartner and Fox. *Canadian Journal of Sociology, 19,* 75-79.

DeKeseredy, W. (1996a). The Canadian national survey on woman abuse in university/college dating relationships: Biofeminist panic transmission or critical inquiry? *Canadian Journal of Criminology, 38,* 81-104.

DeKeseredy, W. (1996b). Making an unsafe learning environment safer: Some progressive policy proposals to curb woman abuse in university/college dating relationships. In C. Stark-Adamec (Ed.), *Violence: A collective responsibility* (pp. 71-94). Ottawa: Social Science Federation of Canada.

DeKeseredy, W. (1996c). Woman abuse in Canadian university and college dating relationships: The contribution of physical, sexual, and psychological victimization in elementary and high-school courtship. In B. Galaway & J. Hudson (Eds.), *Youth in transition: Perspectives on research and policy* (pp. 313-318). Toronto: Thompson.

DeKeseredy, W. (1997). Measuring sexual abuse in Canadian university/college dating relationships. In M. D. Schwartz (Ed.), *Researching sexual violence against women: Methodological and personal perspectives* (pp. 43-53). Thousand Oaks, CA: Sage.

DeKeseredy, W., & Hinch, R. (1991). *Woman abuse: Sociological perspectives.* Toronto: Thompson Educational.

DeKeseredy, W., & Kelly, K. (1993a). The incidence and prevalence of woman abuse in Canadian university and college dating relationships. *Canadian Journal of Sociology, 18,* 157-159.

DeKeseredy, W., & Kelly, K. (1993b). Woman abuse in university and college dating relationships: The contribution of the ideology of familial patriarchy. *Journal of Human Justice, 4,* 25-52.

DeKeseredy, W., & Kelly, K. (1995). Sexual abuse in Canadian university and college dating relationships: The contribution of male peer support. *Journal of Family Violence, 10,* 41-53.

DeKeseredy, W., Kelly, K., & Baklid, B. (1992, November). *The physical, sexual, and psychological abuse of women in dating relationships: Results from a pretest for a national study.* Paper presented at the annual meeting of the American Society of Criminology, New Orleans.

DeKeseredy, W., & MacLean, B. (1990). Researching woman abuse in Canada: A left realist critique of the Conflict Tactics Scale. *Canadian Review of Social Policy, 25,* 19-27.

DeKeseredy, W., & MacLean, B. (1991). Exploring the gender, race and class dimensions of victimization: A left realist critique of the Canadian Urban Victimization Survey. *International Journal of Offender Therapy and Comparative Criminology, 35,* 143-161.

DeKeseredy, W., & MacLean, B. (1993). Critical criminological pedagogy in Canada: Strengths, limitations, and recommendations for improvements. *Journal of Criminal Justice Education, 4,* 361-376.

DeKeseredy, W., & MacLean, B. (1997). But women do it too: The contexts and nature of female-to-male violence in Canadian heterosexual dating relationships. In K. Bonney-castle & G. Rigakos (Eds.), *Battered women: Law, state and contemporary research in Canada.* Vancouver: Collective Press.

DeKeseredy, W., & MacLeod, L. (1997). *Woman abuse: A sociological story.* Toronto: Harcourt Brace.

DeKeseredy, W., Saunders, D., Schwartz, M., & Alvi, S. (1997). The meanings and motives for women's use of violence in Canadian college dating relationships: Results from a national survey. *Sociological Spectrum, 17,* 199-222.

DeKeseredy, W., & Schwartz, M. (1991a). British and U.S. left realism: A critical comparison. *International Journal of Offender Therapy and Comparative Criminology, 35,* 248-262.

DeKeseredy, W., & Schwartz, M. (1991b). British left realism on the abuse of women: A critical appraisal. In H. Pepinsky & R. Quinney (Eds.), *Criminology as peacemaking* (pp. 154-171). Bloomington: Indiana University Press.

DeKeseredy, W., & Schwartz, M. (1993). Male peer support and woman abuse: An expansion of DeKeseredy's model. *Sociological Spectrum, 13,* 393-414.

DeKeseredy, W., & Schwartz, M. (1994). Locating a history of some Canadian woman abuse in elementary and high school dating relationships. *Humanity & Society, 18,* 49-63.

DeKeseredy, W., & Schwartz, M. (1996). *Contemporary criminology.* Belmont, CA: Wadsworth.

DeMaris, A. (1990). The dynamics of generational transfer in courtship violence: A biracial exploration. *Journal of Marriage and the Family, 52,* 219-231.

DeWit, D., Timney, C., & Silverman, G. (1996). A process evaluation of a comprehensive drug education training package. *Journal of Alcohol and Drug Education, 41,* 102-122.

Dobash, R. E., & Dobash, R. (1979). *Violence against wives: A case against the patriarchy.* New York: Free Press.

Dobash, R. E., & Dobash, R. (1992). *Women, violence and social change.* London: Routledge.

Dobash, R., Dobash, R. E., Wilson, M., & Daly, M. (1992). The myth of sexual symmetry in marital violence. *Social Problems, 39,* 71-91.

Doob, A. (1995). Understanding the attacks on Statistics Canada's violence against women survey. In M. Valverde, L. MacLeod, & K. Johnson (Eds.), *Wife assault and the Canadian criminal justice system* (pp. 157-165). Toronto: University of Toronto Press.

Dutton, D. (1986). The outcome of court-mandated treatment for wife assault: A quasi-experimental evaluation. *Violence and Victims, 1,* 163-175.

Dutton, D., & Hemphill, K. (1992). Patterns of socially desirable responding among perpetrators and victims of wife assault. *Violence and Victims, 7,* 29-40.

Edleson, J., & Brygger, M. (1986). Gender differences in reporting of battering incidences. *Family Relations, 35,* 377-382.

Eisenstein, Z. (1980). *Capitalist patriarchy and the case for socialist feminism.* New York: Monthly Review Press.

Ellickson, P., & Bell, R. (1992). Challenges to social experiments: A drug prevention program. *Journal of Research in Crime & Delinquency, 29,* 79-101.

Elliot, S., Odynak, D., & Krahn, H. (1992). *A survey of unwanted sexual experiences among University of Alberta students* (Research report prepared for the Council on Student Life, University of Alberta). University of Alberta: Population Research Laboratory.

Ellis, D. (1989). Male abuse of a married or cohabiting female partner: The application of sociological theory to research findings. *Violence and Victims, 4,* 235-255.

Ellis, D. (1995). *Spousal violence: Who hurts whom, how often and how seriously.* North York, Ontario: York University, LaMarsh Research Centre on Violence and Conflict Resolution.

Ellis, D., & DeKeseredy, W. (1989). Marital status and woman abuse: The DAD model. *International Journal of Sociology of the Family, 19,* 67-87.

Ellis, D., & DeKeseredy, W. (1996). *The wrong stuff: An introduction to the sociological study of deviance* (2nd ed.). Toronto: Allyn & Bacon.

Ellis, D., & Stuckless, N. (1996). *Mediating and negotiating marital conflicts.* Thousand Oaks, CA: Sage.

Elmquist, D. (1995). Alcohol and other drug use prevention for youths at high risk and their parents. *Education and Treatment of Children, 18,* 65-88.

Estrich, S. (1987). *Real rape: How the legal system victimizes women who say no.* Cambridge, MA: Harvard University Press.

Fagan, J., Stewart, D., & Hanson, K. (1983). Violent men or violent husbands? Background factors and situational correlates. In D. Finkelhor, R. Gelles, G. Hotaling, & M. Straus (Eds.), *The dark side of families* (pp. 49-69). Beverly Hills, CA: Sage.

Faludi, S. (1991). *Backlash: The undeclared war against American women.* New York: Crown.

Farr, K. (1988). Dominance bonding through the good old boys sociability group. *Sex Roles, 18,* 259-277.

Fekete, J. (1994). *Moral panic: Biopolitics rising.* Montreal: Robert Davies.

Feld, S., & Straus, M. (1990). Escalation and desistance from wife assault in marriage. In M. Straus & R. Gelles (Eds.), *Physical violence in American families: Risk factors and adaptions to violence in 8,145 families* (pp. 489-505). New Brunswick, NJ: Transaction.

Fenstermaker, S. (1989). Acquaintance rape on campus: Responsibility and attributions of crime. In M. Pirog-Good & J. Stets (Eds.), *Violence in dating relationships: Emerging social issues* (pp. 257-271). New York: Praeger.

Fine, G. (1987). *With the boys: Little League baseball and preadolescent culture.* Chicago: University of Chicago Press.

Finkelman, L. (1992). *Report of the survey of unwanted sexual experiences among students of U.N.B.-F. and S.T.U.* Fredericton: University of New Brunswick, Counselling Services.

Fitzpatrick, D., & Halliday, C. (1992). *Not the way to love: Violence against young women in dating relationships.* Amherst, Nova Scotia: Cumberland County Transition House Association.

Fojtik, K. (1977-1978). The NOW domestic violence project. *Victimology, 2,* 653-657.

Follingstad, D., Wright, S., Lloyd, S., & Sebastian, J. (1991). Sex differences in motivations and effects in dating violence. *Family Relations, 40,* 51-57.

Fossley, R., & Smith, M. (1995). Institutional liability for campus rapes: The emerging law. *Journal of Law and Education, 24,* 377-401.

Fox, B. (1993). On violent men and female victims: A comment on DeKeseredy and Kelly. *Canadian Journal of Sociology, 18,* 320-324.

Fraser, S., & Kar, R. (1996, September 19). The writing on the wall. *Charlatan, 26,* 20-21.

Funk, R. (1993). *Stopping rape: A challenge for men.* Philadelphia: New Society.

Gagné, M., & Lavoie, F. (1993). Young people's views on the causes of violence in adolescents' romantic relationships. *Canada's Mental Health, 41,* 11-15.

Gamache, D. (1991). Domination and control: The social context of dating violence. In B. Levy (Ed.), *Dating violence: Young women in danger* (pp. 69-83). Seattle: Seal.

Gartner, R. (1993). Studying woman abuse: A comment on DeKeseredy and Kelly. *Canadian Journal of Sociology, 18,* 314-319.

Gelles, R. (1974). *The violent home.* Beverly Hills, CA: Sage.

Gelles, R. (1976). Abused wives: Why do they stay? *Journal of Marriage and the Family, 38,* 659-668.

Gelles, R., & Cornell, C. (1985). *Intimate violence in families.* Beverly Hills, CA: Sage.

Ghez, M. (in press). Effective messages. In E. Kine, J. Campbell, & E. Soler (Eds.), *Drawing the line: Changing public perception of domestic violence.* Thousand Oaks, CA: Sage.

Gianini, P., & Nicholson, R. (1994). Hooking your president on prevention. *New Directions for Student Services, 67,* 29-40.

Gibbs, N. (1994). The incidence of rape: An overview. In K. Swisher & C. Wekesser (Eds.), *Violence against women* (pp. 206-211). San Diego, CA: Greenhaven.

Gilbert, N. (1991). The phantom epidemic of sexual assault. *Public Interest, 103,* 54-65.

Gilbert, N. (1994). Miscounting social ills. *Society, 31,* 18-26.

Girshick, L. (1993). Teen dating violence. *Violence Update,* pp. 1-6.

Gomme, I. (1995). Education. In R. Brym (Ed.), *New society: Sociology for the 21st century* (pp. 12.1-12.33). Toronto: Harcourt Brace.

Gondolf, E. (1985). *Men who batter: An integrated approach for stopping wife abuse.* Holmes Beach, FL: Learning Publications.

Goode, E., & Ben-Yehuda, N. (1994). *Moral panics: The social construction of deviance.* Cambridge, MA: Basil Blackwell.

Gorman, D. (1995). Are school-based resistance skills training programs effective in preventing alcohol misuse? *Journal of Alcohol and Drug Education, 41,* 74-98.

Gronau, A. (1985). Women and images: Feminist analysis of pornography. In C. Vance & V. Burstyn (Eds.), *Women against censorship.* Toronto: Douglas and McIntyre.

Grossman, S., Canterbury, R., Lloyd, E., & McDowell, M. (1994). A model approach to peer-based alcohol and other drug prevention in a college population. *Journal of Drug and Alcohol Education, 39,* 50-61.

Gwartney-Gibbs, P., & Stockard, J. (1989). Courtship aggression and mixed-sex peer groups. In M. Pirog-Good & J. Stets (Eds.), *Violence in dating relationships: Emerging social issues* (pp. 185-204). New York: Praeger.

Haggard, W. (1991). The feminist theory of rape: Implications for prevention programming targeted at male college students. *College Student Affairs Journal, 11,* 13-20.

Hahn, E. (1996). Cues to parental involvement in drug prevention and school activities. *Journal of School Health, 66,* 165-170.

Hanmer, J., & Saunders, S. (1984). *Well-founded fear: A community study of violence to women.* London: Hutchinson.

Harmon, P., & Check, J. (1989). *The role of pornography in woman abuse.* North York, Ontario: LaMarsh Research Programme on Violence and Conflict Resolution.

Harris, J., & Ludwin, M. (1996). The trading cards program: An evaluation of use of high school role models for drug abuse prevention. *Journal of Health Education, 27,* 183-186.

Harvey, S. (1995). Factors associated with sexual behavior among adolescents: A multivariate analysis. *Adolescence, 30,* 253-264.

Hay, D. (1993). Methodological review of "The incidence and prevalence of woman abuse in Canadian university and college dating relationships: Preliminary results from a national survey," by W. DeKeseredy and K. Kelly. *Journal of Human Justice, 4,* 53-65.

Henslin, J., & Nelson, A. (1996). *A down to earth approach to sociology: Canadian edition.* Scarborough, Ontario: Allyn & Bacon.

Henton, J., Cate, R., Koval, J., Lloyd, S., & Christopher, S. (1983). Romance and violence in dating relationships. *Journal of Family Issues, 4,* 467-482.

Highfield, R. (1996, October 30). Einstein's terms of endearment show wedded bliss is relative. *Ottawa Citizen,* p. A2.

Hinch, R. (1996). Sexual violence and social control. In L. Schissel & L. Mahood (Eds.), *Social control in Canada: Issues in the social construction of deviance* (pp. 29-58). Toronto: Oxford University Press.

Hippensteele, S., Chesney-Lind, M., & Veniegas, R. (1993). Some comments on the national survey on woman abuse in Canadian university and college dating relationships. *Journal of Human Justice, 4,* 67-72.

Hirschi, T. (1969). *Causes of delinquency.* Berkeley: University of California Press.

Hobbs, D. (1994). Mannish boys: Danny, Chris, crime, masculinity and business. In T. Newburn & E. Stanko (Eds.), *Just boys doing business? Men, masculinities and crime* (pp. 118-134). New York: Routledge.

Holmes, J., & Silverman, E. (1992). *We're here, listen to us!* Ottawa: Canadian Advisory Council on the Status of Women.

Hornosty, J. (1996). A look at faculty fears and needed university policies against violence and harassment. In C. Stark-Adamec (Ed.), *Violence: A collective responsibility* (pp. 31-56). Ottawa: Social Science Federation of Canada.

Hotaling, G., & Sugarman, D. (1986). An analysis of risk markers and husband to wife violence: The current state of knowledge. *Violence and Victims, 1,* 102-124.

Hull, J., & Bond, C. (1986). Social and behavioral consequences of alcohol consumption and expectance: A meta-analysis. *Psychological Bulletin, 99,* 347-360.

Itzin, C., & Sweet, C. (1992). Women's experience of pornography: UK magazine survey evidence. In C. Itzin (Ed.), *Pornography: Women, violence and civil liberties* (pp. 222-235). New York: Oxford University Press.

Jackson, W. (1988). *Research methods: Rules for survey research design and analysis.* Scarborough, Ontario: Prentice Hall.

Jaffe, P., Sudermann, M., Reitzel, D., & Killip, S. (1992). An evaluation of a secondary school primary prevention program on violence in intimate relationships. *Violence and Victims, 7,* 129-146.

James, W., Moore, D., & Gregersen, M. (1996). Early prevention of alcohol and other drug use among adolescents. *Journal of Drug Education, 26,* 131-142.

Jensen, R. (1995). Pornographic lives. *Violence Against Women, 1,* 32-54.

Jensen, R. (1996). Knowing pornography. *Violence Against Women, 2,* 82-102.

Jenson, J. (1991). If only . . . In B. Levy (Ed.), *Dating violence: Young women in danger* (pp. 45-49). Seattle: Seal.

Johnson, H. (1996). *Dangerous domains: Violence against women in Canada.* Toronto: Nelson.

Johnson, S. (1993). *When "I love you" turns violent: Emotional and physical abuse in dating relationships.* Far Hills, NJ: New Horizon.

Jones, A. (1994). *Next time, she'll be dead: Battering and how to stop it.* Boston: Beacon.

Jones, L. (1991). The Minnesota School Curriculum Project: A statewide domestic violence prevention project in secondary schools. In B. Levy (Ed.), *Dating violence: Young women in danger* (pp. 258-266). Seattle: Seal.

Jones, T., MacLean, B., & Young, J. (1986). *The Islington crime survey.* Aldershot, United Kingdom: Gower.

Jouriles, E., & O'Leary, K. (1985). Interspousal reliability of reports of marital violence. *Journal of Consulting and Clinical Psychology, 53,* 419-421.

Junger, M. (1987). Women's experiences of sexual harassment: Some implications for their fear of crime. *British Journal of Criminology, 27,* 358-383.

Junger, M. (1990). The measurement of sexual harassment: Comparison of the results of three different instruments. *International Review of Victimology, 1,* 231-239.

Kalmuss, D., & Straus, M. (1982). Wife's marital dependency and wife abuse. *Journal of Marriage and the Family, 44,* 277-286.

Kanin, E. (1957). Male aggression in dating-courtship relations. *American Journal of Sociology, 10,* 197-204.

Kanin, E. (1967a). An examination of sexual aggression as a response to sexual frustration. *Journal of Marriage and the Family, 29,* 428-433.

Kanin, E. (1967b). Reference groups and sex conduct norm violation. *Sociological Quarterly, 8,* 1504-1695.

Kanin, E. (1969). Selected dyadic aspects of male sexual aggression. *Journal of Sex Research, 5,* 12-28.

Kanin, E. (1985). Date rapists: Differential sexual socialization and relative deprivation. *Archives of Sexual Behavior, 14,* 219-231.

Kasian, M., & Painter, S. (1992). Frequency and severity of psychological abuse in a dating population. *Journal of Interpersonal Violence, 7,* 350-364.

Kelly, K. (1994). The politics of data. *Canadian Journal of Sociology, 19,* 81-85.

Kelly, K., & DeKeseredy, W. (1994). Women's fear of crime and abuse in college and university dating relationships. *Violence and Victims, 9,* 17-30.

Kelly, L. (1987). The continuum of sexual violence. In J. Hanmer & M. Maynard (Eds.), *Women, violence and social control* (pp. 46-60). Atlantic Highlands, NJ: Humanities Press International.

Kelly, L. (1988). *Surviving sexual violence.* Minneapolis: University of Minnesota Press.

Kennedy, L., & Dutton, D. (1989). The incidence of wife assault in Alberta. *Canadian Journal of Behavioural Science, 21,* 40-54.

Kine, E., Campbell, J., & Soler, E. (Eds.). (in press). *Drawing the line: Changing public perception of domestic violence.* Thousand Oaks, CA: Sage.

Kirkpatrick, C., & Kanin, E. (1957). Male sex aggression on a university campus. *American Sociological Review, 22,* 52-58.

Kirkwood, C. (1993). *Leaving abusive partners.* Newbury Park, CA: Sage.

Kivlahan, D., Marlatt, G., Fromme, K., Coppel, D., & Williams, E. (1990). Secondary prevention with college drinkers: Evaluation of an alcohol skills training program. *Journal of Consulting and Clinical Psychology, 58,* 805-810.

Kline, R., & Canter, W. (1994). Can educational programs affect teenage drinking? A multivariate perspective. *Journal of Drug Education, 24,* 139-149.

Klockars, A., & Sax, G. (1986). *Multiple comparisons.* Beverly Hills, CA: Sage.

Koss, M. (1988). Hidden rape: Sexual aggression and victimization in a national sample in higher education. In A. Burgess (Ed.), *Rape and sexual assault* (Vol. 2, pp. 3-25). New York: Garland.

Koss, M. (1993). Detecting the scope of rape: A review of prevalence research methods. *Journal of Interpersonal Violence, 8,* 198-222.

Koss, M., & Cook, S. (1993). Facing the facts: Date and acquaintance rape are significant problems for women. In R. Gelles & D. Loseke (Eds.), *Current controversies on family violence* (pp. 104-119). Newbury Park, CA: Sage.

Koss, M., & Gidycz, C. (1985). Sexual Experiences Survey: Reliability and validity. *Journal of Consulting and Clinical Psychology, 50,* 455-457.

Koss, M., Gidycz, C., & Wisniewski, N. (1987). The scope of rape: Incidence and prevalence in a national sample of higher education students. *Journal of Consulting and Clinical Psychology, 55,* 162-170.

Koss, M., & Oros, C. (1982). Sexual Experiences Survey: A research instrument investigating sexual aggression and victimization. *Journal of Consulting and Clinical Psychology, 55,* 162-170.

Kurz, D. (1995). *For richer, for poorer: Mothers confront divorce.* New York: Routledge.

Kurz, D. (1996). Separation, divorce, and woman abuse. *Violence Against Women, 2,* 63-81.

Laner, M., & Thompson, J. (1982). Abuse and aggression in courting couples. *Deviant Behavior, 6,* 145-168.

Lasch, C. (1977). *Haven in a heartless world: The family besieged.* New York: Basic Books.

Lavoie, F., Vezina, L., Piche, C., & Boivin, M. (1993). *Development et evaluation formative d'un programme de promotion voulant contrer le probleme de la violence dans les relations intimes des jeunes* (Research report). Quebec City: Conseil Quebecois de la Recherche Sociale.

Lea, J., & Young, J. (1984). *What is to be done about law and order?* New York: Penguin.

Ledwitz-Rigby, F. (1993). An administrative approach to personal safety on campus: The role of a President's Advisory Committee on Woman's Safety on Campus. *Journal of Human Justice, 4,* 85-94.

Lenskyj, H. (1990). Beyond plumbing and prevention: Feminist approaches to sex education. *Gender and Education, 2,* 217-230.

Levan, A. (1996). Violence against women. In J. Brodie (Ed.), *Women and Canadian public policy* (pp. 319-354). Toronto: Harcourt Brace.

Levine, E., & Kanin, E. (1986). Adolescent drug use: Its prospects for the future. *Journal of Family Culture, 1,* 4.

Levine, M., & Perkins, D. (1980, August). *Tailor making life events scale.* Paper presented at the annual meeting of the American Psychological Association, Montreal, Quebec.

Lewis, E. (1981). *The effects of intensity and probability on the preference for immediate versus delayed aversive stimuli in women with various levels of interspousal conflict.* Unpublished doctoral dissertation, University of Illinois at Chicago Circle.

Linz, D., & Malamuth, N. (1993). *Pornography.* Newbury Park, CA: Sage.

Lloyd, S. (1991). The dark side of courtship: Violence and sexual exploitation. *Family Relations, 40,* 14-20.

Longino, H. (1995). Pornography, oppression, and freedom: A closer look. In S. Dwyer (Ed.), *The problem of pornography* (pp. 34-47). Belmont, CA: Wadsworth.

Lowman, J., & MacLean, B. (Eds.). (1992). *Realist criminology: Crime control and policing in the 1990s.* Toronto: University of Toronto Press.

MacIvor, H. (1995, April). The biopolitical agenda. *Literary Review of Canada,* pp. 20-21.

MacKinnon, C. (1993). *Only words.* Cambridge, MA: Harvard University Press.

MacLean, B. (1992). The emergence of critical justice studies in Canada. *Humanity & Society, 16,* 414-426.

MacLean, B. (1996). A program of local crime-survey research for Canada. In B. MacLean (Ed.), *Crime and society: Readings in critical criminology* (pp. 73-105). Toronto: Copp Clark.

MacLean, B., & Milovanovic, D. (Eds.). (1991). *New directions in critical criminology.* Vancouver: Collective Press.

MacLeod, L. (1987). *Battered but not beaten: Preventing wife battering in Canada.* Ottawa: Advisory Council on the Status of Women.

Mahlstedt, D., Falcone, D. J., & Rice-Spring, L. (1993). Dating violence: What do students learn? *Journal of Human Justice, 4,* 101-117.

Makepeace, J. (1981). Courtship violence among college students. *Family Relations, 30,* 97-102.

Makepeace, J. (1983). Life events stress and courtship violence. *Family Relations, 32,* 101-109.

Makepeace, J. (1986). Gender differences in courtship violence victimization. *Family Relations, 35,* 383-388.

Manitoba Department of Education and Training. (1993). *Violence prevention in daily life and in relationships.* Winnepeg: Author.

Margolis, G. (1992). Earlier intervention: Confronting the idea and practice of drinking to drunkenness on college campuses. *Journal of College Student Psychotherapy, 7,* 15-22.

Martin, D. (1977). *Battered wives.* New York: Pocket Books.

Martin, P., & Hummer, R. (1993). Fraternities and rape on campus. In P. Bart & G. Moran (Eds.), *Violence against women: The bloody footprints* (pp. 114-131). Newbury Park, CA: Sage.

McMillen, L. (1990). An anthropologist's disturbing picture of gang rape on campus. *Chronicle of Higher Education, 37,* A3.

Megargee, E. (1982). Psychological determinants and correlates of criminal violence. In M. Wolfgang & N. Weiner (Eds.), *Criminal violence* (pp. 81-170). Beverly Hills, CA: Sage.

Mercer, S. (1988). Not a pretty picture: An exploratory study of violence against women in high school dating relationships. *Resources for Feminist Research, 17,* 15-23.

Metz, E. (1993). The camouflaged at-risk student: White and wealthy. *Momentum, 24,* 40-44.

Millett, K. (1969). *Sexual politics.* New York: Avon.

Monahan, J. (1981). *The clinical prediction of violent behavior.* Washington, DC: Government Printing Office.

Mooney, J. (1993a). *Researching domestic violence: The method used and a selection of findings from the North London Domestic Violence Survey.* London: Middlesex University, Centre for Criminology.

Mooney, J. (1993b). *The hidden figure: Domestic violence in North London.* London: Middlesex University, Centre for Criminology.

Muehlenhard, C., & Linton, M. (1987). Date rape and sexual aggression in dating situations: Incidence and risk factors. *Journal of Counseling Psychology, 34,* 186-196.

National Research Council. (1996). *Understanding violence against women.* Washington, DC: National Academy Press.

Nelson, M. (1994). *The stronger women get, the more men love football: Sexism and the American culture of sports.* New York: Harcourt Brace.

Northrup, D. (1985). *Woman abuse pilot study: Sample and field report.* North York, Ontario: York University, Institute for Social Research.

Okun, L. (1986). *Woman abuse: Facts replacing myths.* Albany: State University of New York Press.

Parkinson, G., & Drislane, R. (1996). *Exploring sociology: Pathways in sociology.* Toronto: Harcourt Brace.

Pateman, C. (1988). *The sexual contract.* Cambridge: Polity.

Peterson, S., & Olday, D. (1992). "How was your date last night?": Intimate relationship violence among high school students. *Human Services in the Rural Environment, 16,* 24-30.

Pirog-Good, M., & Stets, J. (Eds.). (1989). *Violence in dating relationships: Emerging social issues.* New York: Praeger.

Pizzey, E. (1974). *Scream quietly or the neighbours will hear.* London: Penguin.

Pollard, J. (1993). *Male-female dating relationships in Canadian universities and colleges: Sample design, arrangements for data collection and data reduction.* Toronto: Institute for Social Research.

Radford, J. (1987). Policing male violence—policing women. In J. Hanmer & M. Maynard (Eds.), *Women, violence and social control* (pp. 30-45). Atlantic Highlands, NJ: Humanities Press International.

Rae, C. (1995). *That macho thing: Social supports of violence against women.* Unpublished doctoral dissertation, Ohio University.

Randall, M., & Haskell, L. (1995). Sexual violence in women's lives: Findings from the women's safety project, a community-based survey. *Violence Against Women, 1,* 6-31.

Renzetti, C. (1992). *Violent betrayal: Partner abuse in lesbian relationships.* Newbury Park, CA: Sage.

Renzetti, C. (1994). On dancing with a bear: Reflections on some of the current debates among domestic violence theorists. *Violence and Victims, 9,* 195-200.

Renzetti, C. (1995). Editor's introduction. *Violence Against Women, 1,* 3-5.

Renzetti, C. (1997). Foreword. In M. Schwartz & W. DeKeseredy, *Sexual assault on the college campus: The role of male peer support* (pp. vii-xiii). Thousand Oaks, CA: Sage.

Reppucci, N. (1985). Psychology in the public interest. In A. Rogers & C. Scheirer (Eds.), *The G. Stanley Hall Lecture Series* (Vol. 5, pp. 125-156). Washington, DC: American Psychological Association.

Reynolds, C. (1995). The educational system. In N. Mandell (Ed.), *Feminist issues: Race, class, and sexuality* (pp. 272-293). Scarborough, Ontario: Prentice Hall.

Ring, T., & Kilmartin, C. (1992). Man to man about rape: A rape prevention program for men. *Journal of College Student Development, 33,* 82-84.

Roberts, C. (1989). *Women and rape.* New York: New York University Press.

Roden, M. (1991). A model secondary school date rape prevention program. In B. Levy (Ed.), *Dating violence: Young women in danger* (pp. 267-278). Seattle: Seal.

Roiphe, K. (1994). *The morning after: Sex, fear, and feminism on campus.* Boston: Little, Brown.

Roscoe, B., & Benaske, N. (1985). Courtship violence experienced by abused wives: Similarities in patterns of abuse. *Family Relations, 34,* 419-424.

Roscoe, B., & Callahan, J. (1985). Adolescents' self-reports of violence in families and dating relations. *Adolescence, 20,* 545-553.

Roscoe, B., & Kelsey, T. (1986). Dating violence among high school students. *Psychology, 23,* 53-59.

Rubin, G. (1993). Misguided, dangerous and wrong: An analysis of anti-pornography politics. In A. Assiter & A. Carol (Eds.), *Bad girls & dirty pictures: The challenge to reclaim feminism* (pp. 18-40). Boulder, CO: Pluto.

Rubin, L. (1976). *Worlds of pain: Life in the working class family.* New York: Basic Books.

Russell, D. (1982). *Rape in marriage.* New York: Collier.

Russell, D. (1990). *Rape in marriage* (2nd ed.). Bloomington: Indiana University Press.

Sanday, P. (1990). *Fraternity gang rape.* New York: New York University Press.

Sanday, P. (1996). *A woman scorned: Acquaintance rape on trial.* New York: Doubleday.

Saunders, D. (1986). When battered women use violence: Husband-abuse or self-defense? *Violence and Victims, 1,* 47-60.

Saunders, D. (1988). Wife abuse, husband abuse, or mutual combat: A feminist perspective on the empirical findings. In K. Yllö & M. Bograd (Eds.), *Feminist perspectives on wife abuse* (pp. 90-113). Newbury Park, CA: Sage.

Schneider, E., & Jordon, S. (1978). Representation of women who defend themselves in response to physical or sexual assault. *Family Law Review, 1,* 118-132.

Schuman, D., & Olufs, D. (1995). *Diversity on campus.* Boston: Allyn & Bacon.

Schwartz, M. (1982). The spousal exemption for criminal rape prosecution. *Vermont Law Review, 7,* 33-57.

Schwartz, M. (1987). Censorship of sexual violence: Is the problem sex or violence? *Humanity & Society, 11,* 212-243.

Schwartz, M. (1991). Humanist sociology and date rape. *Humanity & Society, 15,* 304-316.

Schwartz, M. (Ed.). (1997). *Researching sexual violence against women: Methodological and personal perspectives.* Thousand Oaks, CA: Sage.

Schwartz, M., & Clear, T. (1980). Toward a new law on rape. *Crime and Delinquency, 26,* 129-151.

Schwartz, M., & DeKeseredy, W. (1991). Left realist criminology: Strengths, weaknesses and the feminist critique. *Crime, Law and Social Change, 15,* 51-72.

Schwartz, M., & DeKeseredy, W. (1993). The return of the "battered husband syndrome" through the typification of women as violent. *Crime, Law and Social Change, 20,* 249-265.

Schwartz, M., & DeKeseredy, W. (1994a, November). *Male peer support, pornography and the abuse of women in dating relationships.* Paper presented at the annual meeting of the American Society of Criminology, Miami, FL.

Schwartz, M., & DeKeseredy, W. (1994b). People without data attacking rape: The Gilbertizing of Mary Koss. *Violence Update, 5,* 5, 8, 11.

Schwartz, M., & DeKeseredy, W. (1997). *Sexual assault on the college campus: The role of male peer support.* Thousand Oaks, CA: Sage.

Schwartz, M., & Nogrady, C. (1996). Fraternity membership, rape myths, and sexual aggression on a college campus. *Violence Against Women, 2,* 148-162.

Schwartz, M., & Pitts, V. (1995). Exploring a feminist routine activities approach to explaining sexual assault. *Justice Quarterly, 12,* 9-31.

Scully, D. (1990). *Understanding sexual violence: A study of convicted rapists.* Boston: Unwin Hyman.

Segal, L., & McIntosh, M. (Eds.). (1993). *Sex exposed: Sexuality and the pornography debate.* New Brunswick, NJ: Rutgers University Press.

Shotland, R. (1992). A theory on the causes of courtship rape: Part 2. *Journal of Social Issues, 48,* 127-143.

Smith, D. (1983). Women, the family, and the productive process. In J. Grayson (Ed.), *Introduction to society: An alternate approach* (pp. 312-344). Toronto: Gage.

Smith, M. (1986). Effects of question format on the reporting of woman abuse: A telephone survey experiment. *Victimology, 11,* 430-438.

Smith, M. (1987). The incidence and prevalence of woman abuse in Toronto. *Violence and Victims, 2,* 173-187.

Smith, M. (1988). Women's fear of violent crime: An exploratory test of a feminist hypothesis. *Journal of Family Violence, 3,* 29-38.

Smith, M. (1990a). Patriarchal ideology and wife beating: A test of a feminist hypothesis. *Violence and Victims, 5,* 257-273.

Smith, M. (1990b). Sociodemographic risk factors in wife abuse: Results from a survey of Toronto women. *Canadian Journal of Sociology, 15,* 39-58.

Smith, M. (1991). Male peer support for wife abuse: An exploratory study. *Journal of Interpersonal Violence, 6,* 512-519.

Smith, M. (1994). Enhancing the quality of survey data on violence against women: A feminist approach. *Gender & Society, 18,* 109-127.

Stacy, W., & Shupe, A. (1983). *The family secret: Domestic violence in America.* Boston: Beacon.

Stanko, E. (1987). Typical violence, normal precaution: Men, women and interpersonal violence in England, Wales, Scotland and the U.S.A. In J. Hanmer & M. Maynard (Eds.), *Women, violence and social control* (pp. 122-134). Atlantic Highlands, NJ: Humanities Press International.

Stanko, E. (1990). *Everyday violence: How women and men experience sexual and physical danger.* London: Pandora.

Stanko, E. (1995). The struggle over commonsense feminism, violence and confronting the backlash. In B. Gillies & G. James (Eds.), *Proceedings of the Fifth Symposium on Violence and Aggression* (pp. 156-172). Saskatoon, Saskatchewan: University Extension Press, University of Saskatchewan.

Stark-Adamec, C. (1996a). Collaboration and responsibility. In C. Stark-Adamec (Ed.), *Violence: A collective responsibility* (pp. 143-150). Ottawa: Social Science Federation of Canada.

Stark-Adamec, C. (1996b). Violence and responsibility. In C. Stark-Adamec (Ed.), *Violence: A collective responsibility* (pp. 1-9). Ottawa: Social Science Federation of Canada.

Steinem, G. (1993). Erotica and pornography: A clear and present difference. In S. Dwyer (Ed.), *The problem of pornography* (pp. 29-33). Belmont, CA: Wadsworth.

Stets, J., & Henderson, D. (1991). Contextual factors surrounding conflict resolution while dating: Results from a national study. *Family Relations, 40,* 29-36.

Stets, J., & Straus, M. (1990). The marriage license as a hitting license: A comparison of assaults in dating, cohabiting and married couples. In M. Straus & R. Gelles (Eds.), *Physical violence in American families: Risk factors and adaptions to violence in 8,145 families* (pp. 227-244). New Brunswick, NJ: Transaction.

Stevens, M. (1996). Rural adolescent drinking behavior: Three year follow-up in the New Hampshire substance abuse prevention study. *Adolescence, 31,* 159-166.

Stoller, R. (1991). *Porn: Myths for the twentieth century.* New Haven, CT: Yale University Press.

Stone, S. (1991). They said I was "young and immature." In B. Levy (Ed.), *Dating violence: Young women in danger* (pp. 28-32). Seattle: Seal.

Straus, M. (1979). Measuring intrafamily conflict and violence: The Conflict Tactics (CT) Scales. *Journal of Marriage and the Family, 41,* 75-88.

Straus, M. (1990a). Measuring intrafamily conflict and violence: The Conflict Tactics (CT) Scales. In M. Straus & R. Gelles (Eds.), *Physical violence in American families: Risk factors and adaptations to violence in 8,145 families* (pp. 29-47). New Brunswick, NJ: Transaction.

Straus, M. (1990b). The Conflict Tactics Scales and its critics: An evaluation and new data on validity and reliability. In M. Straus & R. Gelles (Eds.), *Physical violence in American families: Risk factors and adaptations to violence in 8,145 families* (pp. 49-73). New Brunswick, NJ: Transaction.

Straus, M., & Gelles, R. (1986). Societal change and change in family violence from 1975 to 1985 as revealed by two national surveys. *Journal of Marriage and the Family, 48,* 465-479.

Straus, M., Gelles, R., & Steinmetz, S. (1981). *Behind closed doors: Violence in the American family.* New York: Anchor.

Straus, M., Hamby, S., Boney-McCoy, S., & Sugarman, D. (1995). *The revised Conflict Tactics Scales (CTS2-Form A).* Durham, NH: University of New Hampshire, Family Research Laboratory.

Strong-Boag, V. (1996). Too much is not enough: The paradox of power for feminist academics working with community feminists on issues related to violence. In C. Stark-Adamec (Ed.), *Violence: A collective responsibility* (pp. 105-115). Ottawa: Social Science Federation of Canada.

Sudermann, M., & Jaffe, P. (1993, August). *Violence in teen dating relationships: Evaluation of a large scale primary prevention program.* Paper presented at the annual meeting of the American Psychological Association, Toronto, Ontario.

Sugarman, D., & Hotaling, C. (1989). Dating violence: Prevalence, context, and risk markers. In M. Pirog-Good & J. Stets (Eds.), *Violence in dating relationships: Emerging social issues* (pp. 3-32). New York: Praeger.

Surette, R. (1992). *Media, crime and criminal justice: Images and realities.* Pacific Grove, CA: Brooks/Cole.

Taylor, I. (1983). *Crime, capitalism and community: Three essays in socialist criminology.* Toronto: Butterworth.

Thorne, B. (1993). *Gender play: Girls and boys at school.* New Brunswick, NJ: Rutgers University Press.

Thorne-Finch, R. (1992). *Ending the silence: The origins and treatment of male violence against women.* Toronto: University of Toronto Press.

Toby, J. (1957). Social disorganization and stake in conformity: Complementary factors in predatory behavior of young hoodlums. *Journal of Criminal Law, Criminology and Police Science, 48*, 12-17.

Tolman, R. (1989). The development and validation of a non-physical abuse scale. *Violence and Victims, 4*, 159-177.

Tong, R. (1984). *Women, sex, and the law.* Totawa, NJ: Rowman & Allanheld.

United Nations. (1995). *Human development report 1995.* Toronto: Oxford University Press.

Ursel, E. (1986). The state and the maintenance of patriarchy: A case study of family labor and welfare legislation. In J. Dickensian & B. Russell (Eds.), *Family, economy and state* (pp. 150-191). Toronto: Garamond.

Vanier Institute of the Family. (1995, September). Stopping family violence: Steps along the road. *Transition–For Families–About Families,* pp. 4-8.

Vega, W., Gil, A., & Zimmerman, R. (1993). Patterns of drug use among Cuban-American, African-American, and white non-Hispanic boys. *American Journal of Public Health, 83*, 257-259.

Versagi, C. (1996, October 16). Battered, silent—and male: Men as victims of domestic violence. *Cleveland (OH) Free Times,* pp. 2-7.

Walker, L. (1979). *The battered woman.* New York: Harper & Row.

Waller, W. (1937). The rating and dating complex. *American Sociological Review, 2*, 727-734.

Ward, S., Chapman, K., Cohn, E., White, S., & Williams, K. (1991). Acquaintance rape and the college social scene. *Family Relations, 40*, 65-71.

Warshaw, R. (1988). *I never called it rape.* New York: Harper & Row.

Wechsler, H., Moeykens, B., Davenport, A., Castillo, S., & Hansen, J. (1995). The adverse impact of heavy episodic drinkers on other college students. *Journal of Studies on Alcohol, 56*, 628-634.

White, J., & Koss, M. (1991). Courtship violence: Incidence in a national sample of higher education students. *Violence and Victims, 6*, 247-256.

Williams, K., & Hawkins, R. (1989). Controlling male aggression in intimate relationships. *Law and Society Review, 23*, 591-612.

Wyatt, G. (1992). The sociocultural context of African American and white American women's rape. In J. White & S. Sorenson (Eds.), Adult sexual assault [Special issue]. *Journal of Social Issues, 48*, 77-91.

Yllö, K., & Straus, M. (1981). Interpersonal violence among married and cohabiting couples. *Family Relations, 30*, 339-347.

Index

About the Authors

Walter S. DeKeseredy is Professor of Sociology at Carleton University, Ottawa. He has published dozens of journal articles and book chapters on woman abuse and left realism. He is the author of *Woman Abuse in Dating Relationships: The Role of Male Peer Support;* with Ronald Hinch, coauthor of *Woman Abuse: Sociological Perspectives;* with Desmond Ellis, coauthor of the second edition of *The Wrong Stuff: An Introduction to the Sociological Study of Deviance;* with Martin Schwartz, coauthor of *Contemporary Criminology*  and *Sexual Assault on the College Campus: The Role of Male Peer Support;* and with Linda MacLeod, *Woman Abuse: A Sociological Story.* In 1995, he received the Critical Criminologist of the Year Award from the American Society of Criminology's Division on Critical Criminology. In 1993, he received Carleton University's Research Achievement Award. Currently he is coeditor of *Critical Criminology: An International Journal* and serves on the editorial board of *Women & Criminal Justice.*

Martin D. Schwartz is Professor of Sociology at Ohio University. He has written more than 60 articles and chapters and edited books on a variety of topics in such journals as *Criminology, Deviant Behavior, Justice Quarterly,* and *Women and Politics.* A former president of the Association for Humanist Sociology, he has never been convicted of a major felony. He is the coauthor of *Contemporary Criminology, Sexual Assault on the College Campus: The Role of Male Peer Support,* and *Corrections: An Issues Approach,* now in its fourth  edition; the editor of *Researching Sexual Violence Against Women: Methodological and Personal Perspectives;* and the coeditor of *Race, Class, and Gender in Criminology: The Intersections.* He serves as deputy editor of *Justice Quarterly* and on the editorial boards of *Violence Against Women: Race, Class and Gender* and *Teaching Sociology.* He received the award of the American Society of Criminology's Division on Critical Criminology in 1993.